general editor John M. MacKenzie

When the 'Studies in Imperialism' series was founded more than twenty years ago, emphasis was laid upon the conviction that 'imperialism as a cultural phenomenon had as significant an effect on the dominant as on the subordinate societies'. With more than sixty books published, this remains the prime concern of the series. Cross-disciplinary work has indeed appeared covering the full spectrum of cultural phenomena, as well as examining aspects of gender and sex, frontiers and law, science and the environment, language and literature, migration and patriotic societies, and much else. Moreover, the series has always wished to present comparative work on European and American imperialism, and particularly welcomes the submission of books in these areas. The fascination with imperialism, in all its aspects, shows no sign of abating, and this series will continue to lead the way in encouraging the widest possible range of studies in the field. 'Studies in Imperialism' is fully organic in its development, always seeking to be at the cutting edge, responding to the latest interests of scholars and the needs of this ever-expanding area of scholarship.

Engendering whiteness

Manchester University Press

AVAILABLE IN THE SERIES

CULTURAL IDENTITIES AND THE AESTHETICS OF BRITISHNESS ed. Dana Arnold

BRITAIN IN CHINA
Community, culture and colonialism, 1900–1949 Robert Bickers

RACE AND EMPIRE
Eugenics in colonial Kenya Chloe Campbell

IMPERIAL CITIES: Landscape, display and identity
eds Felix Driver and David Gilbert

EQUAL SUBJECTS, UNEQUAL RIGHTS
Indigenous peoples in British settler colonies, 1830s–1910
Julie Evans, Patricia Grimshaw, David Phillips and Shurlee Swain

SCOTLAND, THE CARIBBEAN AND THE ATLANTIC WORLD, 1750–1820
Douglas J. Hamilton

EMIGRANT HOMECOMINGS
The return movement of emigrants, 1600–2000 Marjory Harper

REPORTING THE RAJ
The British press and India, c. 1880–1922 Chandrika Kaul

SILK AND EMPIRE Brenda M. King

LAW, HISTORY, COLONIALISM
The reach of empire eds Diane Kirkby and Catherine Coleborne

COLONIAL CONNECTIONS, 1815–45
Patronage, the information revolution and colonial government Zoë Laidlaw

PROPAGANDA AND EMPIRE
The manipulation of British public opinion, 1880–1960 John M. MacKenzie

THE OTHER EMPIRE
Metropolis, India and progress in the colonial imagination John Marriott

FEMALE IMPERIALISM AND NATIONAL IDENTITY
Imperial Order Daughters of the Empire Katie Pickles

SEX, POLITICS AND EMPIRE
A postcolonial geography Richard Phillips

MARRIED TO THE EMPIRE
Gender, politics and imperialism in India, 1883–1947 Mary A. Procida

IMPERIAL PERSUADERS
Images of Africa and Asia in British advertising Anandi Ramamurthy

IMPERIALISM AND MUSIC Britain, 1876–1953 Jeffrey Richards

THE HAREM, SLAVERY AND BRITISH IMPERIAL CULTURE
Anglo-Muslim relations, 1870–1900 Diane Robinson-Dunn

COLONIAL FRONTIERS
Indigenous–European encounters in settler societies ed. Lynette Russell

WEST INDIAN INTELLECTUALS IN BRITAIN ed. Bill Schwarz

MIGRANT RACES
Empire, identity and K. S. Ranjitsinhji Satadru Sen

AT THE END OF THE LINE
Colonial policing and the imperial endgame 1945–80 Georgina Sinclair

THE VICTORIAN SOLDIER IN AFRICA Edward M. Spiers

MARTIAL RACES AND MASCULINITY IN THE BRITISH ARMY, 1857–1914 Heather Streets

THE FRENCH EMPIRE BETWEEN THE WARS
Imperialism, politics and society Martin Thomas

BRITISH CULTURE AND THE END OF EMPIRE ed. Stuart Ward

Engendering whiteness
WHITE WOMEN AND COLONIALISM IN BARBADOS AND NORTH CAROLINA, 1627–1865

Cecily Jones

MANCHESTER UNIVERSITY PRESS
Manchester and New York

distributed exclusively in the USA
by PALGRAVE

Copyright © Cecily Jones 2007

The right of Cecily Jones to be identified as the author of this work has been asserted by her in accordance with the Copyright, Designs and Patents Act 1988.

Published by Manchester University Press
Oxford Road, Manchester M13 9NR, UK
and Room 400, 175 Fifth Avenue, New York, NY 10010, USA
www.manchesteruniversitypress.co.uk

Distributed in the United States exclusively by
Palgrave Macmillan, 175 Fifth Avenue,
New York, NY 10010, USA

Distributed in Canada exclusively by
UBC Press, University of British Columbia, 2029 West Mall,
Vancouver, BC, Canada V6T 1Z2

British Library Cataloguing-in-Publication Data is available

Library of Congress Cataloging-in-Publication Data is available

ISBN 978 0 7190 6433 3 paperback

First published by Manchester University Press in hardback 2007

This paperback edition first published 2014

The publisher has no responsibility for the persistence or accuracy of URLs for any external or third-party internet websites referred to in this book, and does not guarantee that any content on such websites is, or will remain, accurate or appropriate.

Printed by Lightning Source

CONTENTS

General editor's introduction — vii
Acknowledgements — ix
List of abbreviations — xi

Introduction	1
1 Mapping racial boundaries: gender, race and poor relief in Barbados	13
2 'Worse than [white] men, much worse than the Negroes...': sexuality, labour and poor white women in North Carolina	44
3 'To serve her own desires': white women and property holding in Barbadian plantation society	80
4 'There may be my sphere of usefulness...': the making of a North Carolinian plantation mistress	119
5 White lives, black bodies: Barbadian women and slaveholding	155
6 'She Would Labor Almost Night and Day': white women, property rights and slaveholding in North Carolina	184
Conclusion	217

Bibliography — 226
Index — 233

GENERAL EDITOR'S INTRODUCTION

Studies of white women in colonial societies have unlocked many areas of analysis hitherto closed. Gender is yet another variable in the complex hierarchies of social and economic power that constitute the prime characteristics of multi-ethnic imperial territories. Gendered relationships produce further fields of force in the inflection of authority and influence within both white and black, imperial and indigenous, fractions of such migrant, transplanted and invariably artificial social units. Moreover, despite the obvious and often outrageous privileges of white individuals within such societies, aspects of class divisions were replicated in varying ways across different colonies and continents. Hence, society in each colony needs to be understood in terms of class as well as gender and race, and within this complex mix we also have to observe the operations of elements of miscegenation. There have been a number of highly suggestive analyses of these phenomena in British colonies, including the major unit, the so-called 'Indian Empire'. And, as with so many other aspects of the imperial condition, the patterns and the dynamic of these relationships of gender often reflected back upon the metropolis. Some such studies have already appeared in this series.

But it has been much less common to examine these characteristics in slave-owning societies. In these, the unfree condition of the slaves places white women in further states of tension as the wives of owners, as owners themselves, as nascent entrepreneurs in their own right, and as people to be socially and sexually protected within societies where fear was a notable conditioner of social relations. Moreover, since white women were permitted to slip down the social scale into the condition of 'poor whites', and often did, the position of such disadvantaged females in respect of other whites and of slaves became even more problematical and complex. These nuances of social standing and behaviour are examined with considerable acuteness in this book.

This book's other highly innovative characteristic is to create a comparative study between a colony, North Carolina, which left the British Empire in the 1770s, and Barbados which remained within it throughout the period. Thus additional historical elements are fed into the mix. We have the new legislative arrangements of a state within an emergent and independent federal system and the controversies about the continuation of slavery which were to lead to civil war. On the other hand, we have the enactments of the British Empire in seeking to end the slave trade and, in the 1830s, the institution of slavery itself, albeit through a system of apprenticeship. In each case, efforts to protect the privileges and socio-economic conditions of the whites were even more striking after emancipation almost than before. In each, the position of white women was subjected to much propaganda, legal and political provision, comment in newspapers and in contemporary travel and other

GENERAL EDITOR'S INTRODUCTION

accounts. Indeed, Cecily Jones has produced a notably fresh and enlightening account of these phenomena by isolating case studies and by using a striking range of documents and other sources. Her study offers many pointers to the way in which such research can develop further in the future.

John M. MacKenzie

ACKNOWLEDGEMENTS

This study would truly not have been possible without the generous assistance of a number of grant-making bodies, and the staunch support of very many individuals who have guided and supported me throughout my academic life.

The Economic and Social Research Council provided me with a scholarship, enabling me to fulfil a long-held academic and personal ambition. Generous financial support from the Vice-Chancellor's Discretionary Fund at Goldsmiths College, University of London, made it possible for me to embark on eighteen months' fieldwork in Barbados and North Carolina. Without that assistance, the fieldwork for this study would not have been possible, for it would have entailed a year-long separation from a very precocious pre-teen daughter! Similarly, the A.L.Trust gave generously of their funds and made it possible for my daughter to accompany me to North Carolina. Thanks go also to the Goldsmiths Society, Goldsmiths College, whose financial assistance enabled me to complete the research. At Warwick University the generosity of the Research Development Fund enabled me to return to Barbados to complete some additional research, and the Humanities Research Centre also provided an award to enable publication of this study. The Arts and Humanities Research Council funded a period of study leave from my post at Warwick, allowing me the time and space to turn the thesis into a manuscript.

The fieldwork for this project could not have been completed without the generous assistance of numerous organisations and individuals in both Barbados and North Carolina. In Barbados, Professor Hilary Beckles and his colleagues at the Department of History, University of the West Indies at Cave Hill extended hospitality and support, as well as providing access to libraries, archives and other essential university facilities. Generous thanks also go to the staff of the Barbados Archives in Lazaretto, St Michael, and the staff of the Barbados Museum and Historical Society. Staff in both of these organisations were always unfailingly cheerful and patient as they helped this non-historian to locate and make sense of a bewildering, but fascinating, array of archaic centuries-old documents.

In North Carolina Prof. Jean O'Barr and her colleagues at the Women's Studies Centre, Duke University, welcomed me warmly and extended use of all college facilities to me. The Special Collections Department of the Perkins Library at Duke University offered help and advice to locate materials when, as was often the case, I did not know quite what I was searching for! Grateful thanks also go to the helpful staff at the Southern Historical Collection at the University of North Carolina at Chapel Hill. Other people helped to make the long months of research in Barbados and North Carolina both productive and enjoyable. Special thanks go to Riche Richard who was my enthusiastic guide on a very emotional visit to the Cameron plantation and slave cabins.

ACKNOWLEDGEMENTS

Along the way, I was truly fortunate to have been taken under the wings of some of the most intellectually talented scholars who recognised and nurtured my potential long before it was obvious to me. As an undergraduate student, I was guided by Professor Richard Burton of the School of African and Asian Studies at the University of Sussex who stimulated my passion for the rich histories of the Caribbean region. During my MA studies in the Centre for Race and Ethnic Relations at Warwick University, Professor Annie Phizacklea of the Department of Sociology encouraged me to onwards to pursue a PhD. My doctoral supervisor Dr Caroline Ramazonoglu at Goldsmiths College, University of London, is owed an enormous debt of gratitude; throughout, she believed in me and my project, stayed with me, pushed and prodded me, gave unswerving support, and helped me to retain my sanity when it all got too much. I do not exaggerate when I say that without her unfailing support, I could not have completed my doctoral thesis. Any doctoral candidate would be blessed to have such a wonderfully warm, generous human being possessed of staggering intellectual ability to guide them through the murky seas of postgraduatedom.

Thanks must go to my colleagues at the Centre for Women and Gender Studies, the Department of Sociology at Warwick University, particularly those who covered my teaching commitments while I was on study leave! Professors David Dabydeen and Gad Heuman of the Centre for Caribbean Studies at Warwick University have both mentored and supported me throughout, and to them, and my colleagues in the centre, I owe a great deal.

Many friends – especially Annecka Marshall and Emma Francis – have offered help, advice, strong shoulders to lean on, and kept the white wine flowing well into the night. Hazel Rice, Sharon Clarke and Jonathan Morley gave much needed and much valued help with editing.

Gratitude goes to my family, especially Maxine (especially for giving us Kaylem!!), David Ebanks, Patricia Jones, Eric Jones and Malcolm Jones, and the various assorted members of my large family. Sadly, my brother Adrian died unexpectedly before the book was completed and it is to him that I dedicate this study. Finally, deepest respect and gratitude to Ian Jones, whose unstinting love and support has sustained me throughout.

LIST OF ABBREVIATIONS

BA	Barbados Archives
BMHS	Barbados Museum and Historical Society
NCA	North Carolina Archives
NCDAH	North Carolina Department of Archives and History
SHC, UN-CH	Southern Historical Collection, University of North Carolina, Chapel Hill

Introduction

How did the institution of African slavery penetrate and shape the social worlds of white women in the Americas? What *was* the place of white women within these slave-based societies? What forms of power, if any, did white women exercise? How did the nexus of gender, race and class relations structure their material existences? What strategies did white women deploy in managing their subjugated female status? What did whiteness as a lived identity mean in a racially ordered society? How was whiteness maintained, and what became of women who transgressed the norms of white society? How did whiteness shape the material experiences of white women of different social classes? This work argues that despite the brisk pace of recent scholarship on the complexity of gender as a key organising principle of slave-based plantation societies, there remains a chasm in our understanding of the complex diversity of white women's lives in such societies. More specifically, it seeks to prompt greater reflection on whiteness as a historically constructed racial identity in general, and the gendering of white racial identity in particular. In short, *Engendering Whiteness* seeks to understand the overlapping imbrication of whiteness in shaping the diverse material realities of women of European origin in the English-speaking slave-based societies of the Caribbean island of Barbados, and North Carolina in the American South, between the seventeenth and nineteenth centuries.

Historians of gender and slavery in the United States have significantly enriched our knowledge of the texture of women's everyday worlds in plantation societies of the Southern slaveholding states.[1] Recovering the diverse histories of white women in the colonial Caribbean has, however, proceeded at a sloth-like pace, and white women in the Caribbean colonial context represent one of the least analysed and least understood social categories in the Caribbean colonial world. Given their social proximity to white males, and their membership of and integration into the dominant colonising group, the limited scholarly attention paid to white women in the plantation societies of the Caribbean is striking. Of course, the histories of other groups of women, both colonised and coloniser, remain underresearched. Relatively little is known of the histories and experiences of indigenous Carib or Arawak women, or of later entrants such as Chinese, Indian, or Syrian women on the Caribbean colonial scene. Only recently have historians turned their minds to understanding and explaining the different experiences of the ethnically diverse groups of women who arrived in the Caribbean, either voluntarily or forcibly, in the later colonial era.[2] Newly awakened interest in the gendered experiences of black and white women in the slaveholding societies of the Caribbean, and the continuing proliferation of academic treatises on white women of the Southern slaveholding states of the American mainland, has forged new ways of thinking about colonialism, which we can no longer read as a purely patriarchal, masculine, and gender-blind venture.[3] White European males were indeed the dominant actors driving forward the vehicle of colonialism, but this was a venture that implicated European women at various levels. Especially critical to the reproduction of white male hegemonic rule of the New World colonial societies was the reconfiguration of traditional gender relations and norms, a social process that affected the lives of women and men, white and black, both at home and abroad. Though there is little evidence to suggest that white women acted as a political motivating force driving colonial policy, as a group they were nevertheless important determinants of Britain's success as a colonial and imperial power. In the Caribbean, as in the slaveholding states of the deep South, white women were integral to the formation and development of Britain's colonies. As the biological reproducers of whiteness, they were critical to the maintenance and reproduction of the cultural boundaries of 'whiteness'; and their active agency as slave-owners and participants in diverse sectors of the plantation economy contributed in significant ways to the economic reproduction of slave societies. White women in Barbados and North Carolina aligned themselves with a dominant white male plantocracy, whose social power and authority was legitimated by a patriarchal, racist ideology. In these rigidly stratified societies, where gendered and racialised identity functioned as key organising principles, their social location within the dominant white group afforded all white women, regardless of their class position, not only a privileged status, but also modes of power over others. To deny the privilege and agency of white colonial women as autonomous social actors is to elide the complexity of power relations that structured the material existence of all those enmeshed in the slave societies of the New World.

Power, as postmodern theorists have recognised, is complex and multifaceted. Nancy Hartsock argues that 'any effort to change the subjugated status of women requires a consideration of the nature of power'. In doing so, Hartsock challenges the utility of associating power with male dominance. She suggests that rather than theorising power simply in terms of the ways in which it is used to subjugate women, such theories need to consider also women's 'capacities, abilities and strengths'.[4] African-American feminist bell hooks similarly argues that the exercise of strength by working-class women, for instance, was not previously acknowledged by white feminists to be an exercise of the forms of power valued in society; that is, dominating power.[5] In the same way, I suggest that failure to recognise and acknowledge the capacities and abilities of white colonial women to exercise forms of power has meant that particular forms of 'women's power' have been obscured and remain untheorised. I think, then, that hooks's comments make it possible for us to understand why white women within plantation societies came to be assigned 'victim' status within the historiographies of North Carolina and Barbadian plantation society. If power is conceptualised as the exercise of male dominance within male-dominated institutions, it becomes easy to ignore or overlook the fact that white women within plantation societies also possessed and exercised not only dominating power and control, but also race- and gender-specific forms of power.

These considerations undermine and problematise extant dichotomised conceptualisations of white women as either marginal actors in the processes of colonialism, or passive victims of a patriarchal male-dominated expansionist venture. Instead, it might be more analytically fruitful to interrogate the ways in which white women could be simultaneously socially positioned within plantation societies as both victims and agents. Colonial patriarchy was never so unyielding as to deny white female autonomy entirely; the rights of all white women to exercise authority over all black persons was enshrined in colonial law. I argue, then, that the privileges of whiteness simultaneously constrained white women while allowing them the means to counter their gender subordination.

Whiteness as lived experience that is both gendered and racialised is the underlying theme that runs through this book. The nascent field of critical white studies has stimulated considerable interest in whiteness as a historically and socially contingent racialised identity.[6] Despite its discursive and analytical instability, 'race' served in colonial societies as the most potent basis for individual identity, and white racial identity represented the dominant racial and cultural identity against which all others were measured. But few historians have explored whiteness as a socially constructed racialised identity, and the effect has been to reproduce traditions of knowledge that problematise blackness, while taking whiteness as an unproblematic, naturally occurring category. Richard Dyer highlights what he refers to as the pervasive 'non-racing' of white people, a device that serves to constitute white people as 'just people', a taken-for-granted category bereft of and beyond racial meaning. In contrast, other people are 'something else', always subjected to and identified through perceived racial definitions, as reflected in the naming of racialised identities (e.g. the black slave vs. the [non-racialised] slave master or mistress). Because whiteness is left unnamed, it is represented as the normal human condition, which 'alone defines normal humanity and fully inhabits it'.[7] Frankenberg has similarly pointed to traditions of race theorising that problematise blackness as a subjective identity while ignoring the potency of whiteness in shaping white lives.[8] She refers to the cumulative experiences that shape white identities and realities as 'whiteness'. Whiteness, she argues, has a set of linked conditions. 'First, whiteness is a location of structural advantage, of race privilege. Second, it is a "standpoint", a place from which white people look at others, and at society. Third, whiteness refers to a set of cultural practices that are usually unmarked and unnamed.'[9] Frankenberg argues that as blackness is socially constructed and shaped by a set of material and discursive repertoires, so too is whiteness, though the latter is rendered an invisible category. In rejecting the notion of an essential whiteness, Frankenberg also points to the historicity of whiteness, since the modes of lived whiteness are subject to historical, social, political and economic processes. That whiteness can no longer retain its cloak of invisibility is clear, and the scholarly deconstruction of whiteness has revealed the complex manoeuvres involved in staking secure claims to whiteness. Noel Ignatiev and Theodore Allen, for instance, have respectively argued that the Irish immigrants in America became white only through labour struggles which entailed the displacing of blacks from their formerly held positions in the labour market.[10] The emergence of white studies as an academic paradigm at the end of the twentieth century has been received with equal measures of suspicion and acclaim. Though not without some reservations, I welcome critical inquiries into whiteness for I share with other theorists interested in race the conviction that whiteness must be exposed, recognised and theorised as a historically and socially constructed identity. My intention is to examine the consequences of this critical shift for understanding white women's positions within

INTRODUCTION

the colonising enterprises of the seventeenth to nineteenth centuries. I draw heavily on the problematic category of 'whiteness' as a key theoretical concept to explore tensions between the social significance of women as biological reproducers of the white race – and hence also of the state of freedom – and their potential to dilute whiteness through sexual relations with black men. As will be seen, poor white women in Barbados and North Carolina were defined in ways at variance with constructions of elite white womanhood. Poor white women had to some extent to 'prove' their claims to whiteness if they were to be allowed to retain and enjoy the privileges of that racial identification.

The central argument of this study proposes that white women were integral to the construction and reproduction of whiteness within plantation society. Whatever privileges and benefits white women derived from slavery were linked to the condition of their perceived whiteness. In both Barbados and North Carolina, no white woman regardless of class status was legally denied access to slave labour or the right to own property. Thus whiteness in both North Carolina and Barbados involved a set of political and exclusionary practices. And yet, the very 'naturalness' of that whiteness and its attendant privileges was never questioned by white women, and their personal writings convey little sense of introspection as to what it meant to be a white individual, implicated in the [re]production of racist discourses, practices and structures. As Catherine Hall has pointed out, white women and men experience their gender and race, class status and sexual identities through the lens of race just as black men and women do. The difference, though, is that while black has been a signifier of subjection, white has been a signifier of dominance, and the dominant rarely reflect on their dominance in the ways that the subjected reflect on their subjection.[11] bell hooks underscores Hall's argument with the observation that black people in the US have always reflected on whiteness as a symbol of terror, while white people themselves have imbued whiteness with goodness.[12]

Engendering Whiteness has as its focus the multiplicities of white female experiences and identities in colonial societies; gendered analyses of plantation societies tend to be of the 'plantation mistress' genre, leaving unexamined questions of social class in the shaping of women's lives and identities in the Caribbean colonial context. Concepts of whiteness, womanhood and class cannot be studied in isolation. They are grounded and made meaningful in specific histories, cultures, ideologies and discursive practices, with a variety of struggles to regulate boundaries and to establish difference and dominance. White women have their own histories through being variously positioned in relation to struggles over 'who is white?', and through relations between races, classes and genders. They are conceptualised by how they are regulated in law and in everyday practices. *Engendering Whiteness* attempts to establish how far the white women of Barbados and North Carolina shared common social positions, and in so doing, disrupts the invisibility of white-as-norm. Despite comprising a majority among the white population, poor women constitute a liminal and invisible category within Caribbean historiography. Their continued absence from this historiography is puzzling because, for a variety of reasons, poor white women figured largely in the concerns of colonial authorities, particularly in an era when authorities struggled to demarcate boundaries around the 'white race'.

Neither society could envisage or easily accommodate sexually autonomous white womanhood. Perhaps it is in the arena of sexuality, its regulation and the prohibitions and proscriptions against interracial sex, that the most striking commonalities may be most clearly discerned. While ostensibly proscriptions against interracial sex sought to control the sexual freedoms of *all* individuals, regulation and control of white female sexuality was at all times in both societies the foremost concern. I begin in Chapter 1 by analysing the mechanisms through which the Barbadian authorities strove to regulate and control the sexual freedoms of poor white Barbadian women, whose perceived sexual and social unruliness distinguished them as a potential threat to white hegemony. I argue that the dispensation of poor relief to indigent white women and their daughters could function as a crucial element in the Barbadian authorities' efforts to draw boundaries around whiteness, by imposing stringent qualifications on those women who could be considered deserving of poor relief and exacting sanctions against those women who had, or were perceived to have, transgressed white norms of acceptable social and sexual behaviour. Vestry records and court transcripts are used to explore the interrelations between gender, class and sexuality in the context of Barbadian and North Carolinian slaveholding societies. They also reveal the possibilities of resistance and challenge by poor white women whose social class and socio-sexual behaviour led to their constitution as 'not quite white' women. These themes are further pursued in Chapter 2 which reveals corresponding concerns of North Carolina's authorities over interracial sex; again, the unruly sexuality of poor white women was identified as potentially disruptive of the white social order, and poor white women were made the targets of the Carolina Assembly's punitive legislation intended to prohibit interracial sexual liaisons. Taken together, these chapters reveal the complex intersectionality of gender, race and class on white women's lives in the specific context of slave-based societies.

White women's participation within the economic sphere of colonial societies is of greater significance than has been previously recognised or understood. A critical analysis of the nature and extent of white women's economic functions serves to undermine prevailing representations of white women as an unproductive category reliant on and benefiting from the productive labour of enslaved peoples. Their vital productive and reproductive labour helped create and sustain new societies in practically every single British colony in the Caribbean and on the North American mainland. Despite a patriarchal ethos that insisted on the ideal of dependent womanhood, white women of all social classes in Barbados and North Carolina engaged in a variety of economic pursuits, from waged labour to property investment – that is, property in all its forms, including human bodies. As I argue in Chapter 3, property ownership was imbued with real and symbolic significance for white women of all social classes, and an analysis of property deeds, premarriage contracts, court transcripts and probated wills reveals the diversity of their interests in land, estates, dwellings, and other forms of property both real and personal. Through their investments in property, white women helped to sustain the plantation slave economy in a variety of ways that have hitherto gone unnoticed.

Had they been able to view each other across the Atlantic divide, the white women of Barbados and North Carolina would no doubt have recognised striking similarities in their day-to-day lives, not least their shared confinement to, and responsibility for, the private world of the household and the attendant provision of care, nurture and comfort to its inhabitants young and old, white and black, free and unfree. United by their gender, Barbadian and North Carolinian white women were second-class citizens in patriarchal societies that demanded adherence to ideologies of ideal white womanhood erected on female dependency on, and subjection to, white male authority, constraining restrictions bounding their private lives, and exclusion from the public sphere. Slaveholding mistresses in Barbados and North Carolina wrestled with the problems of managing recalcitrant domestic slaves, worried about their children's education, and fretted about the sexual excesses of their husbands. The omnipresent fear of slave rebellions brought constant unease. But what did it mean to be a plantation mistress and owner of human souls? To paraphrase Simone de Beauvoir, white women were not *born* plantation mistresses, but *became* mistresses – owners of enslaved human property. How then, did individual women become plantation mistresses? How did such women understand their role within the system of slavery? How did slavery shape white women's own sense of self, and their wider understandings about the society and system of which they were a part, and of the various categories of people – free and unfree, poor and elite, white and black, male and female – around them? Chapter 4 charts the gradual transformation of Sarah Hicks Williams, a young Northern-born woman and supporter of abolitionism into a staunch defender of Southern slavery. The journey from newly married, idealistic bride to mature Southern matron took place against the backdrop of Sarah's own reluctant acceptance of her role as the mistress of her husband's extensive plantation holdings. Sarah's story demonstrates the significance of slavery as a powerful determinant in the shaping of her sense of racialised and gendered identity. From yet another perspective, Sarah's story is revealing of the contradictions of the Southern ideology of white womanhood. Forced by her husband's frequent absences to take on the reins of plantation management, Sarah struggled to conform to Southern ideals of true womanhood. Yet, the onerous and unpleasant responsibilities of managing a plantation household and its community of enslaved peoples exposed to her the impossibility of conformity to that model.

In a now oft-cited comment, the late Jamaican historian and pioneer of Caribbean gender history Lucille Mair summarised the different roles of women in the colonial Caribbean with the acerbic observation that 'black women produced, brown women served and white women consumed'.[13] A pithy comment indeed, but it does not fully convey the diversity of material situations experienced by women whether white, brown or black. To be sure, most, if not all enslaved black women were integrated into the productive processes of plantation economies, and numerous brown women, either voluntarily or by coercion, serviced the sexual needs of white males (as did black women). However, although a good many white women led leisurely and desultory unproductive existences, countless others formed the ranks of producers and servers. While Mair's seminal study of gender and slavery in Caribbean plantation society unequivocally represents one of the most important studies of its genre, its representation of white colonial women as a parasitical category requires critical reappraisal and qualification. In Barbados and throughout the Americas, *some* white women produced, *some* white women served and *some* white women also consumed. Women of the elite planter class were locked out of formal economic production by culturally bound ideologies of womanhood that located women's place firmly within the domestic space, but the involvement of plantation mistresses in the

INTRODUCTION

production processes of their plantations represented significant, but rarely acknowledged, contributions to the wider economy. Women of the poorer white classes could rarely rely solely on the economic support of white males, and they too were left with little alternative but to seek waged labour, or to venture into perhaps less savoury and illicit income-generating activities such as prostitution. As the previous discussion of white women's relationships with and to property reveals, numerous white women were active participants in the Barbadian slave economy, and were willing to defend their rights to access and own human property. Many among them refused to accept that the pursuit of wealth remained the prerogative of white males, and strove to secure and improve their own economic circumstances. In Chapter 5, I continue to explore Barbadian women's property interests, though here the focus is primarily on women as slaveholders.

As in Barbados, property ownership provided the basis of wealth, power and individual status in antebellum North Carolina, and like their Barbadian counterparts Southern women, especially when married, struggled to assert their rights to independently own and enjoy property without intervention. Chapter 6 explores the significance of property ownership as a key dimension in shaping gendered social relations in the South, how those social relations structured white women's access to and ownership of property, and in particular, white women's ownership of slaves as property.

Readers may well query the comparative perspective that frames this text. An analysis of aspects of women's lives in North Carolina and Barbados – their sexual subordination and regulation, their roles within production and reproduction, and the limits and nature of white women's access to, and ownership of, property – will provide a comparative framework that might reveal important connections and divergences in the lives of white women in these societies. Though Barbados and North Carolina developed along different trajectories, it seems to me that there are ample historical and intellectual grounds for comparison. Barbados was identified as an appropriate case study through which to explore the problems posed by the specificity of white women's power because although its history as a colonial slave-based plantation society has been well documented, relatively little is known about those white European women who were part of the colonial enterprise, and who were vital to the development and social reproduction of the creole Barbadian plantation society. Barbados provides a suitable site of comparison with the Southern state of North Carolina because of the relatively high ratio of resident white women in both these societies. The existence of strong historical ties provides a link to both societies, and also, I believe, should have produced some areas of structural and institutional continuities in the experiences of white women who made these colonies their permanent home. For all these reasons, a comparative analysis of both these societies seems appropriate. Whilst these two societies may not be typical of plantation societies elsewhere, or at other historical moments, they do provide a productive basis for a critical analysis of the intersection of race, class and gender, and of gender and race relationships as forms of power relationships, at particular historical junctures. The analysis I offer should provide a useful basis for comparative investigation elsewhere. Through explaining both similarities and differences, the specificities and the commonalities of women's social positions and relations can be clarified. Although North Carolina forms the primary centre of analysis for the investigation of antebellum Southern white female experiences, I have on occasion stepped beyond state boundaries to illustrate certain experiences which I believe were common to all white women in the Southern states.

As Bonnie Anderson and Judith Zinsser state, European women have not, despite ideologies of female inferiority and subjugation, been 'victims' of history. In Barbados and North Carolina, 'unable to see beyond their culture's attitudes, they [mastered] the strategies of those in subordinate positions: manipulating, pleasing, enduring, surviving'.[14] At different historical moments some white women dominated, controlled, and disciplined others. Each of these aspects of the exercise of power may be used to illuminate both the specificity of white female power in colonial slave-based plantation societies, and the social differences between women. By rejecting representations of white women as mere victims of male power and authority, it is possible to uncover their agency as legally free, economic actors; as women who struggled daily to define the parameters of their own lives, and in doing so exposed the limits of patriarchal authority.

This work ultimately raises more questions than I am able to provide answers to. Many aspects of the white colonial female experience remain undocumented, largely because of the limited nature of first-hand testimonies by and about white women in the colonial world. This is especially the case in Barbados, where there is a virtual absence of such narratives. Through a critical analysis of public and private documentation, including property deeds, probated wills, court transcripts, women's private journals and correspondence, and slave narratives, I have tried to reveal the complex modes in which gender, race and class relations intertwined to define the contours of white women's lives within the slave societies of Barbados and North Carolina. The historical timeframe spans three centuries: in the case of Barbados, from English settlement in 1627 until the emancipation

INTRODUCTION

of the slaves in the British colonies in 1838; in North Carolina, principally the period between 1730 and the end of the American Civil War in 1865, which culminated in the emancipation of enslaved Black Americans.[15] The study does not, however, pretend to be a chronological history of women in these societies.

Notes

1 Beginning in the 1970s, the challenges by feminist historians of women and gender history for the inclusion of women into the historiography of slavery stimulated immense interest in white and black women's experiences of slavery in the American South. This rich body of scholarship includes Anne Firor Scott, *The Southern Lady: From pedestal to politics, 1830–1930* (Chicago: University of Chicago Press, 1970); Catherine Clinton, *The Plantation Mistress: Woman's world in the Old South* (New York: Pantheon Books, 1982); Deborah Gray White, *Ar'n't I a Woman?: Female Slaves in the plantation South* (New York: Norton, 1985); Jacqueline Jones, *Labor of Love, Labor of Sorrow: Black women, work, and the family from slavery to the present* (New York: Basic Books, 1985); Elizabeth Fox-Genovese, *Within the Plantation Household: Black and white women of the Old South* (Chapel Hill: University of North Carolina Press, 1988); Victoria E. Bynum, *Unruly Women: The politics of social and sexual control in the Old South* (Chapel Hill: University of North Carolina Press, 1992); Patricia Morton (ed.), *Discovering the Women in Slavery: Emancipating perspectives on the American past* (Athens, GA: University of Georgia Press, 1996); Jennifer Morgan, *Laboring Women: Reproduction and gender in New World slavery* (Philadelphia: University of Pennsylvania Press, 2004).
2 Scholarship on Caribbean women in general remains severely undeveloped, though in recent years numerous historical, political and economic studies on women of African origin have helped to undermine the gender blindness of Caribbean scholarship. Some of this scholarship is now attending to the experiences of Indo-Caribbean peoples in general and Indo-Caribbean women in particular. See for instance Rhoda Reddock, 'Indian Women and Indentureship in Trinidad and Tobago, 1845–1917: Freedom Denied', *Caribbean Quarterly* 32 (1986); Verene Shepherd, *Maharani's Misery: Narratives of a passage from India to the Caribbean* (Kingston: University of the West Indies Press, 2002). There remains a dire need for comparative work on Chinese, Syrian, Jewish and other non-European Caribbean women.
3 See for instance Nupur Chaudhuri and Margaret Strobel (eds), *Western Women and Imperialism: Complicity and resistance* (Bloomington: Indiana University Press, 1992); Anne McClintock, *Imperial Leather: Race, gender and sexuality in the colonial contest* (London: Routledge, 1995); Ruth Roach Pierson and Nupur Chaudhuri with the assistance of Beth McCauly (eds), *Nation, Empire, and Colony: Historicizing gender and race* (Bloomington: Indiana University Press, 1998); Clare Midgley (ed.), *Gender and Imperialism* (Manchester: Manchester University Press, 1998).
4 Nancy Hartsock, 'Foucault on Power: A theory for women?', in Linda J. Nicholson (ed.), *Feminism/Postmodernism* (London: Routledge, 1990), p. 158.
5 bell hooks, *Feminist Theory: From margin to centre* (Boston: South End Press, 1984), p. 89.
6 bell hooks, 'Representations of Whiteness in the Black Imagination' in *Killing Rage: Ending racism* (London: Penguin, 1995), p. 45. See also: Ruth Frankenberg, *White Women, Race Matters: The social construction of whiteness* (London: Routledge, 1993); Richard Dyer, *Whiteness* (London: Routledge,1997).
7 Dyer, *Whiteness*, p. 9.
8 Frankenberg, *White Women, Race Matters*, p. 7.
9 Ibid., p. 1.

10 Noel Ignatiev, *How the Irish Became White* (London: Routledge, 1996); Theodore W. Allen, *The Invention of the White Race, Vol. 1* (London: Verso, 1994).
11 Catherine Hall, *White, Male and Middle Class* (Cambridge: Polity Press, 1992).
12 hooks, 'Representations of Whiteness', pp. 31–50.
13 Lucille Mathurin Mair, 'A Historical Study of Women in Jamaica from 1655–1844' (PhD, University of the West Indies, Mona, Jamaica, 1974).
14 Bonnie S. Anderson and Judith P. Zinsser, *A History of Their Own: Women in Europe from prehistory to the present*, Vol. 2 (London: Penguin Books, 1988), introduction, xiv.
15 I use the terms 'Black' and black in two different senses. The capitalised 'Black' refers to non-white women and men of African origin who are, or have been, involved in current political struggles around 'race/racism', and to refer to Black women who identify themselves as feminists. In this sense then 'Black' signifies a political identity. Conversely, I use the term 'black' to refer to enslaved peoples of African origin. During the seventeenth and eighteenth centuries, Black had not yet been employed to refer to the collective political experience that it has come to symbolise since the civil rights movement of the 1960s. Of course, it might be argued that African slaves did not view themselves as 'black', but as African, or even Barbadian or American or even creole. However the concepts of 'black' and 'blackness' were clearly articulated within the related concept of 'Negro', a term used to designate all people of West African origins. In the same way, I use the term 'white' in a general sense to denote membership of the European group, except where the term 'White' is used to denote those women of European origin who struggled politically for white rights. The terms mulatto, brown and coloured, used to refer to individuals of mixed ancestral heritage, are also historical constructions and are also open to contestation. In this text, I have deployed the terms as they appear in public and private documents.

CHAPTER ONE

Mapping racial boundaries: gender, race and poor relief in Barbados

On 27 February 1799, the gentlemen of the Vestry Committee of the northern Barbadian parish of St John convened for the monthly meeting of the parish's Poor Relief Board. As St John was one of Barbados's poorest parishes, its Poor Relief Board received numerous claims from parishioners too old, weak, sick, disabled or poor to support themselves. Deciding just which parishioners were deserving of public assistance was an important part of the Board's remit. Having discussed and decided each individual claim to their satisfaction, the assembled gentlemen turned their attention to the next item on their agenda: a proposal received from Sir Phillip Gibbes, a prominent and wealthy Barbadian. Seven years earlier, in an effort to provide some form of education and training for the many young daughters of poor white families in the parish, the Poor Relief Board had established the St John School for Female Industry, a vocational institution that aimed to provide a rudimentary education, followed by a period of apprenticeship for young white girls. The St John initiative appeared to have been the first of its kind in Barbados, and likely attracted much interest from among public-spirited Barbadians concerned with the welfare of the island's poor whites.[1] A few weeks previously, Sir Phillip Gibbes had sent the Poor Relief Board a letter in which he conveyed his enthusiastic approval of the Board's innovative female vocational educational scheme. As a show of his support for 'this useful establishment' Gibbes proposed to disburse a marriage portion of £50 to the first four 'graduates' to successfully complete their apprenticeship. Gibbes stressed, however, that his gift was to be offered as 'a reward and recompense for good behaviour' on the part of the bride-to-be; moreover, he attached a further condition: that the marriage portion be paid only in the event that the intended marriage received the wholehearted 'approbation of the vestry'. The gentlemen of the vestry could hardly refuse Gibbes's 'liberal and handsome' offer, knowing all too well that few, if any, among the parish's poor white families could afford to provide their daughters with such a generous wedding gift. Indeed, £50 sterling represented a vast sum – far more than the average yearly income of a poor white family.[2] Thus, the Board lost no time in accepting their benefactor's gift.

Eighteen months later, in June 1800, Leah Howard was chosen as the first beneficiary of Gibbes's largesse. The school's headmistress, Mrs Farrell, enthusiastically recommended Leah to the vestry. In her view, Leah had been a model student; she had successfully completed a four-year apprenticeship, and gone on to serve the school for a further four years as a domestic servant. Now, after eight years' dutiful and industrious service to the school that had given her an education, Leah had found a suitor and intended to marry. The Board agreed unanimously with Mrs Farrell's assessment of Leah's 'good and decent behaviour', and moved that she deserved to be 'fairly and justly rewarded'.[3]

There can be little doubt that the vestrymen interpreted Gibbes's offer as evidence of the worthiness of their scheme. Eighteenth-century Barbados afforded poor whites of either gender few waged labour opportunities and, for many, Poor Relief represented their sole means of survival. Presumably, the gentlemen of St John's Vestry intended that their vocational education and apprenticeship scheme would enhance the labour market prospects of young poor white women struggling to survive in an uncertain economy. By equipping young women with the means to learn a trade or occupation, they hoped to reduce the numbers of parishioners dependent on Poor Relief. This is one possible reading of the vestry's rationale for the School's founding. I am proposing, however, another interpretation of their motives, which situates it in a more general concern with the sexual and social freedoms of young, poor, white women in a racially ordered society.

As a poor white woman, Leah Howard's name survives in Barbadian records only because her good behaviour and industriousness brought her to the attention of the Vestry Committee, who with much satisfaction recorded the conferral of her marriage portion in the vestry's Minute Books. But for Sir Phillip Gibbes's philanthropic gesture, Leah Howard, in common with poor white women throughout history, would almost certainly have lived and died without leaving any visible traces of her existence. Yet, brief though they are, the elements of Leah's life revealed to us in the Minute Books – her apprenticeship, her labour as a domestic servant, the reward for a life well lived, and her impending marriage – offer much that is of significance. They may reveal a great deal about the material experiences of poor young white women in eighteenth-century Barbados, and the social class and gender relations that structured their lives. More than this, they offer insight into the processes through which Barbadian authorities constructed and preserved the boundaries of whiteness. This was a period in which dichotomous ideologies of race predicated on beliefs of white superiority gained ground within white society, sharpening race distinctions and making more rigid the social and sexual boundaries between white and black populations. Ruling-class whites deployed perceived racial differences as a means of imposing and strengthening their hegemonic dominance and control of Barbadian society. The maintenance of social distance between whites and blacks required that sexual relations became a matter for regulation. Barbadian legislators stopped short of enacting legislation against interracial marriages, as happened on other colonies, but sexual relations between white and black were rigidly policed. This is not to suggest that sexual relations across racial lines did not occur – indeed, while publicly voicing their opposition to interracial sexual relations, white males throughout the colonial Americas routinely exploited the sexuality of enslaved black women.

At issue was not so much the control of white male sexuality, but the regulation of sexual relations between white *women* and black men, whether free or enslaved. Moreover, patriarchal white male anxieties over the possibilities of sexual relations between white women and black men, and the strategies they deployed to prevent such unions, were arguably directed not so much towards the women of their own class but – for reasons which will become clear – were instead focused on limiting the socio-sexual behaviour of poor white women. Existing on the margins of white society, poor white women represented a potentially threatening category whose socio-sexual behaviour, if left unchecked, could seriously undermine and disrupt the ideologies and practices of the hegemonic white ruling patriarchy.

Critical to the process of regulating poor white female sexuality was the dispensation of Poor Relief. Though ostensibly serving the primary function of providing assistance to indigent whites, Poor Relief also served to maintain socio-sexual boundaries between whites and blacks, while at the same time keeping poor whites within the domain of whiteness. Although all women in Barbados, black, coloured and white, free or unfree, were subject to white male patriarchal authority, poor white women in particular bore the brunt of the regulatory measures of authority in its struggles to construct and police the boundaries of an emerging white identity. These measures included efforts to produce and maintain white racial purity, through controlling the socio-sexual behaviour of poor white women by precluding sexual relationships with black males.

ENGENDERING WHITENESS

The poor whites of Barbados

Variously known as 'red-legs', 'red-shanks' or 'ecky-beckies', the poor white populations of the Caribbean have rarely attracted the attention of historians; the assertion that the discipline of history has been, and continues to reflect, the agency of great and mighty white males may appear to be the weary repetition of a tired old feminist mantra, but it nevertheless remains a reality that, with few exceptions, the world's poor are rarely acknowledged as social actors who make history rather than merely responding to historical events. Caribbean historiography has been no less guilty in representing the major distinctions and social relations of Caribbean slave societies as a dialectic between the plantocracy and enslaved Africans. Until fairly recently, the region's poor whites, who constituted a majority within the white minority, have remained within the historiography a liminal group on the borders of white society, and on the margins of scholarship.[4] Most English-speaking islands witnessed the emergence of this class during the era of colonial plantation slavery, though, perhaps with the exception of Barbados, the poor white community remained numerically limited.[5] The Barbadian census of 1834 reveals an estimated 8,000 poor whites, accounting for over half the total white population of 12,797.[6] Barbados's poor whites were for the most part descendants of indentured servants who made up the bulk of the plantation labour force before the widespread introduction of African slavery. By the mid-seventeenth century, Barbadian planters had began to appreciate the economic advantages of unfree labour, and had largely abandoned the policy of white indentured servitude. As the importation of enslaved Africans rapidly increased, the economic fortunes of the now freed servants severely declined, as most were swiftly displaced from the plantation economy and urban labour markets. Over time, the poor whites developed as a distinct socio-economic category, their white skin the only form of social capital they possessed.

Rather than endure increasing poverty and social marginalisation, the more entrepreneurial among the white poor emigrated either to neighbouring colonies or to the North American mainland. A smaller proportion returned to their homes of origin, leaving behind those either unwilling or unable to carve out new lives elsewhere. Some were fortunate to secure employment as labourers, road and bridge builders, domestic servants, needlewomen or plantation overseers. Others eked out existences close to starvation in the less fertile and marginal lands of the eastern rural parishes, cultivating small plots of land on which they grew subsistence produce. Any surplus produce could be exchanged, bartered or sold in the thriving markets of

Bridgetown and Speightstown. Yet others survived by fishing, hunting game, or working as boatmen, while the numerous taverns and inns that lined the seafront of these port towns employed some men and women as porters, cooks, chamber-maids and serving staff.

The displacement of white servants from the plantations had significant repercussions for poor white women. Many had entered Barbados as plantation labourers, but now enslaved African women had taken their places in the fields. Still, a few waged labour opportunities remained open to white women, both on and off the plantations. Planters employed poor white women as nurses, midwives, housekeepers, washerwomen and needlewomen, while other women travelled the island's roads hawking baskets of ribbons, needles, candles, and a variety of trinkets and sundry household items. And of course, the illicit sectors provided a livelihood for many other women; Hilary Beckles has suggested that many ended up as prostitutes and madams in the island's burgeoning seaport sex industries.[7]

Responding to their abject penury, the Barbadian Assembly endeavoured to create waged labour opportunities for poor whites. Various schemes were mooted to alleviate their misery; a 1770 Act of Assembly attempted to preserve certain occupations for whites, who faced increasing competition from free coloureds. Among these restricted occupations was huckstering, a common mode of petty trading. Hucksters ranged the island selling a variety of small goods, food produce and household wares. The Assembly sought to restrict the trade of huckster to whites by forcing free coloureds to acquire licences before they could engage in trade. The success of this Act must have been limited, for it was overturned in 1799 when it was determined that all hucksters, regardless of colour, were henceforth required to obtain licences before trading, thus in one stroke removing a trading advantage for whites. The consequence of this easing of legislation must have been particularly severe for poor white women, for huckstering was a predominantly gendered occupation conducted primarily by women. Successive governments embarked on a range of employment creation schemes for poor whites, such as road, fort and bridge building projects, which provided work for some skilled poor white males, and a limited number of women. One woman, known only as Sarah, received over £16 for her 'hard work' while employed as a labourer on a fort construction scheme. Another woman, Anne Wade, a slave-owner, successfully tendered a contract with the authorities to provide slaves for construction work, for which she received over £57 in payment.[8] But such work-creation schemes were always inadequate, for they could not accommodate the large numbers of unemployed and unskilled poor whites. Moreover, the majority of these schemes appear to have facilitated employment opportunities for white males, rather than white women. In any case, such work was remunerated at abysmally low wages, and only the most skilled among the white poor could afford to include meat in their diets on a regular basis.

Doubtless, many poor whites believed themselves materially more impoverished than enslaved Africans. The latter at least received regular allowances of food and clothing from their owners. Indeed, it was not an uncommon claim that many poor whites were saved from starvation only by the charity of enslaved blacks and free coloureds. A visitor to Barbados noted in 1825 that 'many of the wretched white creoles live on the charity of the slaves, and few people would institute a comparison on the respectability of the two classes. The lower whites of that island are without exception the most degraded, worthless, hopeless race I have ever met with in my life. They are more pressing subjects for legislation than the slaves, were they ten times enslaved.'[9] The visible presence of so many white indigents represented an embarrassment to elite society, yet few thought that the poor whites merited any special attention. Various philanthropists, among them Joshua Steele, attempted to implement schemes to ameliorate the suffering of poor whites, but in the absence of concerted elite support most schemes were doomed to failure. Elite whites rarely displayed any sense of social responsibility towards less fortunate whites, instead rationalising their disinterest with the argument that the abjection of the poor whites stemmed from their own innate laziness. The contempt with which elite whites regarded poor whites was neatly captured by one doctor who was of the opinion that 'there is no lack of inhabitants in Barbados of the labouring classes – I beg their pardon, of the poorer classes, for labour is a disgrace for a white man in all slave countries, where the poorest wretch is ashamed to submit to it'.[10] So long as both elite and poor white continued to adhere to the belief that certain forms of manual labour were beneath the dignity of free white people, regardless of their class, philanthropists would continue to wage an uphill struggle.

Regarded as outcasts from 'respectable' white society, poor whites nevertheless represented an important, if ambiguous, group, not clearly definable as coloniser or colonised, and at the same, not quite white. Elite white society disparaged the poor whites for their unwarranted hubris, dismissing them as a feckless, work-shy and spendthrift group, but they could not afford to ignore them entirely. Conscious of the imperative to secure the racial loyalty of poor whites in order to assure its own security in the event of black uprisings, elite society attempted to harness the physical resources of the poor whites. The 1671 *Act to Prevent Depopulation* of the whites required planters to hire one white male for every enslaved male engaged in a specific trade, and in the urban towns, slave-owners were required to employ one Christian [white] man or boy for every black male worker.[11]

The incorporation of poor white males into the militia reflected a ruling-class strategy to resolve a number of problems confronting the colony. First, the militia provided employment for poor white males; second, their policing presence on the plantations reinforced order and discipline among the enslaved; and third, the measure answered serious concerns about the weakened numerical state of the island's militia, left depleted in the wake of high levels of white male emigration. But a fourth outcome of these measures was to fix poor white males and their families more securely within the community of whiteness. Yet, despite these 'inducements' to poor white loyalty, elite white society could never be assured of the allegiance of poor whites. And in truth, their distrust was not unfounded; in the early days of settlement, disaffected white servants had shown a willingness to forge alliances with enslaved Africans, and more than one poor white/enslaved conspiracy against the plantocracy had been discovered before it could be put into motion. As the ascendancy of 'King Sugar' in the mid-seventeenth century hastened the continued slide into poverty of the poor whites, Barbadian authorities recognised the potential for poor white revolt. Numerically, they provided much-needed defence strength for the white population, but it was never entirely clear whether their presence undermined or strengthened white hegemonic power.[12] To pre-empt rising disaffection among the poor whites, then, the colonial authority sought to ensure that poor whites remained within the community of whites, even if only as liminal figures on the borders of that society.

To a great extent, the ambivalence of elite whites towards their indigent counterparts stemmed from their uncertainty as to the precise quality of 'whiteness' of this underclass. By the late eighteenth century, white Barbadians were vocal participants in transatlantic discourses about the meanings of whiteness, stimulated by wider debates about the identity of white Barbadians and the nature of their political, cultural and economic relationships with Britain. In the midst of these debates, the debased situation of poor whites assumed prominence. In the early nineteenth century John Poyer, a prominent pro-slavery intellectual, argued that the impoverished state of the poor whites indicated their slippage from the white ideal – poor whites were impoverished, for the most part landless, and unable to enjoy the rights of free men (that is, of white men). Poyer understood freedom and its associated economic, legal and social privileges to be the prerogatives of whites, and lamented the growing social mobility of free non-white peoples as potentially destabilising. Poyer therefore proposed a series of measures including the provision of housing and employment for the island's poor whites, a solution that would not only re-establish the relationship between race and economic power, but would 're-whiten' the poor whites, bringing them back within the boundaries of whiteness, while simultaneously re-imposing legal restraints on the power of free non-whites.[13]

Predictably, Poyer's schemes to elevate and rehabilitate poor whites back into the cultural milieu of whiteness met with apathy from elite society, whose attitudes and responses towards white poverty were framed by their views of poor whites as a class of degenerates who had fallen from white grace, and whose very presence threatened to erode white purity. In Poyer's time, white Barbadians had not as yet fully elaborated a refined discourse of degeneracy – this would come to be wholly articulated during the nineteenth century's recourse to 'scientific' racism – but it is possible to read in their responses to the poor whites a nascent, unformed discourse about the potential degenerative powers of poor whites. As David Lambert points out, Barbadian poor whites were certainly discussed, represented and located within a taxonomy of decline and tropicality. The 'redness' so often drawn on to describe their appearance and complexion was certainly suggestive of some kind of aberration from the white racial normative value, while, on the other hand, conflicting representations of poor whites as 'too pale' or 'albino' suggested almost an ethereal, or supernatural, and thus suspect, quality of whiteness.

The origins of 'whiteness'

When seventeenth-century Englishmen and women spoke about themselves, they rarely employed the term 'white' as a self-descriptor. Commonly, they defined their difference to others in terms that suggested their religion, nationality or status; that is, as Christian, English, or free people. This is not to say that English peoples had not already elaborated a language of race. Indeed, historians have demonstrated that although English society in the sixteenth century had little contact with non-whites, English people already employed a grammar of racial difference to attach racialised meanings to the oppositional categories of 'white' and 'black'. Whiteness symbolically represented all that was good – purity, cleanliness, beauty, goodness, virtue and virginity. Increasingly whiteness represented the marker of civility, a superior cultural state. Blackness, by contrast, signified the base underbelly of human life – alluding to the wicked, evil, dirty, debased, vile, and the sinister. Elizabethans displayed a nascent racism in their attitudes to the 'darker' species, regarding Jews, Africans and Moors with suspicion. Prejudice towards darker-skinned peoples existed, but discourses of black inferiority and white superiority had yet to be elaborately articulated. The Elizabethan language of aesthetics was deeply constitutive of the language of 'race' – fair skin represented both complexion *and* physical beauty – and this language was at once racialised and gendered.[14] The adjective 'fair' was multi-layered, speaking not of maleness, for its internal connotations – virginity, purity, cleanliness, goodness – were qualities that described an idealised feminine state; moreover, the term was class-specific, alluding specifically to elite and middle class women, rather than their swarthy-skinned poor sisters. And finally, the ideal of the 'fair woman' was suggestive of the most important of feminine qualities – modesty and sexual morality, attributes perceived to be lacking among poorer women, who in elite imagination represented actual or potential sexual deviants. Hence, the *idea* of fairness was entangled with notions of racialised sexual difference; at one end of the scale, the fair female body represented sexual morality, and at the lower end of the scale the darker black female body symbolised a debased sexuality. More than this, the black female body represented the physical manifestation of innate racial and cultural inferiority of Africans, and served to establish their 'difference' from civilised English society.

Meanings inherent in the concepts of either whiteness or blackness, then, lacked stability for the seventeenth-century English, either 'at home' or 'out there' in the colonies; indeed, the whiteness of some groups of visibly non-black peoples was often brought into question. Categories of Irishness and Jewishness frequently collapsed with 'blackness' in the literature of the early modern period. Thus the internal meanings of the concept of race as it developed within the English language during this era were highly unstable, in the case of both blackness and whiteness. Where, for instance, should Jewish or Irish people be placed along the spectrum of whiteness – if at all? And should the swarthy-skinned Jews or Irish be considered as members of the same race, or did they represent a separate species of humanity? More intricate understandings of race would emerge in the seventeenth century, assisted by the speculative inquiries of Enlightenment philosophers. As colonialism brought Europeans into ever greater contact with the diversity of global humanity – Native Americans, Africans, Chinese – speculation on the perceived natural, biological differences between the racial groupings of the world, and the social and cultural implications of these differences, increased, reaching its zenith in the nineteenth century with the rise of scientific racism.

European travellers throughout the New World were struck by the distinctive appearance of the Native Americans and Africans they encountered. To some extent, the appearance of Native Americans was not perceived as vastly different from their own, but the darker skin colour and physiognomy of Africans seemed suggestive of a fundamentally different species of human being.[15] Not only were English travellers perplexed by the black skins of Africans, but their social and cultural organisations and practices appeared radically different and inferior to English values and modes of social and cultural organisation. Perhaps the most blatant indicator of African difference could be observed in their sexual attitudes and practices, which – in an era when English sexuality was marked by repression – appeared wild, uncontrolled and promiscuous. In particular, the seemingly 'free', unrestrained sexuality of African women went against the grain of English beliefs about, and attitudes towards, the circumspect nature of female sexuality. The very bodies of African women were representative of a state of dangerous and disarrayed female sexuality, when considered against the perceived modest sexual virtuosity of English womanhood. European travellers' accounts of African women's sexuality were especially lurid, if not fantastical. Descriptions of African women's voracious and insatiable sexual appetite, their penchant for devouring male penises, and their flagrant copulation with the primates of the African jungles, fascinated and repulsed English audiences. Jennifer Morgan has cogently demonstrated the modes through which African women's bodies were represented as animalistic, and therefore *literally* beyond the pale and outside the European framework of femininity. African women represented the absolute otherness of Africans in general and women in particular, their very bodies symbolic of the innate cultural and racial differences between white Europeans and black Africans.[16]

Ideas about the meanings of whiteness were not only inflected with notions of class difference, but intersected with ideas about gender and sexual difference. It would be idle to suggest that these associations sprang solely from eighteenth-century discourses, for it is possible to trace within the literature of the early modern period a growing racialisation of white womanhood. That is to say, the rhetoric of gender became entwined with that of race (whiteness), so that the middle-class white female became the personification of whiteness and civility. But representations of the white female were not, however, without complications, and were always contradictory.

White women had long been suspected of embodying 'a dark side' manifested as an inherent dangerous capricious sexuality that, like Mother Nature, had to be tamed and checked, not only for their own individual good, but for the common good; that is, for white humanity and civilisation in general. Only through their subjection and submission to white masculine authority could white women be compelled to restrain their innate 'black other self' in order to realise their authentic selves as white women. This 'darker' nature resided inherently within the bodies of both black and white women, but whereas the body of the white woman contained a 'black side', Europeans conjectured the absence of a 'white side' residing within the non-white female body. African women were thus wholly 'other'.[17] Even if willing to subject themselves to the norms, standards and behaviours of white women, African women could never truly become white. The discursive construction of the 'white' female body is based, therefore, on the construction of a negative 'black' female body. Lorraine O'Grady has argued that

> The female body in the West is not a unitary sign ... on the one side, it is white; on the other, non-white or, prototypically, black. The two bodies cannot be separated, nor can one body be understood in isolation from the other in the West's metaphoric construction of 'woman'. White is what woman is; not-white ... is what she had better not be.[18]

English introspection about the nature of Africans was as much concerned with attempts to understand just what it meant to be white. If blackness represented a debasedness, then surely whiteness must signify the polar opposite? As evidence, Englishmen pointed to the perceived savagery, heathenism and unbridled sexuality of Africans, qualities that contrasted starkly with the orderly, civilised Christian English. Was it possible, they wondered, to establish a direct correlation between skin colour and civility? The answer was a resounding yes, and perhaps no one made this point more forcefully than the Scottish philosopher David Hume, whose 1748 treatise infamously established a supposed linkage between colour, culture and racial superiority. Hume considered 'the negroes and in general all the other species of men ... to be naturally inferior to the whites. There never was a civilised nation of any other complexion than white, nor even any individual eminent either in action or speculation. No ingenious manufacturers among them, no arts, no sciences.'[19] Hume was certainly not alone in voicing these suspicions. From their musings about the essential natures of black people, then, Europeans derived a sense of themselves as white people – as a white race set apart from, and superior in every aspect to, non-white peoples. Thus it was that colonials in the eighteenth-century Caribbean could draw on a belief in their own innate superiority to justify their dominance over enslaved Africans, and to argue further that slavery was in fact a civilising process that would bring savage Africans into modernity.

But if there was consensus that whiteness represented the pinnacle of the human condition, and the white race the most civilised and superior of all humanity, there was less agreement as to just who could be defined as 'white'. Hume's assertion of the superiority of whiteness was in some ways ironic, for in the eyes of the English not all whites were equally white, and Hume's fellow Scots, along with the Irish and the Welsh, embodied a quality of whiteness that was less certain than was English whiteness. Indeed, some historians have suggested that it was the Irish who were first invoked as a paradigm of inferiority. Ireland had, after all, been England's first colony, inhabited by people the English regarded as primitive and barbaric – analogies that in time would come to describe Africans. Thus Irish people, and in particular, Irish women, were located in a space somewhere between white and black, and it was perhaps no coincidence that Irish women throughout the colonies were described in base terms evocative of European descriptions of African women.

The whiteness of the Irish provoked suspicion, but it was clear also that all English peoples were not equally white. Was the whiteness of poor whites on a par with that of the more cultured English ruling class? If the labouring poor constituted, as they did in the ruling-class imagination, a race apart, could they still be considered white, albeit a lesser class of white people? These questions troubled colonials as much as – perhaps even more so than – they did their counterparts in the metropolis.

By the late seventeenth century, white Barbadians had constructed a society predicated on an ideological belief in their own natural superiority over non-whites. Whites rationalised the enslavement and domination of enslaved Africans by claiming that the latter's innate inferiority rendered them suitable for nothing other than forced labour. In a 1675 speech to the Barbadian General Assembly, Governor Atkins echoed the common view that 'God and Nature' had designated black people as naturally fit for enslavement, and whites to be their natural masters.[20]

Critical to this nascent ideology of white superiority was the notion that white Europeans comprised an easily identifiable, superior and cohesive group. In their imaginings of attaining a discrete, unified white society, the colonial regime in Barbados actively strove to define and maintain social and racial boundaries around the white population. This entailed the imposition of stringent controls over various unruly sections of the white community, whose apparently transgressive behaviour represented a potential threat to white racial purity and solidarity and, by extension, to the entire social order. The plantocracy's goal of white solidarity was achievable only in so far as the entire white community could be drawn into the white ideological, cultural and social domain, which confronted the mass of enslaved blacks with their own inferiority. All whites, irrespective of national origin, ethnicity, social class, religion or status, had to be recognised as the social superiors of even the most prosperous free black person.

Yet claims to white superiority were always vulnerable, and establishing just who counted as white was never straightforward. Ann Laura Stoler's Foucauldian analysis of the nineteenth-century Dutch colonies holds much validity for colonial Barbados. Although claims to whiteness could be generally subsumed under a wider definition of 'European', distinctions between the 'true' Europeans born and educated in Europe, and 'Creoles', persons born and raised in the colonies, produced complicated taxonomies of whiteness.[21] Ethnic, religious and class differences disturbed the easy organisation of whiteness, making claims to a discrete white identity difficult to sustain in practice. How, for instance, were the large numbers of unruly Catholic Irish to be defined? And what of Quakers and Jews? Just how *white* were these groups?

Despite efforts to represent white society as a cohesive category, at no time did white Barbadians represent a homogenous group. White Barbados represented a melting pot of European settlers of French, Portuguese, German, Dutch and other European origins. The presence of Welsh, Irish and Scottish nationals, each pursuing their own economic, political, religious, ethnic and cultural interests, ensured a continual state of unease. Protestantism represented the dominant religion, and until the late eighteenth century Catholics, Quakers and Jews endured significant discrimination, including disqualification from certain political offices. Social class and status position intervened to create yet further strata of distinction. Between the planter elite at the top, and the generality of the poor on the bottom rungs of the white hierarchical ladder stood other classes of whites – senior plantation employees, lawyers and accountants, doctors and clergy, artisans, shopkeepers and tradespersons. White Barbadians may have thought of themselves as a distinct class set apart from the mass of enslaved blacks, but the diversity of ethnic, religious and social differences among them undermined white racial unity.

In practice, white unity was always fragile, but in the face of potential threats to white hegemonic power, differences among whites could be tolerated, accommodated or set aside. Threats to white ruling-class power could arise from sources both internal and external to the island. Internally, white society lived with the ever-present fear of black rebellion, while the prospects of external attacks by French or Spanish invaders kept the island's militia in a permanent state of readiness. Especially heightened in the wake of the successful 1791 Saint-Domingue enslaved revolution, fear of black rebellion led colonial regimes throughout the Caribbean to draft a diverse array of slave codes intended to maintain the subjection of enslaved Africans. But while it was one thing to legislate against the social freedoms of enslaved peoples, it was quite another matter to bring the full weight of the law down upon the heads of potential challengers to white authority from among the white community itself. The Barbadian authorities were well aware that threats to white power, white identity, white purity and white solidarity could also emanate from within its own ranks. Watchful surveillance had always to be kept over those disaffected whites who might disturb the social order, particularly the freed Irish servants who had earlier united with enslaved Africans against ruling-class whites. Poor white women, whose claims to whiteness were always tenuous, were to figure among those identified as actual or potential transgressors against white dominance and cohesion.

The innate blackness of white women – especially poor white women – meant that they were always in danger of never being quite white enough.[22] Hence white women had to strive to *achieve* whiteness, and that whiteness was performed through expressions of piety, morality, modesty and sexual virtue, and the careful application of often dangerous cosmetics to produce the desired 'whiter than white' complexion. This was the ideal womanhood: white in body, grace and spirit, representing, embodying, and symbolic of the cultural superiority of the English nation. Colonial expansionism simply intensified this relationship between white female subjectivity and the state of civilisation. White women throughout the colonies came to be represented as the reproducers of the state of whiteness, civility, and hence freedom. Yet, colonial womanhood was at all times an ambiguous state, and white women of all classes always inhabited the condition of otherness. They were at once objects and subjects of colonialism – objectified because of their gender; made subject because, as mistresses of enslaved peoples, they functioned as 'others' to the master. As members of the colonising group, they must be considered as social agents who struggled to maintain a subject position in the patriarchal discourse of slavery through the appropriation of enslaved bodies, and the denial of the subjectivities of those bodies.[23] Yet strong words of caution are needed here. Not all white women were members of the slaveholding elite, and poor women experienced their 'otherness' in ways qualitatively different from their elite and middle-class 'sisters'. Collectively, the majority of white women and children in Barbados enjoyed the social benefits that accrued from slavery. This does not imply that those benefits were distributed equally among white women, for numerous women of the lower classes led daily existences that were not so far removed from those of the enslaved.

That the sexuality of poor white women in particular should have been identified by the Barbadian authorities as requiring regulation was a product of contemporary attitudes towards the status of lower-class women. English society had always viewed poor women as occupying a lower place on the scales of morality and respectability, and English settlers took to the Caribbean the same rigid and derogatory class-bound views of lower-class women as sexually immoral and slovenly beings.

Servant women were held in especially low regard, as attested to by an anecdotal tale revealing the disrespect with which poor white women were regarded. According to Richard Ligon, a planter wanted to buy a woman servant, and hearing that his neighbour had one such woman for sale, agreed to pay the planter one pound of hog's flesh for every pound of the woman's flesh. The sale concluded, the planter discovered that he had purchased a woman who was to all intents and purposes 'extremely fat, lazy and good for nothing'.[24] Travellers and other observers often alluded to poorer-class white women in terms that suggested a debased, blackened character; representations of poor white colonial women as 'sluts', 'loose wenches', or 'white niggers' abounded.[25] Undoubtedly, unease about white female transgression was rooted in anxieties about the possibility of sexual relations between poor white women and black men, and the consequences that interracial unions posed for white racial purity and superiority.

Despite their ambivalence towards the enslaved Africans among them, the Barbadian authorities at first displayed a degree of tolerance towards marriages between whites and blacks, and surviving parish registers of the eighteenth century indicate some defiance of the sanctions against interracial relationships.[26] But as slave society matured, ideologies asserting white superiority gained the ascendancy and interracial marriages were no longer tolerated. Barbadian legislators publicly censured interracial sexual unions, yet – mindful of provoking antagonism among powerful white males who expected unrestrained sexual access to black women – stopped short of actually legislating against interracial sex. It is doubtful, though, that such legislation could entirely curtail such unions, for while sexual relations between white women and black men were at all times socially proscribed, white males strenuously asserted their rights to enjoy sexual relationships with black women. White Barbadians stood firm against interracial marriage, but were prepared to sanction informal sexual relations between black women and white men. In any case, outright prohibition of interracial sex would have proven difficult, if not impossible, to enforce. Planters wielded absolute power on their plantations, and this included the rights to the sexuality of the enslaved. Moreover, anxiety over interracial sex was directed not towards the sexual behaviour of white men, but towards the sexual freedoms of white women. Thus as Barbara Bush has noted, a hypocritical double standard flourished, for white males regularly sexually abused and exploited black women, while at the same time endeavouring to inhibit sexual relations between 'their' white women and black males.[27]

White males' freedom to access black women's sexuality without invoking fears of racial contamination was facilitated by a matrilineal inheritance principle that tied the legal status of children to the legal identity of their mother. In 1658, a recently freed black woman described as 'Mary, a negro' sued her former master, a Lieutenant-Colonel John Higginbotham, on the grounds that her status as a free woman meant that her own children should enjoy the same status. The Barbadian Council thought otherwise, however, and adjudicated that since Mary was enslaved at the time of her children's birth, then Higginbotham should retain ownership rights over them.[28] This ruling fixed the status of children securely to that of their mothers, and directly subverted longstanding English patrilineal principles through which individual status derived from the father. This departure from English common law, first established in Virginia in 1662, was a peculiar feature of slaveholding colonies throughout the Americas.[29]

The revised legislation carried significant implications for mothers, fathers and children, white and black. From the perspective of slave-owners, any child born to an enslaved woman, regardless of its father's race, social standing or legal status, became the property of its mother's owner, thus augmenting the enslaved community. White males were therefore free to engage in sexual relationships with enslaved women with impunity. Conversely, white mothers passed on free status to their children, a state of affairs that potentially threatened white hegemonic dominance. Faced with the prospects of a class of free coloureds who might conceivably demand a greater share of political power, the authorities found it imperative to limit both the growth and freedoms of this class. Hilary Beckles has noted that the small community of free coloured people that had emerged by the early eighteenth century soon became a target for the legislature.[30] Thus while white males could indulge freely in exploitative sexual relations with black women, white female sexuality had to be regulated. Indeed, controlling the sexuality of all women, white and black, rich or poor, was a fundamental component of the power of white colonial males.[31]

In particular, the long-held belief in the promiscuity of poor white women made this socially disadvantaged group the primary target for regulation. Left unchecked, the authorities feared, the unruly sexuality of poor white women made them liable to succumb to the pernicious sexual attentions of black men. Such relationships could not be given legal or social sanction, for they would erode the boundaries of freedom and whiteness, undermine white claims to superiority, threaten the social order, and tarnish the cherished ideals of pure white womanhood. Perceiving white women as the biological reproducers of freedom, the authorities found it necessary to deter white women from forming sexual relationships with black men.[32] This was imperative if the purity of the white race was to be preserved. The potential instability of whiteness and the challenge to white rule thus prompted a powerful mechanism for the social and sexual regulation of poor white women.

Policing the sexual and social freedoms of elite and middle-class white women probably proved easier to enforce, partly because of their closer proximity to ruling-class white males, and also because they stood to lose their racial privileges and social status if they transgressed. But poor white women, existing on the periphery of the plantations, and often without the economic support of white males, were thrown into more intimate daily contact with the slave community. Their socio-economic position on the margins of white society made poorer white women a less manageable group than white women of the planter class.

English settlers took with them to Barbados old-world cultural values that assumed the necessity of women's subordination to male patriarchal authority. Among the elite and middle classes, the planter asserted his mastery and authority over every single member of 'his' household, free whites (his wife, children, overseers, and other white plantation employees) and enslaved blacks. All were expected to submit to his mastery, and his wife no less so. The plantation household was his 'domain', the source and site of his power, and the authorities of the plantocracy refrained as far as possible from interfering with the power of the master. But as Michel Foucault reminds us, the exercise of power is never smooth or one-way, nor located within a single group, but instead is an ever-changing flow between different interest groups and institutions; most importantly, power invariably invites resistance. Hence power is not to be regarded as a purely negative force, for it is first and foremost productive, in so far as it inevitably produces resistance.[33] Though given legal force, the master's power was never secure, and his subjects, black and white, male and female, waged a seemingly relentless challenge to his authority; enslaved African women and men attempted with varying degrees of success to burn down his house, set fire to his cane fields, break his tools and machinery, lie to and steal from him, poison his food and drink, and even wrest power from his hands through armed insurrection. The planter's wife also – though perhaps more subtly – challenged the limits of his power; through prenuptial contracts she tried to retain control of whatever property she had brought to the marriage, she sued for inefficient management of her estate, filed for separation, divorce, and custody of 'his' children, conducted extramarital affairs, refused his sexual advances, spent 'his' money, and in perhaps the greatest challenge to his authority, sided with the enslaved in disputes against him. White male patriarchal power was never so universal or absolute as to preclude the possibilities of resistance from his subjects.

Ruling-class males sought to assert their authority over women of all races and of all classes. Increasingly from the seventeenth century, the sexual and social regulation of white women came to represent a major concern for the colonial patriarchy. Their efforts to regulate the socio-sexual behaviours of women did not, however, go unchallenged. Throughout the colonial era, women of all races and classes resisted the imposition of white male power. Collectively and individually, enslaved women engaged in anti-slavery activities that would eventually help secure their freedoms. Poor white female servants joined forces with men of their class – and sometimes with the enslaved community – to protest against the ill-treatment meted out by planters, or defied social strictures against interracial sex, and boldly formed sexual partnerships with black males. Colonial authorities strove to create docile bodies of women – white and black, elite and poor – but their efforts met with rebuttal as numerous women of all races and classes displayed equally strong wills to resist.

Ruling the unruly

Poor white women remain among the most elusive and invisible within Caribbean historiography. Few women of any class left behind firsthand accounts of their experiences, and existing narratives are invariably those of elite temporary residents. For the most part white Barbadian women, whether wealthy or poor, possessed little more than rudimentary literary skills. A few enlightened white families sent their daughters to be educated in England, but most young women were taught at home by governesses and tutors.[34] Some parishes provided an elementary schooling for children of the poor, but young white girls rarely gained access to the limited educational opportunities. In any case, the rudimentary education that the parish vestries offered poor young women emphasised the acquisition of domestic skills such as spinning and weaving; reading, writing and arithmetic remained the preserve of a few fortunate elite women. Much of our knowledge about white Caribbean women, then, necessarily derives from the comments of male observers, but their representations of white colonial womanhood are largely informed by misogynistic, class-bound perspectives, and must therefore be approached with caution. However unsatisfactory these texts, and whatever their limitations, we cannot afford to ignore these sources simply on the basis of their male authorship. In seeking to understand the relationship between class, gender, race and sexuality in seventeenth-century Barbados, in the absence of women's own testimonies, I have of necessity relied on official sources, specifically, the seventeenth- and eighteenth-century Minute Books of the Vestry Committees of the parishes of St John and St Michael respectively. These records provide insight on the distribution of Poor Relief to 'deserving' parishioners, the majority of whom were poor, landless white women. Of greater significance to this work, the Minute Books also provide the most tangible evidence of the conflictual relationship between Barbadian authorities and poor white women. As such they represent important sources on the poor white female experience in Barbados, revealing as they do the role of the Barbadian vestries in sustaining the dominant patriarchal system, and the mechanisms through which the vestry structured and controlled the lives of those socially marginalised women who were forced to rely on its charity.

It is at the level of the Poor Relief Boards, operating under the aegis of the parish vestry, that we can find traces of authoritarian efforts to regulate unruly poor women, through their incorporation into the white domain. Public relief helped soften the harsher edges of white poverty but government provision for the white poor always fell short of actual requirements, leaving parochial Poor Relief Boards heavily reliant on inadequate and often infrequent donations from the more public-spirited among the wealthy.

The provision of poor relief also served to delineate the social and sexual boundaries between free whites and unfree blacks. The prevalence of white women among the claimants of poor relief may be interpreted in two ways: either as the result of efforts by Barbadian authorities to alleviate their miserable poverty, or as the consequence of the colonial authority's attempts to incorporate disenfranchised poor whites in general, and poor white women in particular, into a white ruling-class cultural sphere that rested on an ideology of white superiority. This entailed efforts to limit the possibilities of 'white slippage', by preventing the social status of poor whites from slipping below that of black people, and to prevent also the blurring of the boundaries of whiteness, by limiting the possibilities of sexual partnerships between white women and black males. Poor relief also served to maintain a semblance of solidarity and cohesion within the white population, through the construction of boundaries that clearly demarcated both the racial identities of, and social spaces between, the black and white populations. The control and policing of poor white women's sexualities and social existence formed a principal component of the authority's strategy to maintain social and sexual distance between the white and black populations.

It is unclear when poor relief was first established in Barbados. In the early colonial days most whites were in servitude, and their welfare was the concern of their employers. Hence, initially there was probably little perceived need for an island-wide system of public relief. By 1650, however, as slavery accelerated and numerous ex-indentured white servants found themselves displaced from the labour market, some parishes had already instituted a system of poor relief under the auspices of the parochial vestries. Larry Gragg has suggested that the vestries' concern to improve the material conditions of poor whites represented a pragmatic response to dampen down elite fears of possible social unrest; the growing numbers of listless, landless and disenfranchised poor whites posed a potential threat to the stability of the social order.[35] As time passed without discernible improvement in the economic situation of ex-servants, Barbadian vestries were increasingly consumed by the problem of the white poor, and the dispensation of poor relief occupied a great deal of the vestries' attention. Relief assumed a number of forms. In the early years claimants received a quantity of sugar, which could be bartered for other goods or sold. A needy parishioner might receive free medical care or housing, while small landowners could claim a tax exemption for a specified period. Other claimants received assistance to help them establish a trade, as did Ellin Ridley, who received ten shillings from the St Michael vestry to 'set her up in market'.[36] St Michael parish provided an almshouse for the most needy, but other parishes did not follow suit for many years. Instead, most parishes favoured a policy of placing their homeless in the households of better-off parishioners, who in turn received an allowance. Children of poor families, orphans and the 'bastard' children of the elite were bound out as apprentices, until aged 21 when they were recognised as free adults. As white unemployment rates continued to climb, Poor Relief Boards had to balance the problem of limited resources against the competing demands of large numbers of claimants. Where possible, they attempted to conserve their meagre resources by identifying those with familial, moral or legal responsibilities towards claimants and forcing them to contribute to the upkeep of claimants.

Modelled on the English design – as was so much of the colonial society's infrastructure – Barbadian vestries functioned as local authorities for each of the eleven parishes into which the island was divided. Each Committee was charged with the levying and collection of local taxes, the passing of local byelaws, the defence of the parish, the appointment of local clergy and churchwardens, the care and repair of the parish church, and the dispensation of poor relief. Responsibility for the administering of poor relief rested with the Vestry Committee of each parish. The Committee's membership comprised Protestant men of property and wealth, among them many who nursed ambitions for political office. Jews, Quakers, minors and women, regardless of social standing or wealth, were excluded from membership, although some prominent local women fulfilled supportive advisory roles. Typically however, women received no public recognition for their vestry work, for their involvement was informal in scope. An individual woman might be called upon to find a home for an orphan child, or to assist with fund-raising efforts, but white women were otherwise excluded from the formal decision-making processes of the Vestry. White female involvement in vestry matters, however, was crucial, for it was often on the recommendation of respectable women that claims for poor relief would be decided, particularly when the character of a claimant was doubtful, and when the Poor Relief Board needed to establish a claimant as deserving – or otherwise – of poor relief.

White women represented the principal claimants of poor relief, the majority of whom were widowed, deserted or unmarried mothers. In the mid-seventeenth century the majority of Africans were enslaved, and responsibility for the welfare of the old, sick and infirm among them rested with their owners. The extent to which individual planters fulfilled their responsibility varied, and many a disabled or elderly slave was thrown back on to their own resources for their survival. Despite this, no black person, free or unfree, could claim relief, and the authorities refused to extend poor relief to non-whites until well after emancipation in 1838.[37]

The main criterion for receiving poor relief was therefore not poverty *per se*, but that the individual was identifiably white. Besides this primary consideration other factors were considered in establishing a claimant's eligibility. No claimant could expect to have their application approved until the Board was first satisfied that they were indeed deserving of public assistance – being poor or unemployed did not automatically qualify an individual as deserving. While the Board accepted some civic responsibility towards a few categories of female claimants (the widowed, abandoned mothers of young children, the elderly and the sick), other women had to first establish their claims to be deserving of relief. It is clear that the concept of 'deserving' was closely aligned to perceptions of personal character and conduct. Ultimately, whether a woman was assessed as 'deserving' or 'undeserving' rested with a patriarchal all-male committee which undoubtedly held ideas about appropriate standards of behaviour for white womanhood.

In August 1693, the Poor Relief Board of St John Parish agreed that Mary Seeley was eligible to receive the sum of 10 shillings per month, 'for as long as the Churchwarden thinks she shall deserve relief from this parish'.[38] However, the precise criteria used to judge whether an individual claimant was suitably deserving (or not) remain unclear. Only through a close reading of the Minute Books is it possible to discern some conditions that defined a claimant as deserving or otherwise. In this racially stratified society, white women who formed sexual relations with black men could clearly not be regarded as deserving.

Victoria Bynum has noted that in the antebellum Southern slaveholding states, Poor Relief Boards inflicted punishment on white women who transgressed sexual boundaries through the forced removal of their coloured children from their homes. Such children would be forced to serve out their minority as apprentices in the homes of respectable white members of the community.[39] This action effectively relieved the authorities of responsibility towards 'unruly' white women, who would henceforth be left to fend for themselves. Colonial authorities in Barbados also adopted this measure, forcibly separating poor white children from their families. Clearly, poor relief could then work as a powerful disincentive to white female-black male relationships, and by extension, can be seen to have functioned as an institutional weapon of the authorities in maintaining racial and sexual boundaries.

Among women considered 'deserving' were those willing to accept responsibility for the care of the sick, elderly and infirm, and the illegitimate and orphaned children of the parish. In the absence of formal welfare provision, poor white women performed a vital service to their parish by keeping and caring for destitute whites (and hence maintaining them within the boundaries of whiteness), while at the same time obtaining an income. Katherine Williams of St Michael earned her living by taking into her home and caring for Elizabeth White, an orphan whose mother had been executed for murder.[40] As a foster mother, Katherine was granted 150 lb of sugar per month, and clothing was provided for the child.[41]

By the 1660s, the vestries had come to rely heavily on the informal care services provided by poor white women. At times, women also took into their homes the illegitimate children of wealthy parish residents. At their meeting in 1678, the St John Vestry Committee reported that the Governor of Barbados had himself ordered Colonel Walrond, a prominent Barbadian planter, to pay the parish '200lbs of sugar towards the maintenance of Thomas Rich, his bastard child', being cared for in the home of a poor white woman.[42] Barely a year later, the Poor Relief Board agreed to pay Elizabeth Connell 1200 lb quarterly 'for the maintaining of the bastard child of William Drinkwater', brother of Richard Drinkwater, the parish clerk. Furthermore, the Churchwarden was ordered to prosecute the errant father for recovery of parish funds expended on the maintenance of his 'bastard child'.[43] At the time Elizabeth took over the care of Drinkwater's illegitimate child, she was already the carer of another indigent, Dormand Kelly, for whom she received 100 lb of sugar a month.[44]

Although poor women made up the largest group of claimants, poor white men could, in certain circumstances, also receive public assistance. The dispensation of poor relief to these male claimants – those too sick or old to work – indicates that men as well as women, who could have slipped easily out of white society, were being maintained. In their roles as carers of these men, poor white women served a double function, of keeping both the carers and the cared-for white. In some cases, poor white males also received an allowance for their care services. Thomas King received £5 sterling 'for taking into his care and charge, Mary daughter of John Forde'. On the same day, King was also allowed a retrospective payment of £5 for caring for Mary's sister Elizabeth, shortly to be apprenticed to Mrs Collyton, a widow. Under the terms of apprenticeship, Mrs Collyton would receive an annual payment of £5 for which she was expected to keep, maintain and train Elizabeth in domestic service until her charge reached 21 years of age.[45]

Unsurprisingly, widowed women comprised a significant majority of claimants. On 24 November the Poor Relief Board voted to allow the widow of Hugh Hall a one-off payment of 500 lb of sugar, 'for relief of herself and children, she having promised this parish to be no further chargeable to them'. On the same day the widow of John Miles also received 500 lb of sugar, 'on the same terms'.[46]

Abandoned and deserted wives also appeared with depressing regularity on poor relief books. That many men chose migration as an opportunity to abandon their families is evident from an Act of 1672 which required the names of any individual (excluding married women and children under the age of fourteen years), intending to leave the island to be published, and explicitly demanded that security be posted for any dependents left behind on the island.[47] This Act had the function of preventing the desertion of wives and children by their husbands and fathers, who in 1679 represented 88 per cent of applicants for tickets to depart Barbados, thus exposing the gendered nature of emigration. Of 583 passengers granted tickets to depart the island, fewer than seventy were women.[48]

Women's responsibilities for their families both restricted their mobility and left them vulnerable to desertion when their husbands left the island. While wealthy women could look to the courts to claim a proportion of the property of deserting husbands, many poorer women were forced on to public assistance. In August 1681 Anne Hibbert successfully applied for poor relief on the grounds that her husband had deserted her, leaving Anne and her children destitute. The St Michael vestry ordered that a search be made for the errant husband, but until he could be found, Anne was to receive 12/6d towards her relief.[49] At the best of times, the vestry funds, raised primarily through taxes levied on the property owners of the parish, were always limited, and were further strained by the demands of abandoned women and children.

Claimants continued to receive poor relief only so long as the Vestry Committee considered them deserving of public assistance. Any perceived transgression could result in the removal of these women from the parish list of deserving poor. In the economic crisis that befell the poor white population in the years after the institutionalisation of slavery, the threat of being struck off the parish roll acted as an effective deterrent to transgressive behaviour.

Some time in early 1790, the St John Poor Relief Board decided that measures had to be taken to increase employment opportunities for poor white women of the parish. Their solution was to establish a vocational school for young girls of poor families, and a special sub-committee was set up with a remit to 'carry into execution the plan of the school'.[50] A suitable house was identified, and its widowed owner Sarah Coombes induced to sell the property to the vestry for the sum of £17.10. A headmistress, Mrs Farrell, was appointed to oversee the preparations for the school's opening. Assisted by enslaved Africans, she set about making the required improvements before the school could open. Suitable pupils were identified from the list of the parish poor families. A suit of new clothing was promised for each new student, which must have been an attractive inducement for prospective pupils. It is not quite clear how the school was to be funded, but it is probable that the vestry expected its operational costs to be met from revenue levied from local taxpayers. Additionally, local benefactors also provided support, and the Governor of Barbados was sufficiently impressed by the scheme to contribute financial assistance in his personal capacity.[51]

The St John School for Female Industry opened its doors in 1792. It was a unique institution, apparently the first parochial school in Barbados established solely for the purpose of educating poor young women and girls. The school's first entrants were a group of twelve young girls whose parents were in receipt of poor relief. Pupils were boarded under the tutelage of Mrs Farrell, who was responsible for the day-to-day running of the school, while the sub-committee remained in overall control. The school's curriculum, devised by the sub-committee, ordained that the school day begin with morning assembly for all pupils, who should 'first be made to read the psalms for the day, and a chapter in the Bible, with some short prayer, in which they should beg a blessing from God for the success of their labours'.[52] How this particular objective was to be achieved is not quite clear, given that most, if not all, of the girls were illiterate, and there is no suggestion that literacy or numeracy training would form part of the curriculum. Instead, as befitting their status, pupils were to be trained for domestic service and their education limited to the acquisition of spinning, knitting, weaving and other domestic skills.

It is difficult to know with certainty the Vestry Committee's rationale for establishing the school at this period. However, I think it could be convincingly argued that their decision was based primarily on the need to widen employment prospects for poor white girls and young women, recognising that poor white women who had independent livelihoods were less likely to seek out black men as providers; second, to reduce parish expenditure on poor relief; third, to draw those women considered deserving into a white cultural milieu, thereby securing the boundaries of whiteness, and at the same time reinforcing white unity; and fourth, to impose a degree of control over the lives of poor mothers and their daughters. I am concerned here primarily with the first, third and fourth aspects.

In theory young women could enter the school only with the consent of their mothers – existing records suggest that the majority of pupils came from poor households headed by single mothers. In practice however, school attendance was closely tied to the receipt of poor relief; mothers could claim relief only as long as they agreed to their daughter's remaining in school. This requirement effectively deterred recalcitrant mothers from opposing the parish authorities, who were quick to invoke the threat of removal from the poor roll at the first signs of discontent.

Nonetheless, linking poor relief to what many probably viewed as a welcome opportunity for their daughters to acquire even a limited education proved unacceptable to many mothers and their daughters. The Board encountered strong and vociferous opposition from some mothers over what they interpreted as their daughter's enforced attendance at the school. Elizabeth Howard's mother provoked the Committee's wrath when it was reported at a meeting in February 1796 that Elizabeth had been 'insolently taken from the school by her mother'. When Camilla Phillips similarly removed her daughter from the school, she was ordered to be sent out of the parish.[53] Banishment represented a particularly cruel punishment for her forced removal cut the mother off from the network of family and friends in the parish on whom she relied for support and comfort. Moreover, it was highly unlikely that Camilla Phillips could expect public assistance from any neighbouring parish, especially given the circumstances of her banishment. In sending Camilla Phillips from the parish, the Vestry Committee must have realised that she faced a precarious and lonely future – possibly without her daughter. Henceforth, the committee brooked no maternal challenges to their authority, ordering that in future, 'no girls shall be admitted to the [school] unless their parents will agree to bind them to the churchwarden and his successors for the term of eight years, of which eight years they shall be kept four at the school, and the remaining four to be bound out in such families as the Committee will approve of'.[54]

For many mothers, it was the issue of indentureship that generated the greatest and most prolonged conflict between the vestry and claimant mothers.[55] After four years' schooling, girls aged fourteen and over were required to serve a four-year apprenticeship in the households of wealthier parishioners. For some mothers and their daughters apprenticeship was no doubt regarded as an opportunity to acquire marketable skills that would in the long term enhance the family income. In this sense, the apprenticeship scheme could be regarded as a positive measure. Yet it is apparent from the Minute Books that many claimant mothers, and their daughters, strenuously opposed the system of apprenticeship.

Quite why parents should have resisted the vestry's apprenticeship scheme is unclear. Several possibilities offer themselves. Geoffrey Oxley noted a comparable opposition to the apprenticeship of young children in England during the same period. In rural England, parents criticised the apprenticeship on the grounds that their children were often bound out to sweated or unskilled trades, and sometimes placed in households where they were exploited and subjected to abuse.[56] Many children were also placed in households outside the parish, therefore forcing their separation from their families. For some white Barbadian mothers, the forced apprenticeship of their daughters may have evoked the spectre of servitude, which had initially brought so many poor white women to the colonies. It is also possible that the four-year apprenticeship represented to mothers both the loss of a daughter's domestic labour, and the removal of a potential source of family income. Whatever the reasons for the widespread objections to apprenticeship, one fact remains clear; apprenticeship served to maintain patriarchal control over poor white mothers and their daughters.

The response of some dissenting mothers to the introduction of the scheme was, understandably, then, to remove their daughters from the school on completion of their vocational training, but before they could be bound out as apprentices. Some mothers actively encouraged and aided daughters to abscond from the school or to desert their place of apprenticeship. In response, the sub-committee exacted the most stringent punishment at their disposal – the denial of poor relief to mothers. This step proved an effective deterrent to some disgruntled mothers, but others persisted in their opposition. In August 1797, Ursula Marshall was dismissed from the school 'for misconduct of her mother and self . . . and her mother taken off the parish list'.[57] In March the following year, the Sub-Committee was still concerned about the number of girls who were being encouraged to abscond from the school before their apprenticeship, and reiterated the condition that poor relief would only be given to mothers on condition that they agreed to their daughters serving a future apprenticeship. This warning appears to have gone unheeded, for mothers continued to collude with their daughters to abscond from the school and from their place of apprenticeship. Well into the nineteenth century, the apprenticeship system continued to represent a major site of struggle between the Poor Relief Board and poor white women. In June 1803, the Rector of St John reported that 'two of the three girls last put out [to apprenticeship] Mary Brooks and Sarah Charge had run away from their masters at the encouragement of their parents'. Mrs Charge was ordered to be struck off the poor list, and her daughter to be 'given up'. Additionally, Mary Brooks was to be 'corrected and returned to her master, if he will receive her'.[58] We have no way of knowing the fate of those women who were removed from the poor lists, but it is certain that in the stricken economy of Barbados, removal from the parish list and the loss of their pensions could only serve to push poor white women even further to the margins of white society. Women who failed to conform to dominant racial and moral norms were ostracised by 'decent' white society, and when this happened, having little else left to lose, many probably forged more intimate relations with free black or coloured men. Hence, removing white women from the poor rolls represented a contradictory position for the maintenance of the boundaries of whiteness.

The efforts of the vestries to regulate the lives of poor white women in St John and St Michael point to some ways in which new conceptions of white dominance developed and shaped the lives of all those enmeshed in the institution of slavery, delineating the contours of white women's lives as surely as it structured the lives of the planters and the slaves. Fragmented as they are, the Minute Books of the St John and St Michael vestries do offer some partial glimpses into the material realities of the poorest white women, though they are unable to provide much insight into the experiences of those women who were not considered sufficiently poor or deserving to warrant public assistance.

Struggles between poor white women and the Poor Relief Boards illustrate only one strategy implemented by the white supremacist, planter-dominated authorities to control white women's lives and sexualities. The 'success' of such strategies remains in doubt, however. Although threatened with removal from the parish list, numerous poor white women in St John parish chose to challenge, or were propelled into challenging, the colonial regime.

As biological and social reproducers of the ruling white group, white women constituted a strategically important group, critical to the formation and maintenance of a newly emerging white identity. Poor white women figured in the white imagination as a degenerate category, necessitating control in the interests of white purity and hegemony and the long-term stability of the social order. In St John's parish, the School of Female Industry not only offered vocational training to young white women, but also functioned as a crucial institution through which the socio-sexual behaviour of poor young women and their mothers might be monitored and controlled. Leah Howard exemplified the success of this strategy. Leah was chosen as the recipient of Sir Phillip Gibbes's largesse because she symbolised conformity to standards of white womanhood. Regardless of her proven capacity for industry, had Leah chosen a black male as her intended husband, her forthcoming marriage would certainly not have received the approbation of the vestry. But Leah apparently represented a singular success, for she appears to have been the sole recipient of Gibbes's four awards.

When poor white women had little to lose, even the withholding of material incentives was insufficient to deter them from forging sexual relations with black men. Although their economic opportunities were limited, they strove to secure a livelihood by whatever means they could. Self-sufficiency therefore enabled poor white women to defy the social or racial mores of plantation society. This in no way implies that poor white women resisted their racially elevated status as members of the ruling white group. Regardless of their impoverished state, as members of the white community, poor white women enjoyed the ultimate human state – freedom.

Valuable sources though they are, the Minute Books raise more questions than they answer about what it meant to be a poor or wealthy white woman in a society in which race rather than gender functioned as the principle mode of social stratification. A more critical reappraisal of the position of white women is needed in order to clarify further the inter-relations of race, class and gender in Barbados.

Notes

1 'Poor white' was and remains still a commonly used designator to describe the class of whites who were situated on the lowest rungs of white society. Poor whites represented a separate social category, distinct from other non-elite/non-slaveholding groups such as the yeomanry and tenant farmers, not only because of their economic impoverishment, but also because they were deemed to fall short of the cultural standards of the dominant elites. In both Barbados and North Carolina, poor whites came to be a marginalised group relegated to the fringes of white society, and increasingly, denigrated as a genetically inferior people. Throughout, I use the term 'poor white' as a descriptive, rather than a derogatory term.
2 This sum was greater than the salary paid to Mrs Farrell, the school's first headmistress, who received an annual salary of £30.
3 *St John Vestry Minute Book, June 1800*, Barbados Museum and Historical Society (hereafter BMHS).
4 David Lambert, 'Liminal Figures: Poor whites, freedmen and racial reinscription in colonial Barbados', *Society and Space*, 19 (2001), pp. 335–350.
5 Jill Sheppard, *The 'Redlegs' of Barbados: Their origins and history* (New York: KTO Press, 1977).
6 Ibid., p. 63.
7 Hilary Beckles, 'White women and slavery in the Caribbean', *History Workshop Journal* 36 (1993), pp. 66–82.
8 See Beckles, 'Class formation in slave society: the rise of a black labour elite and the development of a white lumpen-proletariat in seventeenth century Barbados', *Journal of the Barbados Museum and Historical Society* 37:1 (1983).
9 Sheppard, *'Redlegs' of Barbados*, p. 49.
10 Ibid., p. 48.
11 Ibid., p. 39.
12 Lambert, 'Liminal Figures', p. 335.
13 Ibid., p. 342.
14 Kim Hall, *Things of Darkness: Economies of race and gender in early modern England* (Ithaca: Cornell University Press, 1995).
15 Jennifer Morgan, *Laboring Women: Reproduction and gender in New World slavery* (Philadelphia: University of Pennsylvania Press, 2004).
16 Ibid. p. 49.
17 Hall, *Things of Darkness*, p. 53.
18 Quoted in Brigitte Kossek, 'Power, Dread and Desire: The remaking of anybody during slavery', unpublished paper (University of Vienna 2001).

19 Footnote to 'Of National Characters' (1754) cited in E.C. Eze (ed.), *Race and the Enlightenment: A reader* (Oxford: Blackwell, 1997), pp. 30–33.
20 Governor Jonathan Atkins, cited in Gary Puckrein, *Little England: Plantation society and Anglo-Barbadian politics, 1627–1700* (New York: New York University Press, 1984), p. 169.
21 Ann Laura Stoler, *Race and the Education of Desire: Foucault's history of sexuality and the colonial order of things* (Durham: Duke University Press, 1995).
22 Brigitte Kossek, 'Representing self/otherness and "white women" slave owners in the English speaking Caribbean', unpublished seminar paper presented to the Institute of Commonwealth Studies (March 2000).
23 Ibid., p. 4.
24 Richard Ligon, *True and Exact History of the Island of Barbados* (London: Frank Cass, reprinted 1970), p. 59.
25 Hilary Beckles, *Natural Rebels: A social history of enslaved black women in Barbados* (London: Karnak House, 1988).
26 Beckles's claim is based on the discovery of an entry in the St Michael Parish Register for 1685 which records the marriage of Jane Long, a white woman, to Peter Perkins, described as a Negro. This is not the sole instance of legal unions between black men and white women, but few other such marriages are recorded, which leads to the suggestion that they were in fact quite rare events.
27 Barbara Bush, *Slave Women in Caribbean Society 1650–1838* (London: James Currey, 1990).
28 Larry Gragg, *Englishmen Transplanted: The English colonization of Barbados 1627–1660* (Oxford: Oxford University Press, 2003), p. 126.
29 Kirsten Fischer, *Suspect Relations: Sex, race and resistance in colonial North Carolina* (Ithaca: Cornell University Press, 2003), p. 124.
30 Hilary Beckles, *A History of Barbados: From Amerindian settlement to nation-state* (Cambridge: Cambridge University Press, 1990).
31 Bush, *Slave Women in Caribbean Society*, p. 26.
32 Beckles, 'White Women and Slavery in the Caribbean', p. 69.
33 Michel Foucault, *The History of Sexuality, Vol. 1* (Harmondsworth: Penguin, 1987).
34 Carl Bridenbaugh and Roberta Bridenbaugh, *No Peace Beyond the Line: The English in the Caribbean, 1624–1690* (New York: Oxford University Press, 1972).
35 Gragg, *Englishmen Transplanted*. p. 84.
36 *St Michael Vestry Minute Book, February 1680*, BMHS.
37 Sheppard, *'Redlegs' of Barbados*, p. 81.
38 *St John Vestry Minute Book, 14 August 1693*, BMHS.
39 Victoria Bynum, *Unruly Women: The politics of social and sexual control in the Old South* (Chapel Hill: University of North Carolina Press, 1992).
40 *St Michael Vestry Book, 1661*, BMHS.
41 Sugar remained the unit of currency in Barbados until the late decades of the seventeenth century. St John Parish paid its claimants in sugar until 1679/80, after which ayments were usually made in cash (or in kind). The amount of relief paid varied between 100 and 1200 lb of sugar, depending on the individual's circumstances. In 1681, 1200 lb of sugar was roughly equivalent to £6 in value.
42 *St John Vestry Minute Book, February 1678*, BMHS.
43 *St John Vestry Minute Book, January/February 1679*, BMHS.
44 *St John Vestry Minute Book, February 1679*, BMHS.
45 *St John Vestry Minute Book, August 1687*, BMHS.
46 *St John Vestry Minute Book, November 1679*, BMHS.
47 Richard Hall, *Acts Passed in the Island of Barbados, 1643–1762, Vol. 1* (William Clowes and Sons, 1875).
48 Richard Dunn, *Sugar and Slaves: The rise of the planter class in the English West Indies 1624–1713* (New York: W.W. Norton, 1972), p. 110; see also J.C. Hotten, *The Original Lists of Persons of Quality; emigrants; religious exiles; political rebels; serving men sold for a term of years; apprentices; children stolen; maidens pressed;*

and others who went from Great Britain to the American plantations, 1600–1700 (New York: G.A. Baker & Co, 1931), pp. 345–418.
49 *St Michael Vestry Minute Book, August 1681*, BMHS.
50 *St John Vestry Minute Book, July 1792*, BMHS.
51 *St John Vestry Minute Book, July 1795*, BMHS.
52 *St John Vestry Minute Book, July 1793*, BMHS.
53 *St John Vestry Minute Book, February 1796*, BMHS.
54 *St John Vestry Minute Book,* February *1797*, BMHS.
55 St John and St Michael parishes were not the only Barbadian parishes to establish an apprenticeship system. In 1799, the Barbadian authorities ruled that any boy or girl under the age of 21 who had been educated at the expense of the parish should be put out to apprenticeship.
56 Geoffrey Oxley, *Poor Relief in England and Wales 1601–1834* (London: David and Charles, 1974).
57 *St John Vestry Minute Book, August 1797*, BMHS.
58 *St John Vestry Minute Book, June 1803*, BMHS.

CHAPTER TWO

'Worse than [white] men, much worse than the negroes...'[1]: sexuality, labour and poor white women in North Carolina

On an April day in 1772, Sarah Herring Wiggins appeared before the New Bern District Court of North Carolina, charged with the murder of her newborn infant. According to witnesses, the child was healthy and of 'full size' at birth, suggesting that it had been carried to term. Two days later, however, the child was discovered dead, 'the scull bones... broken and fractured', and the finger of blame soon pointed at its mother. Sarah was summarily charged with infanticide and a month later faced trial in court.

It is impossible to know the exact circumstances surrounding the death of Sarah's child. Quite possibly, the alleged murder was intended to cover up evidence of an adulterous and illicit relationship between Sarah and Will, an enslaved man owned by Sarah's father. Sarah, it emerged, had borne another mulatto child, also allegedly fathered by Will. So why then did Sarah apparently kill this second mulatto child? Sarah's defence against the charge of infanticide was astonishing. In her testimony, Sarah admitted mothering two mulatto children but steadfastly denied a consensual sexual relationship with Will. Instead, she insisted, over a period of years Will had subjected her to a regime of fear, and coerced her into a sexual relationship. According to Sarah's deposition, three years earlier Will had come to her house, and over her protests, forced her to drink some rum. Days later he came again with another bottle of rum, and tricked Sarah into drinking it. Will had taken advantage of her inebriation, 'and by that means had carnal knowledge of her body'. She had fallen pregnant, but Will had threatened to poison her if she publicly revealed his paternity of the child, even went so far as threatening to force his sexual attentions on Sarah's sister, and boasting of previous sexual conquests of 'the best of [white] women'.[2]

Were Sarah's accusations against Will a desperate attempt to cover up her own complicity in an illicit sexual relationship? How could

Will, an enslaved black male, exert such a powerful hold over Sarah for so many years? Would their sexual relationship – coerced or otherwise – ever have come to light had Sarah not borne a second mulatto child? How did Sarah explain the birth of her first mulatto child? Why did the 'facts' of Will's rape not emerge after the birth of that first child? Even if, as Sarah claimed, Will had silenced Sarah for so long by threatening to poison her family, it still somewhat stretches credulity that she could have been so thoroughly intimidated by an enslaved male that she endured his abuse, even after the birth of their first child.[3] Most intriguingly, Sarah was not an unmarried woman, but the wife of Gershum Wiggins, a man twelve years her senior. How did Sarah explain to Gershum, her family and friends the birth and paternity of her first mulatto child?

Sarah Herring married Gershum Wiggins in 1767 when she was seventeen. A year later she gave birth to John, and a daughter followed two years later. It is not known when the first mulatto child was born– perhaps Sarah miscarried or the child was stillborn; perhaps the child was concealed among the enslaved community. We know of the child's birth only through Sarah's confession, and we can only speculate as to its whereabouts in 1772. Perhaps Gershum was aware of the child's birth, but, enthralled by his wife's youth (and her father's wealth), chose to forgive her indiscretion. If this was the case, it might explain Sarah's alleged act of infanticide. Perhaps, unable to endure the combination of Gershum's anger at a second betrayal, and the inevitable scandal that would follow once the child's paternity became public knowledge, Sarah murdered her mulatto child. To comprehend Sarah's actions in the alleged infanticide more fully, it is necessary to look beyond this seemingly isolated tragedy at the wider, complex social relations that structured Sarah's world, and to understand how the dynamics of gender, race and class race in North Carolina could lead to an act of infanticide.

For a white woman in colonial North Carolina, bearing illegitimate children represented a serious transgression of Southern moral and sexual codes. In engaging in adulterous sex Sarah had violated these codes, which confined white female sexuality to the institution of marriage. As if her adultery was not sufficiently damning, Sarah further compounded her 'crime' by giving birth to two mulatto children, visible evidence of her transgression of the South's rigid racial boundaries. And then she had, allegedly, murdered at least one of those children. Yet still, Sarah was freed from court to return to the bosom of her family. The loyal Gershum supported his wife throughout the trial and afterwards, and the couple went on to have more children.

Other Southern husbands found their wives' transgressions harder to forgive, especially when their faithless spouses mothered mulatto children. Catherina Limbaugh's serial adultery with white and black men drove her husband Christian to petition for divorce. Christian told the Rowan County Court in 1805 that he had left his wife after a short and miserable marriage, 'a state of the most poignant misery' caused by Catherina's 'ungovernable temper'. His wife's sexual 'incontinency' proved even harder to bear, 'for [Christian] frequently had reason to believe, that her immoral & indecent turn of mind led her to be connected with other men than [himself]'.[4] Christian further claimed that Catherina had borne 'one or more mulatto children'. The Assembly heard further evidence that Catherina had appeared before the Salisbury Superior Court the previous year, charged with 'the barbarous murder' of one of her mulatto children. Found guilty and convicted of the crime, Catherina was sentenced to death by hanging, but received a last-minute reprieve from Salisbury Governor James Turner, who, swayed by a supporter's argument that the murder of a mulatto child was 'not an example so dangerous to society as most others', pardoned Catherina as she stood beneath the gallows.[5]

Sarah Wiggins's alleged act of infanticide, as she attempted to conceal an illegitimate birth, was by no means uncommon. Many white Southern mothers of mulatto children also sought to conceal the evidence of their sexual transgressions. Unmarried Rachel Fields of New Bern killed her 'bastard child' in 1783, and she and the child's father were both charged with its murder. In 1790, widow Sarah Bryan of Jones County stabbed to death her illegitimate baby daughter, and over in Wayne County in 1793, spinster Rachel Roberts also killed her illegitimate child. In February the same year, unmarried Sarah Simpson of Craven County also murdered her newborn infant.[6] Court records of the eighteenth and nineteenth centuries are replete with indictments against unmarried mothers charged with the murder of illegitimate children, though the majority of women in this situation probably did not resort to such extreme measures.

When white women mothered mulatto children they did so in the certain knowledge that they would be made to suffer the consequences of cross-racial sex. This was especially true for poor white women. Sarah Wiggins escaped conviction, but this was most likely because in the first place, juries rarely attached much value to the lives of mulatto children, and second, Sarah was a member of the slaveholding class. While her family could not be counted among the county's wealthiest, Sarah's husband and father owned several slaves and nearly 300 acres of land. Sarah's husband and male relatives therefore enjoyed a measure of status and power in New Bern, and it was unlikely that a jury would return a guilty verdict for the wilful death of an unwanted and illegitimate mulatto child. As Victoria Bynum and others have shown, however, Southern courts frequently punished deviant poor white women by forcefully removing and apprenticing their children to planters or other businesses or tradespersons.[7]

In common with other Southern slaveholding states, North Carolina's legislature had passed a series of acts explicitly prohibiting interracial marriages. The first of these Acts, passed in 1715, was subsequently amended throughout the colonial and antebellum years.[8] Yet, while they could legislate against marriage, the authorities could not legislate against emotions, and whites and blacks continued to defy racial boundaries, though not without consequences.

Southern Assemblies routinely manipulated the apprenticeship scheme to punish women of all races – free blacks and mulattoes, and poor white women deemed to have transgressed moral and racial codes – by forcibly removing their offspring from their homes, and binding them out as apprentices in the households of more 'respectable' white residents. That children of all races were forced into apprenticeship against their parents' wishes is clear, though the lawmakers explicitly sought to punish white mothers of mulatto children. Section 15 of the 1715 'Act Concerning Servants and Slaves', which also regulated apprenticeship, specifically empowered churchwardens to bind out as apprentices any children born from a union between a white woman and a black man, until they reached the age of 31 years. This was blatantly discriminatory, for the legitimate children of same-race parents could be bound out only until they reached 21 years. As Karin L. Zipf argues, apprenticeship gradually became an instrument deployed by the patriarchal state seeking to establish control of households headed by white women and free blacks. By the time of the Civil War, the Southern apprenticeship system had emerged as an institution steeped in presumptions about gender, race, and class to deny single, poor and widowed white women, free blacks and mulattoes their rights as parents.[9]

In November 1774, the Bertie County Court of Pleas and Quarter Sessions ordered that sisters Jemima and Mary Beth Wiggins, 'bastard Mulattos of Sarah Wiggins',[10] be apprenticed to one John Skinner. However, six months later, the strenuous objections of Edward Wiggins, their free black father, forced the court to enquire more closely into John Skinner and being 'convinced of Skinner's ill and deceitful behaviour' the order was subsequently rescinded.[11] In this instance, Edward Wiggins successfully secured the return home of his young daughters, reuniting them with their mother. Other mothers and their children were less fortunate.

The apprenticeships of free black and mulatto children, as well as illegitimate and orphaned white children, neatly combined a variety of functions. Primarily, the intrusion of the patriarchal state into the homes of poor white mothers represented a powerful mechanism for the social and sexual control of women deemed as deviant – women who engaged in interracial sexual liaisons, and the mothers of illegitimate children. Illicit interracial sex not only disturbed white racial hegemony, but in their relationships with black men, white women also challenged Southern ideals of womanhood, motherhood and the sanctity of the white family. The forced separation of mothers and children served as a stern admonition to women who violated Southern codes of race, morality and womanhood, and sent a salutary warning to other wayward women that the state would not condone interracial sex.[12] On another level, the forced apprenticeship of the children of poor whites performed another civil function. In the absence of a comprehensive welfare system, impoverished poor whites had to rely principally on county poor relief provision. At the best of times, poor relief was limited in scope and nature, and apprenticeship represented a cost-effective method of addressing the welfare problems posed by indigent white families. Apprenticeship of children meant the county could spend less on providing pecuniary assistance to needy poor whites.[13] Not surprisingly, while recognising that apprenticeship could be the means through which their children acquired trade skills, many regarded it with a measure of ambivalence. Not only did it compel the separation of children from their homes, and the undermining of parental rights over their children, but it also deprived parents of their children's much-needed household labour.

Southern white males considered free sexual access to black women the outward expression of their mastery over enslaved men and women, and routinely enjoyed voluntary and coerced sexual relationships with free and enslaved black women with limited social censure. The same society that sanctioned the widespread sexual abuse of black women by white males was not, however, prepared to tolerate the possibility that black males might enter sexual relationships with white women. Social and sexual distance between white women and black males was to be rigorously enforced, and in the main was achieved through legislation, the systematic terrorisation of black males and their subordination under patriarchal white male power. Yet unknown numbers of enslaved and free black men and white women defied Southern prohibitions against interracial sex, forming unions, cohabitating in common-law marriages and raising families. While some communities might show a degree of tolerance towards interracial couples, the state took a firmer stance, imposing sanctions against transgressors. Invariably, the general acceptance of white male-black female sexual relationships meant white women were more likely than white males to be identified as transgressors. Moreover, poor women, rather than elite women, bore the brunt of the authorities' efforts to deter interracial sex.

The historiography of Southern slavery has tended to privilege the material experiences of the slaveholding elite. Yet North Carolina's slaveholding class represented a minority among the white population. The 1860 census, collated on the eve of the Civil War, recorded the numerical dominance of non-slaveholding whites, who represented 70.8 per cent of the state's white population, while the politically dominant planter class represented a mere three per cent of the white population.[14] Non-slaveholders were by no means a homogeneous social group, but comprised several distinct socio-economic groups. The top echelons were occupied by a small class of wealthy professionals and merchants. Below them, and numerically the largest group, was the yeomanry – small farmers who worked their land with family and/or hired white or black labour. At the bottom of the non-slaveholding group was the class of poor whites, who accounted for an estimated twenty-five per cent of the white population. Generally unpropertied, North Carolina's poor whites eked out a subsistence existence on the margins of 'respectable' society. Like their Barbadian counterparts, the poor whites of North Carolina were viewed contemptuously by propertied whites and enslaved blacks alike. To the latter, they were 'white trash' or 'poor buckra'; to the propertied they were 'rednecks' and 'the dregs of civilisation'. In a society that insisted on the superiority of whiteness, and in which ownership of land and property was the foremost indicator of social status, poor white men and women represented a liminal group. To be white and poor meant to lack honour, respectability and status. In particular, poor white women were suspiciously regarded by elite Southerners as base women, 'little better than negroes' (as one nineteenth-century Southern judge opined), and like the blacks in their midst, possessed of an inherent sexual depravity. Certainly, their economic circumstances militated against their conformity to the Southern idealised notions of dependent domestic-bound womanhood.

That poor white women of colonial and antebellum North Carolina should remain 'overlooked and underestimated' is to obscure their vitality as social actors who, in diverse ways, played critical roles in the development of the Southern economy and culture, and in doing so, challenged Southern race, class and gender norms. With this in mind, this chapter explores two interrelated themes: the sociosexual control of poor white women, and their participation in North Carolina's colonial and antebellum economy.

Early American colonists viewed Africans as an inferior species of being, but for some time refrained from taking legal steps to institutionalise race distinctions between black and white. Cross-racial marriages were tolerated, perhaps because such partnerships were rare. Non-marital or informal sexual relations, however, occurred with more frequency, as evidenced by the numbers of mulatto progeny of these unions. Tolerance of interracial unions does not, however, signal the acceptance of blacks as true equals of whites; rather, it should be read as indicative of a certain ambivalence by whites towards blacks. However, by the late seventeenth century, as slavery increasingly dominated the Southern economy, the sharpening of racial attitudes led legislators to take a decisive stand against interracial unions. It is in this period that Southern colonies, led by Virginia, began to enact laws against marriages between whites and blacks.

Southerners' increasing concerns to prohibit interracial sexual relationships were grounded in several related fears, but primarily that of the emergence of a sizable and potentially powerful class of free coloured people who could challenge white hegemony, and fear of the erosion of the supposedly distinct racial categories of whiteness and blackness. To permit racial intermarriage would lead inexorably to the gradual blurring of racial categories, a phenomenon that raised uneasy questions in white minds about the basis on which individuals could rightfully claim entitlement to freedom. Southern slavery rested on the assumption that only white people possessed inalienable rights to freedom. The emergence of the South's mulatto population not only provided ample evidence of the corruption of white racial purity, but disturbed the categories of black and white: just who could be counted as white? Who were to count as free or unfree? The free mulatto children of white mothers posed for white Southerners the troublesome question of just how these categories were to be defined, how freedom was to be distributed, and the boundaries of that freedom. The 'problem' of mulatto status was eventually resolved following a high-profile lawsuit brought by Elizabeth Key, the enslaved illegitimate mulatto daughter of an enslaved woman and a white man. In 1655, Elizabeth sued for freedom on the grounds that because her father was a free man, she should therefore inherit his status.[15] Elizabeth won her freedom, but in 1662 the Virginian Assembly moved decisively to clarify matters. Henceforth, the status of all children would be secured through the subversion of a longstanding English legal principle that established individual status through the father, by replacing it with the peculiarly colonial principle of *partus sequitur ventrim* (literally, 'progeny follows the womb'). Not only did this principle give white males *carte blanche* to sexually abuse enslaved women with impunity, but, significantly, it also ensured that children born of illicit unions between white men and enslaved women followed the condition of the mother. The Act not only inscribed black enslaved women's bodies as the literal reproducers of unfreedom, but, moreover, served to naturalise and to racialise slavery.

That colonial lawmakers were reluctant to place constraints on white male sexual behaviours was borne out by further legislation that specifically targeted white women. In 1691, Virginia required that any white woman who bore a mulatto child pay a fine or face indentured servitude of five years for herself and 30 years for her child. At the same time, marriage between blacks and whites was proscribed, as indicated by the declaration that any white man or woman who married a 'Negro, mulatto, or Indian' would be banished from the colony forever. White males could be prosecuted for marrying black women but, crucially, attracted no punishment for informal sexual unions with them, and black women who bore children with white males were not criminalised.[16] Neither white nor black, the offspring of illicit interracial sexual relationships between white women and black men could not be forced into enslavement, but Southern authorities nevertheless insisted that their freedoms be policed and curtailed, and their mothers punished.

In 1715 concern over growing levels of social disorder – reportedly excessive cases of illicit sex, illegitimate births, fornication, adultery and prostitution, and interracial marriages, all acts that were believed to threaten moral and social wellbeing – forced matters to a head. The general belief that the cause of much of this disorder was the free and easy social and sexual intercourse between whites and blacks prompted the authorities to legislate that henceforth marriages between whites and all non-whites would no longer receive legal sanction, and that those who challenged the letter of the law, including officiating clergy, could expect to be severely dealt with. This legislation signalled a significant sea-change in white attitudes and tolerance towards blacks. By regulating interracial unions between 'inferior' blacks and 'superior' whites, colonial authorities sought to establish the hegemonic dominance of the white ruling class, and the reinforcement of a racialised social order founded on beliefs of innate racial differences.

The impact was far-reaching, affecting the lives and social interactions of every individual, free and unfree, black and white, male and female. Furthermore, it marked the historical moment when ideologies of white racial supremacy began to attain ascendancy. Racial and legal categories became inextricably tied to colour, the intended consequence of which was to racialise slavery by defining clearly just who could or could not be enslaved. No white person, regardless of status, could be forced into slavery, which henceforth was to be understood as a permanent and inheritable condition.[17] In establishing the principle of black slavery and white freedom, the Act effectively secured white racial dominance and privilege. It cannot simply be understood as the outcome of governmental impulses to impose order and authority over the enslaved population; rather it was an attempt to define and limit the boundaries of race, gender and class relations of every individual within the society. By the mid-eighteenth century, North Carolina had evolved into a patriarchal hierarchical social order founded on distinctions of race, gender and social class.

Yet punitive legislation did not summarily end casual or permanent sexual unions between the various racial and cultural groups. That interracial marriages continued unabated is borne out by the passing of successive legislation in 1723 and 1741, which imposed punitive fines and additional tax levies on whites who married non-whites, reiterating the colonial authorities' continuing intolerance towards cross-racial marriages. Further, numerous surviving transcripts of court proceedings against white women with black spouses during the colonial era attests to the willingness of some couples to subvert the law. But such couples always did so in the knowledge that they might be called upon to answer for their 'crimes'.

In truth, most sexual relations that occurred across colour lines involved illicit sexual relations between white males and free and enslaved black women. Yet, what is most striking about the 1715 laws is their inherent gender and class biases. While seeking to regulate the sexual freedoms of all the colony's population, the 1715 Acts evidence a particular concern to control and limit the sexual freedoms of all white women in general, and lower class women in particular. As the literal bearers of freedom, white women were targeted for regulation. There can be little doubt, however, that legal force was directed towards women of the poorer classes rather than elite women.

Few women who crossed racial boundaries did so lightly, especially if they mothered black children. Indentured mothers of mulatto children were forced to pay a fine of six pounds and had their servitude extended by two years for having 'a Bastard child by a Negro, Mulatto, or Indian'. Free white women also could be made to pay a fine, or forced into servitude.[18] As Dorothy Roberts has argued, since only white women could produce white children, they were charged with the responsibility of maintaining the purity of the white race, and when they transgressed, mother and children both paid the penalty.[19] Some states, including North Carolina, went so far as to sentence the illegitimate children of white women and black men to terms of servitude for the first two to three decades of their lives.[20]

The meanings and effects of white racial identity shaped the contours of white women's lives throughout the colonies. But, as the ways in which whiteness was played out differed across colonial sites, the strategies devised in the pursuit of maintaining white racial purity, and the ways in which white women were drawn into these strategies, differed also.[21] White male anxieties that 'their' women might be 'led astray' were directly related to their fear of the racial contamination of the white race. In a society that promoted white supremacist ideologies, fear of the dissolution of the white race was the leitmotif that ran through Southern society. As the biological reproducers of the white race (and hence of freedom), white women – especially poor, single women – represented the foremost potential threat to white racial purity. So long as white women were dependent on white men, fears of white racial dilution could be partially allayed. Of course, their anxieties about the consequences of interracial sex did not prohibit white men themselves from having sexual relationships with free and enslaved black women. Clearly, it was white racial purity that was at stake, for Southern whites did not define blackness as a pure racial category that could also be contaminated.

As we saw in Chapter 1, colonial patriarchs took to the Americas a tradition of inherent distrust towards lower class women who appeared in elite imaginations as sexually loose and immoral creatures. Southerners adhered to the belief that poorer-class women were always potential sexual and racial transgressors, for poor women had ample opportunity to meet black males. The productive roles of poor white women and black men within the Southern economy frequently brought them together in circumstances that heightened the possibilities for cross-racial relationships. In rural communities, poor white women worked alongside enslaved men and women on farms and plantations. Enslaved people and poor whites frequently traded goods and produce, providing further opportunities to bridge the racial line, and Southerners commonly complained that many taverns run by poor white women provided a social space for illicit liaisons between black men and white women. Thus, black men and poor white women met in a variety of social spaces in both urban and rural contexts. Perhaps inevitably, as they worked alongside each other, traded with each other, or socialised together, white women and black men developed close, and sometimes intimate, friendships in the face of over-arching racial ideologies and legal constraints that sought to maintain social and sexual distance between them.

Southerners might pretend otherwise, but it was known that some middle-class white women had enjoyed adulterous affairs with black males. Some elite women subverted accepted norms of respectable feminine behaviour, as did the young daughter of North Carolina's highest-ranking revolutionary general who, before she was eighteen years old, had allegedly given birth to two mulatto sons.[22] Perhaps overstating his case, an antebellum North Carolina court official noted that bastardy cases were heard regularly by the courts, but wryly suggested that these children were not exclusively the offspring of poor white women. 'Mulattos are not a rare article, and wives and daughters of slave-holders are oftener the mothers of them, than are poor women.'[23] As recently as the 1930s, in a WPA interview, Millie Markham insisted that she was the freeborn child of Tempie James, the daughter of wealthy slaveholders who owned a plantation on the Roanoke River. When Tempie's affair with Squire James, the family's 'tall and light-coloured' coachman, was exposed, Tempie ran away from her parent's house, purchased Squire's freedom from the new owners to whom he had been sold, and after swearing an oath that she was of mixed blood, married her suitor. Tempie was subsequently disowned by her family.[24] Adorah Rienshaw of Raleigh also recalled that her mulatto father was the 'issue' of a wealthy plantation mistress and 'a coal-black nigger man' on her husband's plantation. The affair between Adorah's grandfather and his mistress was discovered when she later gave birth to a mulatto child.[25] Many more ex-enslaved lay claim to white mothers, many of whom were allegedly the daughters of wealthy slave-owning families.

Slander cases brought by and against propertied women often involved accusations of sexual intimacy with black males. Such was the case when the planter husband of one Mrs Reid was forced to bring a suit after a rash of rumours circulated in the neighbourhood asserting that his wife had been caught *in flagrante delicto* with one of her slaves.[26] A few years later, in an 1858 case, unmarried Candace Lucas of the Piedmont region was forced to sue her neighbour, Gilbert Nichols, for his slanderous claims that she had been romantically involved with several local slaves, and had given birth to illegitimate mulatto children.[27]

Husbands from all socio-economic groups filed divorce petitions alleging their wife's adulterous behaviour with black men.[28] As Dorothy Roberts notes, in the racialised society of the South, female marital fidelity was doubly important, for while it assured white men of their legitimate paternity, it also ensured white racial purity. By being faithful to their husbands, white women were also faithful to their race.[29] Adulterous white wives could therefore hardly be tolerated either by their injured husbands or by their community. Ultimately though, their close familial proximity to white males, and their racial privileges, limited elite women's opportunities and motives for engaging in cross-racial sex. White men could pass their illegitimate coloured children off as slaves, but white women who bore coloured children were situated very differently. Still, court records do reveal instances of elite women's sexual relationships with black males.

The volumes of journals and correspondence of elite Southern women indicate that they shared with white males the belief of the undesirability of interracial sex, and embraced dominant valves that normalised white males as potential partners. For Southern ladies tempted to cross racial boundaries, the social consequences were severe. They faced not only losing their racially derived status and privilege, but also possible ostracism from their families (leading to certain impoverishment) and exclusion from elite society. Poor white women had much less to lose in their relationships with black males. Indeed, for the most impoverished, sexual relationships – whether common law or, more rarely, marriage – probably represented a commonsense, if illicit, route to relative economic security.[30]

Marriage for white women purportedly offered economic security and protection from the vicissitudes of life, and for many it represented the source of their deepest satisfaction; but for countless others, marriage brought great unhappiness and disaffection. Husbands committed adultery, wasted women's property, drank heavily, gambled, beat, abused and murdered wives. Ex-enslaved Dave Lawson remembered with awe his grandpappy's master, Drew Norwood, 'de meanest white man de Lawd ever let breath de breaf of life', who brutalised his slaves and his wife in equal measure. Following a particularly vicious whipping by Norwood, the pregnant Mrs Cary died after prematurely giving birth to a stillborn child.[31] In 1853, *The Raleigh Register* reported the case of Revd. George Washington Carrowan, wealthy planter, preacher and community stalwart, who 'on some frivolous pretext, knocked his wife down with a chair, and beat her ... until the chair broke to pieces, and then seized a large stick and continued to beat her'. Mary Carrowan's life was saved only by the timely intervention of Clement H. Lasssiter, their boarder. Carrowan, known to have enjoyed multiple affairs with married and unmarried women of his congregation, had previously accused Lassiter of paying untoward attention to his wife. When Lassiter's murdered body was found days later, Carrowan was charged with his murder. During the trial, it emerged that Carrowan had had two previous marriages, and evidence suggested that his former wives, now both deceased, had met their deaths probably by Carrowan's hands.[32] Mary Carrowan was not called upon to give evidence, but supported her husband throughout the trial. When a guilty verdict was announced, the condemned man shot and wounded the prosecutor before taking his own life. Unbeknown to her neighbours, Mary Carrowan had endured years of abuse from her husband. The mother of Carrowan's children and stepmother to the children of his previous marriage, Mary had scant choice but to remain in a marriage to a violent man on whom she was economically dependent.

Despite the prevailing belief that marriage was women's natural destiny, unfulfilled and unhappy unions led some women to break their marriage vows and, to the chagrin of their husbands, many forged sexual relationships with black males, often compounding their offences by bearing mulatto children. Such was the case of Sarah Dickson, who married Alexander Smith of Ashe County, North Carolina, in 1784. The couple enjoyed a few years' 'domestic peace and pleasure', but in 1801, Sarah abandoned husband and five daughters to elope with 'a Mullatoe [sic] man Nearly as Black as an Negro'. Smith's divorce petition was granted in 1809, and the Assembly further prohibited the errant Sarah from asserting claims to any part of her ex-husband's estate.[33] The 1824 divorce petition filed by Lewis Tombereau, a French shoemaker of Martin County, vilified his wife Nancy Jolly as 'one of the most frail, lewd, and depraved daughters of Eve'. Nancy had not only audaciously abandoned her husband for a mulatto barber, but further inflamed Tombereau's anger by giving birth to a mulatto child.[34] Jonathan Bryan, of New Hanover County, also sought a divorce from his wife, Ann Jane Anders, who not only attempted to kill him but also incited 'an Insurrection' among his slaves. Ann Jane had left him on several occasions, and in 1827 when the suit was filed, had been absent from the marital home for nearly two years, and was known to be living in 'a Negro house... with Negros'.[35]

Lacking in social status or racial privileges, many poor white women – married or otherwise – openly violated Southern legal codes and taboos against interracial sex, often becoming the subjects of county and state newspaper reports, court proceedings and petitions to the Legislature. In 1803, the illiterate poor white Isaac Bracewell of Edgecombe County sought a separation from wife Nancy after she had deserted him 'without just cause, or provocation'. Nancy, he claimed, had enjoyed extramarital relationships with various men 'without distinction of colour'.[36] Young Utley of Wake County, a self-described man of 'obscure birth & condition' but nevertheless possessed of 'high principles', was granted a divorce from his wife Mary Woodward. The couple had married when Mary 'was in an advanced stage of pregnancy', and Young confessed that 'he had reason to believe that he himself was the cause of her situation'. Shortly after the marriage, to Young's surprise and distress, 'the wife he so tenderly loved was delivered of a mulatto child'. In 1810 Mary left the marital home and moved to Tennessee, where she now allegedly cohabited with 'a man of Colour (the supposed author of her shame) in the character of a wife'.[37] In 1813, Wayne County Court heard the divorce petition of Joseph Hancock, whose wife Tabitha had, '[A]bandoned herself to the most vile prostitution and debauchery', and had further insulted her husband's sensibilities by giving birth to children 'of various colours and complexions'.[38] In 1832, the legislature received a divorce petition from John Johnson of Orange County, who testified that when he, 'being destitute of Land of his own, was induced to become a Partner in a farm with a free negro', his wife Peggy 'formed an attachment to said negro and consequently treated your Petitioner in such a way that he was forced to abandon her'.[39] Wayne County wife Ann Borden challenged her husband Jesse's 1827 divorce petition brought before the Legislature. Ann insisted that she had left her husband because she could no longer tolerate her husband's ill-treatment of her. At the heart of the matter was a 'mulatto child, the fruits of a negro', born to Ann about a month prior to her marriage to Jesse Borden. Ann testified that contrary to her husband's intention to plead otherwise, he had known that he was not the child's father, and she had not, as he claimed, tried to pass it off as his, as attempts to do so 'would have been unavailing as the child would unavoidably have shown for itself'. Jesse Borden issued a counter-claim, alleging instead that he had believed the child to be the consequence of a pre-marital sexual relationship he had enjoyed with Ann, only to discover 'to his mortification and astonishment' that the child was a 'mulatto'.[40]

Between 1800 and 1835, an estimated 7.5 per cent of all divorces in North Carolina were granted to petitioners alleging a spouse's interracial adultery.[41] Invariably, a proportion of wives charged with adulterous interracial sexual relations were the subjects of false accusations. Winny Manning's 1805 divorce petition, considered by Edgecombe County Court, conveyed barely suppressed outrage at the discovery by this 'young and healthy woman' that she had been duped into marrying a man unable to satisfy her sexual needs. Eli, she charged, was 'absolutely impotent'. Worse still, Eli attempted to displace blame on to his wife, accusing her of having 'illicit connection with every man, both white and black that may have seen her'. Interestingly, Eli 'freely and sincerely' joined Ann in her petition, perhaps a tacit admission as to the truth of his wife's claims.[42]

Divorce law in North Carolina was certainly more liberal than in other Southern states, but the sanctification of the patriarchal family as the bedrock of Southern society invariably made it difficult for married couples to obtain divorces. Victoria Bynum has shown that in all but three of fifteen divorce suits appealed to the state's superior court between 1830 and 1861, petitioners were denied a divorce even in the face of compelling evidence of adultery or wife-beating. Even proven allegations of interracial sex brought against an adulterous spouse were not necessarily accepted as sufficient cause for dissolving a marriage. Marvin Scroggins's petition, laid before the Superior Court of Buncombe County, alleged that his wife's adulterous relationship with a black man had resulted in the birth of a mulatto child. The petition was denied, on the grounds that the plaintiff had been an accessory to his own dishonour by marrying a woman he knew to be of lewd character.[43]

That the majority of petitions alleging adulterous interracial relationships emanated from white males reflected the South's more hardened stance against white women who transgressed racial lines. White males commonly enjoyed sexual unions with free and unfree black women, but these relationships attracted less opprobrium. In 1816 an indignant Iredell County wife petitioned for divorce after her husband had 'abandoned her, and his children, and in violation of the laws of God, and man', had taken up 'with a negro woman, and still continued to live and cohabit with her'.[44] In the same year Harriet Laspeyre, a slave-owner of New Hanover County, requested legal separation and protection from claims made on her property by her wastrel husband, alleging that he had married her solely for her property. Harriet's petition charged that her husband Bernard 'would urge in the most pressing manner, for her consent to sell the Negroes secured to her by said settlement, upon her refusal he would fall in to the most violent paroxysms of rage, and abuse her in the most virulent language ... too gross and indecent to be repeated'. Eventually, 'wearied out by his reiterated ... importunities ..., intimidated by his ... threats and fondly hoping that a compliance with his wishes, might purchase her kinder treatment', Harriet consented to the sale of three of her slaves. The aggrieved Harriet further alleged that she had been usurped in Bernard's affection by a negro mistress, whom Bernard encouraged to take Harriet's place as the legitimate mistress of his household. Harriet complained that she was

> at length stripped of the right that every woman claims and is so very tenacious of the direction and superintendance [sic] of her house hold affairs [,] divested of her keys, deprived of the authority of a mistress [,]

her negroes forbidden to obey her orders under penalty of the severest punishment, exposed to contumely and want and every attempt made to render her an object of detestation to her own Children.

Perhaps Harriet could have borne her suffering in silence, but Bernard's romantic liaison threatened the security of Harriet's children, for according to his wronged wife, Bernard had appropriated 'the profits arising from the labor of her Slaves, which ought to have been appropriated, to the support and education of her Children, she had the extreme vexation to see wantonly lavished on his black and mulatto mistresses'. As Harriet continued,

> while subject to his authority, [she] suffered the most degrading and humiliating treatment, [was] abused in the dirtiest language such as a well-bred man would blush to apply to the worst of Servants, actually threatened with manual chastisement, and frequently order'd [sic] to leave his House . . . the said Bernard Laspeyre in violation of every law human or divine and setting publick [sic] opinion at defiance has lived for a long time in the Town of Wilmington in open adultery with a negro wench taken her in to his House and permitting her to exercise all the rights and authorities of a Wife – The atrocity of his character has been recently developed by his absconding and bearing off the greatest part, and most valuable of her Negroes . . . Your Memorialist no longer capable of enduring such accumulated wrongs in hourly expectation of violence to her person and seriously apprehensive of an attempt upon her life she left his House, with a fixed and immutable determination never again to subject herself to his tyranny.[45]

In a counter-petition, Bernard vigorously contested his wife's accusations, claiming that she had brought a 'virulent and Infamous Libel' against him, and requested that the Assembly repeal its decision to grant Harriet control of her property.[46] Bernard's behaviour towards his wife was especially cruel; not only had he wantonly abused his wife before abandoning her, but in bringing his black mistress into the marital home, and allowing her to assume the mantle of mistress, he had struck directly at Harriet's sense of womanhood.

So long as their husbands did not flaunt their sexual infidelities, most white Southern wives might have silently accepted their husband's marital peccadilloes with enslaved women, but Bernard's outrageous behaviour in divesting his wife of authority and placing it in the hands of his black mistress represented a step too far, and one that could not be quietly endured. No white wife could be expected to tolerate the usurpation of her household authority by a black woman – an event that so undermined and demeaned Harriet's sense of self as a white woman that she was finally forced to bring a suit against her husband. Bernard's behaviour was not an isolated incidence. In Halifax County Mary Reid, alias Polly Read, also sought divorce in 1832 after her husband Elias had cruelly 'banished her to the Negro quarters, beat her and abandoned her, eventually taking her slaves out of the state, and vowing never to return during her lifetime'.[47] And in 1845 a divorce petition filed by Ruthey Ann Hansley, the wife of another New Hanover County planter, Samuel G. Hansley, reached the Supreme Court. The petitioner claimed that her husband had taken up with a slave woman on his plantation and that he had allowed his mistress 'to treat his wife with contempt, depriving her of all authority as mistress of the house and conferring it on the negro'. Hansley heaped further cruelty and embarrassment on his wife by forcing her to 'sleep in bed with said negro Lucy, when he would treat the said Lucy as his wife, he occupying the same bed with the petitioner and the negro Lucy'.[48] Numerous wives unwilling to countenance their husband's adultery turned to the divorce courts, but a few took rather more drastic action. Ex-enslaved Jacob Manson of Raleigh recalled after emancipation the shooting to death of local planter Jimmie Shaw by his enraged wife, after she had caught him *in flagrante delicto* with his enslaved mistress. Cursed by her guilty husband, who told her to 'tend to her own damn business and he would tend to his', the angry wife 'grabbed de gun and let him have it. She shot 'im dead in the hall.'[49]

White women invariably found it harder than males to conceal their involvement in cross-racial affairs. Often these illicit relations remained clandestine, only discovered by husband and community when the birth of a mulatto child bore witness to an interracial affair. In 1825, just months after their marriage, John Chambers of Haywood County sought an annulment from Riney O'Neal, charging that his wife had given birth to a mulatto child. Riney had attempted to conceal the child's birth and racial heritage by giving the child to an enslaved woman owned by her father, but Chambers had discovered his wife's deception.[50] In some instances, when the facts of concealment became known, the white community reacted with sympathy to the plight of the child. Such was the case with the enslaved woman Lucy Selph and her daughter Laura, whose suit for freedom was laid before the Assembly on her behalf by her owner Gurdon Deming. Deming had purchased Lucy and her daughter after the death of her previous owner, a Mr Selph. According to Deming, he had discovered from 'a number of the most respectable citizens of Fayetteville, that it was always the intention of Mr Selph to manumit the Said Lucy at his death'. After Mr Selph's sudden death his estate was declared insolvent, and to clear his debts Lucy and her daughter were sold by the estate's administrator. 'She was purchased at a mere nominal Sum by

Several Gentlemen with the View to Carry out the wishes of Mr Selph; Owing however to the insolvency of the person delegated to bid her off, occurring soon after, She was again Sold and has subsequently fallen into the hands of your petitioner.' Deming not only pleaded that Lucy be manumitted in accordance with the wishes of her deceased owner, but further argued that he '[had] reason to believe... from diligent inquiries made, that the Said Lucy ought not to be held longer in bondage.' According to local rumour, Lucy was in fact the illegitimate mulatto daughter of a white mother who, desperate to protect her reputation, had placed the infant Lucy 'in [the] charge of a woman, a slave of one John Selph'. Though conceding that he '[was] aware that legal proof cannot be made of the fact' he was 'fully satisfied, that the Said Lucy is the daughter of a free white Woman'. As proof of Lucy's maternal heritage, Deming pointed to the lightness of Lucy's skin which 'in colour is perfectly White, and cannot be distinguished from the purest of the race'. Though Lucy's case received support and sympathy from members of the white community of Cumberland County, the Assembly was not convinced of Lucy's claims to whiteness, and Deming's petition was dismissed.[51]

In defiance of state laws against interracial marriages, a few whites did attempt to put their intimate relationships with black partners on to a legitimate footing. John Waters, 'a very poor [white] man' of Wilkes County, intended to marry his lover Elisabeth Culms, a 'woman of colour', but knowing that interracial marriages were not legally permitted, the couple instead cohabited together. The couple had 'six fine children', and lived together in apparent peace until a malicious neighbour brought them to the attention of the authorities. In 1809, John and Elisabeth were indicted for contravening the laws against interracial marriages and each fined $100. Neither spouse could afford the fine, so Waters petitioned the Legislature for relief on the grounds of his impoverishment. He admitted his 'unlawful and irreligious' cohabitation with Elisabeth and their children, but hoped they as providers and protectors of their own wives and children would understand his masculine desire to 'do a fatherly and Husbands part' by his family, 'as time or circumstances cannot alienate them from me'.[52] Waters' impassioned plea for aid was rejected. In August 1840, the Supreme Court also considered the case of free black Joel Fore and Susan Chesnutt, a white woman of Lenoir County. Fore was accused of having taken 'into his house Susan Chestnutt and they did live and bed and cohabit together without being legally married – they did have children as a result of the cohabitation'. Fore produced a Marriage Licence authorising the marriage before 1838, when the General Assembly made cross-racial marriages illegal. For some reason, their marriage had not been solemnised until 1840, and the Court objected to the marriage and their cohabitation.[53]

Sexual liaisons between white women and free black men held particularly worrying implications for the Southern authorities, not only because they undermined white male patriarchal power over 'their' white women and black males, but also because they threatened existing property relations which stipulated that white males alone could hold unquestionable rights to property ownership. Fearing the potential economic and political power of a property-owning class of free coloureds and blacks, Southern authorities were at all times concerned to limit the property rights of non-whites. In 1820 Samuel Love, a free Negro of Burke County, having acquired, 'by the blessing of divine providence and his honest industry and care... some property both real and personal', petitioned the Legislature to legitimise his son Samuel Jr, so that he might inherit his father's property. Love received an unsympathetic hearing. The committee noted that 'the petitioner is quite a Black man, and the mother of his Son a white woman', before summarily dismissing his petition. To do otherwise would, they reasoned, 'not only encourage immorral Turpitude [sic]', but would also 'lessen the opprobrium now attached to a licentious entercourse [sic] between persons of opposite colours'. In Love's case, the court's refusal to legitimise his mulatto son signalled not only the public reaffirmation of the state's unwillingness to sanction an illicit interracial marriage, but in refusing to recognise Samuel Jr as his father's legitimate heir, curtailed his rights to own and freely dispose of whatever property he possessed. Moreover, the court used the opportunity to remind Samuel Love that though he might be legally free, he was nevertheless an inferior species of being and unworthy of the inalienable rights of white males. The message to Samuel Love was clear. Though his status as a free man moved him beyond the immediate control of a slave-owner, he was to remain nevertheless a subject of white, male authority as represented in the body of the Assembly.[54]

The fact that Samuel Love owned property surely stood out in a society in which few free blacks could acquire or maintain a sure hold over property. Love's status as property owner almost certainly created unease in the minds of elite whites in an era when many poor whites were themselves landless and propertyless, and dependent on public assistance for their survival. Poor relief helped alleviate the dire poverty of North Carolina's indigent white community but, in its dispensation, helped reinforce existing social hierarchies.[55] It represented a crucial mechanism through which the patriarchal state could exert control over the social and sexual freedoms of poor white women, especially those women who were deemed to have transgressed.

The absence of a comprehensive Southern welfare system left many of the poorest whites with no other means but poor relief. By mid-nineteenth century, however, a number of benevolent and charitable associations provided additional support, primarily to poor white women and their families. Formed in 1820, the Raleigh Female Benevolent Society had as its objective the raising of

> a fund to be applied to the relief of aged widows and other distressed females who may be considered fit objects of charity; to provide employment to such females as are able and willing to work, and who cannot meet with employers; to give articles of clothing to orphans and other destitute children; to promote the education of poor children, and cause them to be instructed in some of the most useful domestic employments; to promote order and industry among the poorer classes of society, and to discourage idleness and vice as far as practicable.[56]

Philanthropic societies such as that established by the elite women of Raleigh generally operated within religious and moralistic frameworks. Poverty was a scourge on society, regarded as symptomatic of the innate failings of the poor, especially the twin evils of idleness and vice, rather than the consequence of structural inequities. Given this logic, few benevolent societies were driven by a social reform agenda. Poverty could be ameliorated only through the adoption of a sober and industrious work ethic.

The creation of employment opportunities for impoverished women, and training in religious instruction for poor children, represented the foremost functions of the social work of benevolent societies. Within two years of its inception, the Raleigh Female Benevolent Society could proudly count as a major achievement the establishment of a school for young girls of poor families. In addition to religious and basic instruction in reading, writing and arithmetic, young girls were also taught 'all kinds of plain work' – weaving, spinning and a range of other domestic skills that would later enhance their employment prospects, and thereby '[enable them] to repay, by their industry, some part of their Debt to Society, while they are acquiring that knowledge which may rescue them from poverty, and render them useful and respectable in the human sphere which God has placed them'.

While the Society's endeavours to provide schooling for children of poor families met with considerable success and widespread approval, its efforts to induce poor women to embrace 'habits of industry' were not consistently fruitful. Subscriptions, donations and other fundraising activities enabled the Society to procure vast quantities of cotton and wool which were then turned into clothing, bedding and sundry household items, and sold by the Society to the public. Income from the sale of the finished products was paid as wages – often the sole source of familial income – to the women who manufactured them. Most pleasing to the Society, this income enabled the married women among their poor beneficiaries to 'assist their husbands in the performance of a sacred duty'.

While reporting considerable success in its income-generating objectives, the Society's managers nevertheless admitted that attempts to provide employment for women had encountered some resistance. At the 1821 Annual Meeting they announced with regret that some 'individuals have been found, who refused the work offered, either from a false pride, or other motive equally unwarrantable'.[57] That the managers attributed poor women's rejection of employment to a sense of 'false pride' is revealing of their inability to appreciate fully the grim realities of seamstresses in the Southern labour market. Granted, some poor women were genuinely work-shy, preferring instead to secure a livelihood through other less respectable avenues, such as prostitution. But a variety of factors informed women's wide-scale refusal of this needlework. As Mari Jo Buhle suggests, needlework inspired one of the earliest forms of female benevolence, in large part because needlework was assumed to be an essential domestic skill undertaken by women of all classes.[58] No doubt the benevolent ladies of Raleigh rationalised that encouraging poor women to turn their hands to needlework was, after all, simply a matter of transforming a staple of women's labour from a domestic vocation to a wage-earning occupation. But it was one thing to sew, knit, weave, and spin clothing, bedding and household items for one's own family, and quite another to take up the same tasks as an occupation. In the first place, while such employment schemes provided some poor white women with an income, the wages received by women for their long hours of work proved insufficient to support women and their families. Though the Society stressed that the women would be engaged in 'plain work', a survey of their records reveals that much of the sewing completed by needle-workers was in fact intricate and labour-intensive. In an 1823 accounting of sundry items produced by the needlewomen, we find hundreds of pairs of socks and stockings, but also '3 suits Bed Curtains, 25 Table Cloths, 35 Toilet Cloths, 30 Napkins, 7 Coats and Vests, 18 Counterpanes, and 2 bed quilts' – items demanding fine embroidery skills.[59] Securing decent rates of pay for the high-quality handiwork of poor seamstresses represented a considerable challenge for the Society. When they weighed up their options, many poor women no doubt rationalised that the paltry wages offered by such schemes were insufficient to offset the amount of labour expended. Worse, accepting the charity of middle-class women, however well meaning, invariably entailed accepting their intrusion into their homes and private lives. Raleigh's Female Benevolent Society certainly expected that the poor 'objects of charity' make significant adjustments to their lifestyles, urging poor women to adopt temperance, sexual purity and adherence to religious values, and indeed some poor women proved receptive. In 1823, the managers proudly reported that they had:

> the happiness to believe, that some have embraced habits of industry, which this Society has furnished them with the means of acquiring, who before trod the path which leads to destruction. They had erred, and were conscious of it, and have sought a refuge from guilt and woe, in constant employment and reformed habits. They have wept in contrition, and have exulted in the means of returning from the now detested paths in which they formerly walked.[60]

Most charitable female employment schemes displayed less concern with tackling the sources of root sources of poverty than with bringing about the moral improvement of poor women. As the Raleigh Society was careful to explain to its subscribers: 'the most deserving may not be the most *necessitous* and although evil may previously have been committed, yet who shall say what has been *resisted*'.[61] While some poor women were rescued from their former lives of depravity, not all embraced middle-class morality, especially when it demanded the sacrifice of small comforts that made their miserable lives bearable. How, after all, could middle-class women who had never suffered from deprivation appreciate that the grim realities of poverty could drive many poor women to seek comfort in alcohol or illicit sex? That many benevolent middle-class women were naive, to say the least, about the vicissitudes of poverty undermined their authority to dispense advice to their poorer sisters, many of whom chose to reject charity rather than accept the moralistic self-improvement imperative driving middle-class women's philanthropic endeavours. Doubtless many poor women regarded these 'do-gooders' with equal measures of suspicion, distrust and scepticism, viewing them as the feminine representatives of a patriarchal state that sought to control their social freedoms. And it could not have escaped the attention of poor white women that many middle-class female philanthropists acted from self-interested motives.

The charitable work of the Raleigh Female Benevolent Society was informed by a commitment to the ideology of the sanctity of the white family. In targeting women and young girls, the Society positioned itself as a vehicle for the social upliftment of the poorest white families. That these middle-class societies placed poor white women at the centre of their strategies was a reflection of their acceptance of the dominant ideology that stressed women's central roles and responsibilities within the family, especially in a climate with high levels of male unemployment that militated against men's ability to fulfil their socially expected role of familial provider. As the Society's managers recognised, the wages earned by poor white women for whom they found employment were often their household's sole income. 'Too frequently it happens', they reported in 1823, 'that the companions of these necessitous females lay not their hands at the labouring oar, or perhaps that their united exertions may not be adequate to provide the positive necessaries of life'.[62] In acknowledging the vital importance of women's waged labour to their familial income, the Society unwittingly exposed contradictions in Southern ideologies. The existence of labouring white women revealed the fallacies of Southern gender conventions: the myth of dependant white womanhood, the ideology of separate spheres, and the gender division of labour. More than this, they revealed the uncomfortable reality of poor white women's critical roles in sustaining the family economy.

According to the ideology of separate spheres, the private domestic household represented the natural and proper place for white women. In reality, however, the need to secure an independent income or to contribute to the family finances often pushed women of the poorer classes into the public sphere, and often beyond the patriarchal reach of males. The doctrine of separate spheres held less meaning for poor women whose survival necessarily depended on their movement between the domestic sphere and the public world of waged labour. To be sure, most working women did not experience labour as a liberating force, but for many their participation in the market economy nevertheless secured a degree of social and sexual agency. Southern societies had no place for such independent women, elite or poor. The very public visibility of labouring women offended Southern conventions of dependent womanhood, while exposing flaws in the ideology of males as familial providers.

Expectations of white female domesticity and economic dependence on white males were evident from the early colonial period. Seeking to maximise the colony's income from tobacco production, Virginian lawmakers in 1643 redefined the population of all those liable for taxes. Under the new schema, 'youths of sixteen years of age [and] upwards' *and* all black women aged sixteen and over were to be included in the category of 'tithables'. As Kathleen Brown and Jennifer Morgan have respectively noted, the inclusion of black women among the category of male tithables for the first time created a legal distinction between black and white women; not only was black women's labour now taxable, but the exemption of white women from taxation implicitly negated recognition of their roles as productive labourers, while confirming their supposed economic dependence on white males.[63] Henceforth, the black female body would be legally and socially configured primarily as a labouring body, a definition that served to underscore African women's racial distance from the ideal of dependent domestic-bound white womanhood. Other colonies followed Virginia's discriminatory tax laws; a North Carolina statute of 1715 defined as tithable all negroes, male and female, of twelve years or more, while defining as taxable among the white population only those white males of sixteen years.[64] Yet, in clarifying white women's status as dependent non-taxpayers, colonial Assemblies could not entirely escape the unpalatable reality that poverty forced many poor white women into productive labour. Certainly, in succeeding years many colonies would wrestle with the problem of how to classify the tithable status of labouring white women, while still retaining the ideal of non-productive white womanhood, thus revealing their determination to maintain racial distance between black and labouring white women. How poor working women negotiated the difficult criss-crossed terrain of class, gender, race and sexuality in the rigid hierarchy that was Southern society is still not fully appreciated.

Though the economic roles of white husbands and fathers as familial providers conferred on males ultimate authority, Southerners nevertheless regarded white women as pivotal to the welfare and reproduction of the white family. Southern males insisted that marriage and motherhood represented the natural destiny of white women. In 1835, the *Southern Literary Messenger* published a long essay by pro-slavery professor Thomas R. Dew, in which he emphasised the domestic world as white women's natural sphere. Dew argued that white women's biologically determined roles as wives and mothers militated against their participation in politics and business, for the demands of white motherhood were incompatible with political life. White women, Dew urged, should therefore apply themselves spiritedly to the fulfilment of this duty.[65] While Northern feminists took umbrage at Dew's conservatism, Southern women embraced his message. Essays, letters and articles in the popular *Southern Ladies Companion* stressed women's responsibility for the 'peace and happiness of the home'.[66] As one Southern woman correspondent enthused, '[in] her home is woman's influence most profoundly felt. There is her limitless sphere – there is her holy mission, in all the beautiful relations of daughter, sister, mother, wife. There she blesses or she curses.'[67] Revd Thacker used the pages of this periodical to reinforce the message of his sermon whilst preaching to a Southern church congregation: 'A Wife, A Mother, How sacred and venerable these names!

What nobler objects can the most aspiring ambition propose to itself, than to fulfil the duties these relations imply! Instead of arguing that your field of influence is so narrow, should you not rather tremble at the magnitude and sacredness of your responsibilities?'[68]

Only within the folds of marriage and motherhood could white women expect to find fulfilment as they discharged their caring and nurturing roles as wives and mothers. Marriage therefore represented the most normative state for elite white women, and Southerners viewed spinsters with a good deal of suspicion. To exist outside of marriage was to exist beyond patriarchal authority, and thus outside the social order – and Southerners could ill-countenance any perceived threats to that social order. As Southern males such as George Fitzhugh were wont to declare, white women *needed* the controlling authority of white men, without which they would be led astray.[69] Southern society could not accommodate women who were neither the wives nor slaves of white men: 'Such women had no place or function in white society. Unmarried, property-less white women were not the vessels through which white male progeny and property passed.'[70] For white women living in households independently of white men, the state assumed the patriarchal role of the non-existent husband, father or brother, exerting its influence over the most private areas of women's lives.[71]

This was especially the case when unmarried, poor white women offended the gender sensibilities of the South. The rigid patriarchal ideology and power structures of North Carolina rendered married women of the elite and middle classes economically dependent on white males, and effectively locked white women into a powerful ideology of womanhood that severely constrained their participation and behaviour in the public sphere. Yet, numerous women of all social classes lived in households without male kin, and for many a sedentary, leisured domestic existence could not be their reality – insofar as it was the reality of *any* white Southern woman. Some fortunate elite white women living in non-male households may have had independent incomes that enabled them to hire domestic labour, thus freeing them from domestic drudgery or the necessity to secure an income. Impoverished Southern white women were, however, forced by their economic circumstances to adopt survivalist strategies that took them into the masculine-dominated public sphere. For these women waged labour, whether formal or informal, legal or illegal, represented their sole means of survival.

Southern rhetoric might insist on the domestic sphere as white women's rightful place, and on the virtuousness of dependent white womanhood, but such sentiments could hardly be upheld by poor class whites. Regardless of marital status, few impoverished white women could look to their husbands or fathers for economic security, and their labour, both within and beyond their household, was essential to the family's welfare and survival. Unlike their 'sisters' in elite households, poor women were expected to contribute to the household income, and according to Charles Bolton, it was not unusual for poor white women to engage in extra-domestic waged labour.[72] Rowan Hinton Helper acknowledged the centrality of poor white women's waged and non-waged labour to the family economy: 'Time and again, in different counties in North Carolina have we seen the poor wife of the poor white husband following him in the harvest field from morning till night, binding up the grain as it fell from the cradle. In the immediate neighbourhood from which we hail, there are not less than thirty women, non-slave-holding whites... who labour in the fields every summer.'[73]

Southern white women of all classes performed a diverse range of waged and unwaged labour. Extant gender historiography has focused on the unwaged, domestic labour of plantation wives and mistresses, revealing the complex integration of women into the plantation economy. By contrast, relatively little attention has been brought to bear on women's labour beyond the boundaries of the plantation household, perhaps in itself an indicator of the pervasiveness of the Southern ideology of dependent womanhood, and we do not as yet fully appreciate the nature and extent of white women's waged and non-waged participation within the domestic and market economies. To a great extent, the invisibility of white female labour was a product of several discourses on which Southern cultural norms rested – prevailing beliefs in the separation of domestic and public spheres, the gendered division of labour, the household as white women's natural space, and a nascent ideology of the centrality of the white male as family breadwinner. All these factors conspired to render invisible the extent and nature of women's domestic and extra-domestic labour.

Scholarship on the yeoman farmers of North Carolina has gone some way towards illuminating the working lives of women of this class. By far the majority of North Carolina's non-elite white women were members of the yeomanry. In the class hierarchy of the state, the yeomanry fell somewhere between the elite planters and the poor, landless whites. Yeoman farmers cultivated small to medium sized tracts of land, producing both subsistence foods and cash crops. The value of female yeomanry has been noted by Keith Bryant, who argues that on these subsistence farms the women were most often engaged specifically in the cultivation of cash crops.[74] In general, few yeoman farmers could afford to invest in slaves, and family members of both genders therefore constituted the primary labour force. At busy times of the year, yeoman farmers hired slave labour, but most yeoman farmers relied primarily on family labour. Despite Southern cultural and racial norms that stressed field labour as suitable only for white males or enslaved peoples, it was common but shameful knowledge that yeoman farmers frequently employed poor white women as field hands, and many ex-slaves recalled working alongside poor white women in the fields.[75] Certainly, the spectacle of free whites and enslaved blacks working together on plantations and yeoman farms was not an uncommon sight in the rural south. Thomas, an ex-slave of Chatham County, remembered that his owners Baxter and Katie Thomas had sometimes hired 'both men and women of the poor white class to work on the plantation. We all worked together.'[76] The spectacle of labouring white women muddied racially coded gendered understandings of white and black womanhood. In the white Southern imagination the figure of the labouring woman was black, not white. Indeed, distinctions between women who laboured and those who did not underpinned the differential constructions of black and white womanhood. Whilst black women's identity was inextricably linked to their roles as labourers, white women's privileged status as 'ladies' was secured through their removal from these same processes. White female respectability derived from women's willingness to accept their relegation to the domestic sphere; and with few exceptions, white women labourers who ventured into the masculine-dominated public sphere risked becoming the objects of male opprobrium. As the editor of the *Weekly Post* opined superciliously in 1852, '[W]e do not doubt our lady readers will pardon us for the opinion that their proper position is not in the full glare of public observation ... not in the general practice of what are called the learned professions, nor in any employment which would compel them to violate the delicate modesty in which their virtue is enshrined.'[77] Southerners could accept a limited range of occupations for white women – hotel keeping, millinery, dressmaking, midwifery and teaching – but only because these roles drew on women's supposed innate domestic qualities, and equally importantly did not threaten white male dominance of the learned professions.

Besides their often unacknowledged participation in field labour, yeoman wives and daughters engaged in more gender-specific labour within and beyond the farm household. Janet Schaw, who visited Wilmington in pre-revolutionary days, was particularly struck by the industriousness of white women of all classes. She was especially impressed by Mrs Cornelius Harnett, wife of a local politician, who kept a garden 'from which she supplies the town with what vegetables they use, also with melon and other fruits . . . minced pies, cheesecakes, tarts, and little biskets which she sends to town once or twice a day, besides her eggs, poultry and butter, . . . all her little commodities are contrived so, as not to exceed one penny a piece and her customers know she will not run tick'.[78] In addition to domestic cleaning, cooking, laundering and raising children, yeoman women tended poultry and livestock, cultivated vegetable gardens, butchered and smoked meats, preserved foodstuffs, spun and wove wool, sewed clothing and bed-linen, milked cows, churned butter and cheese, baked bread, fetched water, and made candles, soap and sundry other household necessities.

Prior to the 1850s, the relatively undeveloped state of Southern manufacturing and the high costs of manufactured products combined to instil in yeoman farmers an ethos of independence and self-sufficiency. Nothing was to be bought that could be made or produced on the farm, and the responsibility for subsistence production and the marketing of surplus produce rested most heavily on the shoulders of yeoman women. As Stephanie McCurry has noted, a farm household without a farm wife was a disadvantaged one indeed.[79] Women's labour was therefore an essential component in the yeoman farmer's quest for self-sufficiency. In 1860, Elizabeth Thomas contributed to the household economy $90 from the sale of home-produced goods, along with 150 lb of butter. Elizabeth and her husband owned neither land nor slaves, and were dependent solely on family labour. Elizabeth's income from the sale of her home-made goods probably represented the bulk of the family's annual income for that year.[80]

Most yeoman farms were owned by males, but some poor women also owned and farmed small tracts of land, growing cash crops and raising livestock and poultry.[81] The widespread practice of hiring out enslaved people meant that even female farmers with smallholdings could appropriate the labour of enslaved women and men. Smallholding enabled less wealthy white women to pursue independent and autonomous livelihoods, and their use of hired enslaved labour drew them into the property relations of the Southern slave-based economy. The economic importance of the women and men who comprised the yeomanry of North Carolina has, until recently, drawn little attention from Southern historians, who placed the plantation unit at the centre of Southern economic production. Without further research, the nature and extent of women's independent participation in this sector of the North Carolinian economy remains hidden. Such research would illuminate critical aspects of the differentiated lives of poor white women, from those of the elite and planter classes. It would also enable examination of the independent accumulationist strategies and agency of such women.

As had occurred in the Caribbean, the Southern plantocracy's reliance on slave-production narrowed employment opportunities for poor whites of both sexes, though they did offer limited employment for some white women, especially in regions where slaves were less numerous. When, in 1858, ill-health deprived Stephen A. Norfleet of his wife Frances's domestic labour, the wealthy planter of Bertie County employed Miss Virginia Vaughan to housekeep for six months. Following Frances's death in 1859, Norfleet again resorted to a white housekeeper, Miss Renny Wooten, at an annual salary of $60, and he also employed white female weavers and seamstresses on his plantation.[82] Why Norfleet chose to employ free white labour is unclear. Bertie County was one of sixteen counties where the enslaved population outnumbered whites, and Norfleet was reckoned among the most substantial planters in the county. In 1860 he owned numerous plantations worked by over 150 slaves. Norfleet was reputedly a public-spirited citizen, and the employment of local white labourers on his plantations was probably driven by his concern for the welfare of the county's poor whites.

Some plantation mistresses employed poor white women as nurses and midwives, washerwomen, governesses for their young children, or as casual labourers to assist with the production of sundry household goods. At times, the employment of poor white women by the planter elite could serve rather more expedient purposes. Mary Norcott Bryan recalled that before the Civil War her parents often employed Bettie, a white maid, to accompany them on 'pleasure trips' to the North. Bryan's parents regarded themselves as humane slave-owners, and though convinced that their slaves preferred bondage to freedom, the Norcotts nevertheless took the precaution of hiring white maids to accompany them on their northern journeys, fearing that taking 'one of our own slaves would have produced unpleasant complications'.[83] Generally however, slave labour remained the bedrock of plantation production, and few planters employed white, waged labourers. A few whites even went to work in the homes of free blacks.[84]

Beyond the plantations, poor white women took in boarders and plied trades as seamstresses and milliners, washerwomen or domestic servants, while others grew foodstuffs and manufactured home-produced goods for sale or barter in local markets. Ex-slaves often recalled that they had traded a variety of foodstuffs and sundry goods with local poor whites. Indeed, in some areas white women marketers found themselves trading alongside enslaved people, in wilful defiance of legislation. Southerners frequently complained of such illicit trading between poor whites and blacks, and more than one white woman fell foul of the law. Around 1830, Hannah Mozingo of Wayne County was rudely awoken one night by neighbours Nathan Lassiter and William Waters, who burst into her home and, in front of her daughters Harriet and Anne, beat her with a stick while hurling accusations of her unlawful trading with local blacks. The following day Hannah was visited by a county official, who also subjected her to a tirade of violent abuse, before taking possession of her hogs and serving her with a warrant for negro trading. Hannah brought a lawsuit against the men involved, but lost her case and was fined $100 for illicitly engaging in trade with negroes.[85]

The numerous taverns, hostels and hotels throughout the state represented a popular means of self-sufficiency for poor white women. Yet women hostel owners and inn-keepers often attracted the suspicious attention of the law, who feared that these were little better than brothels, as indeed some undoubtedly were. That many impoverished white women entered, or fell into, the sex industries is evident because their illegal activities frequently brought them into contact with the authorities, and so into surviving court records. Perhaps because it supposedly drew on women's domestic qualities, hotel-keeping proved an attractive and respectable venture for white women, who in 1851-52 owned an estimated twenty-six hotels throughout the state. Among them was Mrs Beach of Wilmington, owner of the Commercial Hotel, while Mrs Pearce managed the nearby Courthouse Hotel, and Mrs Brothers enjoyed a lively trade at the Franklin Hotel. Most likely these women were widowers, as hotel-keeping was considered one of the most respectable occupations for widowed women. Other white women owned dry goods or grocery stores. In Newcastle, Wilkes County, Mrs Hunt owned a small dry goods and grocery store, and in Columbus and Cherokee Counties, Eliza Herbert and Alva Smith both traded as independent store-owners. Women owned all of the state's three confectionery stores in 1851-52. The confectionery in Ashville, Buncombe County, was managed by Madam Couche, a Frenchwoman, and in Wake County, Mrs Hardie Moxon and Mrs Woltering both operated confectionery stores.[86] Nancy Harbinson, of Lincoln County, appears to be among the first women to own a business there before 1800. She and her brother William Jr owned and operated a tavern in Lincolnton, North Carolina.[87] Alan Watson has also highlighted the prevalence of women among the state's ferry-keepers. Between 1762 and 1764, five women were known to have operated ferry services in Cumberland County, while in Tyrell County another four widows successfully applied for permission to take over the running of their deceased husbands' ferry-keeping businesses.[88]

By the mid-nineteenth century the South's gradual integration into industrial capitalism had fostered the growth and expansion of a cotton textile manufacturing sector – a development that impacted significantly on white women. Technological innovations in textile production aided the manufacture of cheap mass-produced products, against which women who had previously survived by weaving and spinning in their homes could not compete. Indeed, by the 1820s domestic manufacturing had declined to such an extent that Rowan County legislators felt compelled to pass a motion urging members of the House of Commons to 'appear clothed in Homespun, for the purpose of encouraging domestic industry and promoting a spirit of economy in our State'.[89] Factory-based production significantly increased waged labour opportunities for poor white women. Following the general pattern already established by Northern textile manufacturers, Southern factory owners preferred to employ female and child labour in the new textile mills. Edwin Holt, owner of Alamance Textile Factory, specifically favoured employing female-headed families. Holt's preference for a female-dominated labour force had less to do with his concern to improve poor women's material conditions than with economic factors. Women and children were cheaper to employ than male workers, and given the dearth of employment opportunities available to white women, Holt could be assured of an inexpensive, acquiescent, and easily controllable labour force.[90] On the eve of the Civil War, North Carolina's cotton textile industry was decidedly feminised and overwhelmingly white, although mill-owners also employed a few free black women. The South's progress to industrialisation was tremendously significant, for the shift from home production to factory manufacturing substantially increased opportunities for waged labour and independence for poor white women who relied on the factories and mills for their very survival.[91]

As Southern labour historian Bess Beatty has commented, 'In the fictional ante-bellum world of Scarlett O'Hara the only women who worked were slaves'.[92] Yet, as Beatty's work reveals, all but the most elite among North Carolina's white women were engaged in some form of productive labour. Ownership of slaves freed numerous plantation mistresses from the drudgery of field and domestic labour, but few were entirely exempted from involvement in the domestic management of slaves. Beyond the plantations, out of sheer economic necessity or in a spirited quest for independence, white women of all social classes participated in diverse ways and at different levels within the Southern economy. Ex-slave Mattie Curtis remembered that just before the Civil War his mistress, Miss Fanny Long of Franklin County, had owned a tobacco factory 'where tobacco was stemmed, rolled and packed in cases for selling. They said that she had got rich on selling chewing tobacco.'[93] As wives, daughters, widows or spinsters, white women managed households, cultivated vegetable gardens, planted and harvested diverse crops, spun cotton and knitted wool into clothing and sundry household items, repaired clothing, raised poultry and livestock, laundered clothing and linen, picked cotton, tobacco, rice and indigo, nursed and reared children, family, slaves and community members, taught in Sunday and public schools, fetched water, trimmed wicks, made soap and candles, marketed produce and goods, split logs, baked bread, worked in mills and down mines.[94] Whether waged or unwaged, white Southern women's labour made a significant contribution to the South's economic success, and was increasingly essential as the South embraced industrial capitalism. Yet, much of Southern women's industriousness remained unremunerated and unacknowledged by Southern white males whose tenacious insistence on the twin ideals of dependent white womanhood and male-as-provider, required the denial of white women's productivity.

The devaluation and invisibility of white women as workers – sustained within antebellum censuses which rarely recorded women's labour activities – has, not surprisingly, been reproduced in traditional labour histories of the south. Traditional Southern labour history has given scant regard to the diversity and economic significance of Southern white women's labour. Since the 1990s, gender and labour historians of the south have begun a critical re-evaluation of the place of labouring white women within the Southern economy. In doing so, they have forced re-definitions of the concept of work, traditionally associated with waged labour performed usually by males in the public sphere. Widening the concept of work to include forms of non-waged labour enables historians to analyse more comprehensively the myriad forms of women's integration into the Southern economy. Moreover, greater attention must be paid to the roles of class, age, race, marital status and geographical location in determining patterns of white, Southern women's labour activities.

This chapter has demonstrated some contradictions within Southern discourses of ideal white womanhood. It has revealed how white women of all classes – but especially poor white women – disrupted Southern gender and racial ideologies through their intimate sexual relationships with black males, and in their labour participation in the Southern economy. Labour represented a fundamental component of the lives of *all* Southern white women. Whether white women worked out of necessity, to achieve a measure of autonomy or a sense of personal satisfaction, or for all of these reasons, their rarely acknowledged labour substantially girded the development of the Southern economy, especially after the mid-nineteenth century. Only after the Civil War would Southerners begin to recognise women's vital labour contributions.

Notes

1 Virginia slaveholder to Frederick Law Olmstead, cited in V. Bynum, *Unruly Women: The politics of social and sexual control in the Old South* (Chapel Hill: University of North Carolina Press, 1992), p. 7.
2 New Bern District Court Minutes, May 1772, *The King* v. *Sarah Wiggins*, North Carolina Archives, New Bern Court, Miscellaneous Records, Box DSCR 206.928.3 (see also Box 206.306.1).
3 The fate of Will, Sarah's alleged seducer, is unknown.
4 Race and Slavery Petitions Project, Petition of Christian Limbaugh, PAR 11280515, NCDAH, Raleigh, NC.
5 Pleading for mercy, supporter Ed Jones wrote to Governor James Turner 'She was convicted on clear full testimony but she is a woman – was left unprotected desolate and in poverty by her vagabond husband, it is said she expected his return and that her crime was caused by such expectation.' Governor Turner (1766-1824) granted the pardon on 12 April 1804. Ed Jones to James Turner, 28 March 1804, Papers of Governor James Turner (G.P. 27), 202, NCDAH.
6 See Lenoir County, NC – District Supreme Court Abstracts for Dobbs, Lenoir, Greene, Wayne, Craven, Onslow and Jones counties, 1762–1806. (www.rootsweb.com/~usgenweb/copyright.htm (21 August 2005)).
7 Bynum, *Unruly Women*, p. 89; Martha Hodes, *White Women, Black Men: Illicit sex in the nineteenth-century South* (New Haven: Yale University Press, 1997), p. 116.
8 Guion Griffis Johnson, *Ante-bellum North Carolina: A social history* (Chapel Hill: University of North Carolina Press, 1937).
9 Karen L. Zipf, *Labour of Innocents: Forced apprenticeships in North Carolina, 1715–1919* (Baton Rouge: Louisiana State University, 2005).
10 The Sarah Wiggins mentioned here is not the same Sarah Wiggins whose case is discussed at the beginning of this chapter.
11 Weynette Parks Haun, Bertie County, North Carolina County Court Minutes, Court of Pleas & Quarter Sessions, Book IV (Durham, NC, 1984).
12 Bynum, *Unruly Women*, pp. 88–92.
13 Timothy J. Lockley, 'Public Poor Relief in Buncombe County, North Carolina', *North Carolina Historical Review* 80: 1 (January 2003).
14 Bill Cecil-Fronsman, *Common Whites: Class and culture in Ante-bellum North Carolina* (Lexington: University of Kentucky Press, 1992).
15 Warren S. Billings, 'The Cases of Fernando and Elizabeth Key: A note on the status of blacks in seventeenth century Virginia', *William and Mary Quarterly* 3rd Ser., 30:3 (Jul. 1973), pp. 467–74.
16 Peter Bardaglio, '"Shameful Matches": The regulation of interracial marriage and sex in the South before 1900' in Martha Hodes (ed.), *Sex, Love, Race: Crossing boundaries in North American history* (New York: New York University Press, 1999), p. 115.
17 Some historians have argued that some poor whites were abducted and sold into slavery. See Carol Wilson and Calvin D. Wilson, 'White Slavery: An American paradox', *Slavery and Abolition* 19:1 (April 1998), pp. 1–23.
18 Courts usually charged the white partner; for it was whites, not blacks, who were guilty of transgressing the boundaries of whiteness. Invariably too, it was white women, rather than men, who were the defendants in such cases.
19 Dorothy Roberts, *Killing the Black Body: Race, reproduction and the meaning of liberty* (New York: Pantheon Press, 1997), pp. 104–149.

20 Hodes, *White Women, Black Men*, pp. 29–30.
21 Vron Ware, *Beyond the Pale: White women, racism and history* (London: Verso Books, 1992), p. 39.
22 Marvin L. Michael Kay and Lorin Lee Cary, *Slavery in North Carolina, 1748–1775* (Chapel Hill: University of North Carolina Press, 1996), pp. 61–62.
23 Hodes, *White Women, Black Men*, p. 50.
24 Narrative of Millie Markham, in George Rawick (ed.), *The American Slave: A composite autobiography. Vol. 15, North Carolina Narratives, Part 2* (Westport, Greenwood Publishing Co., 1941), p. 106.
25 Ibid., Narrative of Adorah Rienshaw, p. 213.
26 Ibid., pp. 80–81.
27 Ibid., p. 53.
28 Though, given the costs of divorce, it is likely that the majority of these petitions originated from among the wealthier sectors of society.
29 Roberts, *Killing the Black Body*, pp. 104–149.
30 Timothy J. Lockley, 'Crossing the Racial Divide: Inter-racial sex in ante-bellum Savannah', *Slavery and Abolition* 18: 3 (December 1997), pp. 159–173.
31 Narrative of ex-enslaved Dave Lawson in G. Rawick, *The American Slave*, p. 43.
32 Extracted from *People's Press* (Salem, NC) 2:46 (January 1853) (www.fmoran.com/pphyde.html).
33 Divorce Petition of Alexander Smith to General Assembly, Divorce Petitions Session November to December 1809, held on deposit at North Carolina Department of Archives and History (hereafter NCDAH), Petition Analysis Record (hereafter PAR) No. 1128092. For reasons of brevity, I refer to these sources hereafter as Race and Slavery Petitions Project and cite the petitioner's details as given in the Project Analysis Record (PAR). Visit the Project's Website at http://library.uncg.edu/slavery_petitions/index.asp.
34 Race and Slavery Petitions Project; Petition of Lewis Tombereau to General Assembly, Session Records, PAR No. 11282403, NCDAH.
35 Race and Slavery Petitions Project; Divorce Petition of Jonathan Bryan to General Assembly of North Carolina, PAR No 11282712, NCDAH.
36 Race and Slavery Petitions Project; Petition of Isaac Bracewell to General Assembly of North Carolina, PAR No 11281105, NCDAH.
37 Race and Slavery Petitions Project; Petition of Utley Wake to the General Assembly of North Carolina, PAR No 11281010, NCDAH. See also August 1996 issue of *North Carolina Genealogical Society*. Visit the website at http/freepages.genealogy.rootsweb.com/~fcharper/RichardWoodward.html.
38 Race and Slavery Petitions Project; Petition of Joseph Hancock to General Assembly of North Carolina, PAR No 11281304, NCDAH.
39 Cecil-Fronsman, *Common Whites*, p. 91, see also Race and Slavery Petitions Project; Petition of Ann M. Borden, PAR No. 11282708, NCDAH.
40 Ibid.
41 Cecil-Fronsman, *Common Whites*, p. 90.
42 Race and Slavery Petitions Project, Petition of Ann M. Borden to General Assembly of North Carolina, PAR No 11282708, NCDAH.
43 Bynum, *Unruly Women*, p. 69.
44 Griffis Johnson, *Ante-bellum North Carolina*, p. 589.
45 According to the docket page, the Senate rejected the request for divorce but apparently agreed to Harriet Laspeyre's request to control any property she might acquire in the future.
46 Race and Slavery Petitions Project; Petition of Harriet Laspeyre to General Assembly of North Carolina, PAR No 11281601; see also counter-petition of Bernard Laspeyre, PAR No 11281703, NCDAH. See also L. Schweninger (ed.), *The Southern Debate over Slavery, Vol. 1, Petitions to Southern legislatures, 1778–1864* (Urbana: University of Illinois Press, 2001).
47 Race and Slavery Petitions Project; Petition of Mary Read alias Polly Read to the General Assembly of North Carolina; PAR No. 11283204, NCDAH.

48 Willie Lee Rose (ed.), *A Documentary History of Slavery in North America* (Athens: University of Georgia Press, 1999), p. 427.
49 Narrative of ex-enslaved Jacob Manson, in G. Rawick, *The American Slave*, p. 98.
50 Race and Slavery Petitions Project; Petition of John Chambers to the North Carolina General Assembly; PAR No 11282504; NCDAH.
51 Petition of Gurdon Deming to the North Carolina General Assembly, December 1800, Records of the General Assembly, Session Records, NCDAH. No act was passed. PAR No. 11280005.
52 Cecil-Fronsman, *Common Whites*, p. 92; see also Hodes (1997) for a discussion of the limits of community tolerance for illicit cross-racial relationships.
53 *State v. Fore & Chesnutt*, 1841, Lenoir County, North Carolina Archives (hereafter NCA).
54 Griffis Johnson, *Ante-bellum North Carolina*, p. 590.
55 Ibid.
56 'Revised Constitution and By-Laws of the Raleigh Female Benevolent Society', Adopted 23 July 1823. With the Reports of the Society From its Commencement, p. 3. Available on the website *Documenting the American South*, http://docsouth.unc.edu/result.phtml?lcsh = Female+Benevolent+Society+(Raleigh%2C+N.C.
57 Ibid., p. 6.
58 Mari Jo Buhle, 'Needlewomen and the Vicissitudes of Modern Life: A study of middle-class construction in the antebellum Northeast', in Nancy A. Hewitt and Suzanne Lebsock (eds), *Visible Women: New essays on American activism* (Urbana and Chicago: University of Illinois Press, 1993), pp. 145–65.
59 Raleigh Female Benevolent Society, *The Report Of the Managers and Treasurer, read at the Annual Meeting*, 28 July 1823.
60 Ibid., p. 11.
61 Ibid., p. 11.
62 Ibid., p. 10.
63 Kathleen M. Brown, *Good Wives, Nasty Wenches, and Anxious Patriarchs* (Chapel Hill: University of North Carolina Press, 1996), pp. 116–121; Jennifer L. Morgan, *Laboring Women: Reproduction and gender in New World slavery* (Philadelphia: University of Pennsylvania Press, 2004), p. 74.
64 Col. W.L. Saunders, *Colonial Records of North Carolina*; ten volumes, 1886–1890. Col. Recs., II., p. 889. cited in J. B. Spencer, *Slavery and Servitude in the Colony of North Carolina* (Baltimore: Johns Hopkins Press, 1896).
65 Thomas. R. Dew, 'Dissertation on the Characteristic Differences Between the Sexes, and on the Position and Influence of Women in Society', *Southern Literary Messenger* 1: 11&12 (July & August 1835), pp. 621–632, 672–691.
66 *Southern Ladies Companion*, October 1852.
67 Catherine Clinton (ed.), *Half Sisters of History: Southern women and the American past* (Durham: Duke University Press, 1994).
68 *Southern Ladies Companion*, December 1852.
69 George Fitzhugh cited in Ann Firor Scott, *The Southern Lady: From pedestal to politics* (Chicago: University of Chicago Press, 1970), p. 17.
70 Bynum, *Unruly Women*, p. 89.
71 Ibid., p. 57.
72 Charles C. Bolton, *Poor Whites of the Ante-bellum South: Tenants and labourers in central North Carolina and Northeast Mississippi* (Durham: Duke University Press, 1994), pp. 38–39.
73 Hinton Rowan Helper, *The Impending Crisis of the South: How to meet it* (New York: Burden Press, 1957).
74 Keith. L. Bryant Jr., 'The Role and Status of the Female Yeomanry in the Ante-bellum South: The literary view', *Southern Quarterly* 18:2 (Winter 1979–80), pp. 73–88.
75 Carol Wilson and Calvin Wilson have argued that many white women field labourers may have been abducted and enslaved on Southern plantations. See Carol

POOR WHITE WOMEN IN NORTH CAROLINA

Wilson & Calvin. D. Wilson, 'Whites Slavery: An American paradox', *Slavery and Abolition* 19:1 (April 1998), pp. 1–19.
76 Ex-slave Elias Thomas, cited in Belinda Hurmence (ed.), *My Folks Don't Want Me to Talk About Slavery: Twenty-one oral histories of former North Carolina slaves* (Winston-Salem: John F. Blair, 1984).
77 *Weekly Post 1852* cited in Griffis Johnson, *Ante-bellum North Carolina*, p. 248.
78 J Andrews, E. Walker Andrews, C. McLean (eds), *Janet Schaw's 'Journal of a Lady of Quality: Being the narrative of a journey from Scotland to the West Indies, North Carolina, and Portugal, in the years 1774 to 1776'* (New Haven: Yale University Press, 1921).
79 Stephanie McCurry, *Masters of Small Worlds: Yeoman households, gender relations and the political culture of the antebellum South Carolina low country* (Chapel Hill: University of North Carolina Press, 1995), p. 75.
80 Cecil-Fronsman, *Common Whites*, p. 9.
81 Bynum, *Unruly Women*, p. 17.
82 Cited in Griffis Johnson, *Ante-bellum North Carolina*, p. 247.
83 Mary Norcott Bryan, *A Grandmother's Recollection of Dixie* (New Bern: Owen G. Dunn, 1912).
84 Bolton, *Poor whites of the Ante-bellum South*, p. 39.
85 *Hannah Mozingo v. Nathan Lassiter and Wm. Waters*, John Heritage Bryan Collection (NCA).
86 Thompson's *Mercantile and Professional Directory 1851–1852*, North Carolina http://www.ls.net/~newriver/nc/ncthom.htm.
87 Lincoln County Court, North Carolina, April 1786. See: http://www.rootsweb.com/~nccmaide/fam_indx-harbinson.
88 Alan Watson, 'Women of Colonial North Carolina: Overlooked and underestimated', *North Carolina Historical Review* 58 (January 1981), pp. 1–22.
89 Legislative Report, *Raleigh Register*, 16 December 1828.
90 Bess Beatty, '"I can't get my bored on them old lomes": Female textile workers in the Antebellum South', in Susanna Delfino and Michele Gillespie (eds), *Neither Lady nor Slave: Working women of the Old South* (Chapel Hill: University of North Carolina Press, 2002).
91 Bess Beatty has argued that poor white women were not alone in seeking mill-work. Mill owners employed freed black women, but Beatty's research also reveals a surprising number of white women of middling wealth who also sought waged labour in North Carolina's textile mills.
92 Beatty, 'Female Textile Workers' in Delfino and Gillespie (eds), *Neither Lady nor Slave*, p. 250.
93 Mattie Curtis, in Hurmence, *My Folks*, p. 36.
94 Susanna Delphino, 'Invisible Women: Female labour in the Upper South's iron and mining industries', in Delfino and Gillespie, *Neither Lady nor Slave*, p. 285.

CHAPTER THREE

'To serve her own desires': white women and property holding in Barbadian plantation society

For centuries, property relations stood at the heart of social relations throughout the world. Until the early modern period there could be no greater indicator of an individual's social and political status than his or her rights to access, own and control property. As historians have noted, until well into the nineteenth century the relationship between political rights and property rights could not be disentangled; in short, the extension of political rights was closely tied to property qualifications.[1] In England, gender and social class had for centuries represented the foremost determinants defining the individuals' relationship to property. Though some elite women owned and exercised autonomy over property, ownership of property represented a privilege largely confined to ruling-class males. The relationship of persons to property was particularly attenuated throughout the colonial world. In Barbados, as was the case throughout anglophone colonial America, race, rather than gender, was the principal rationale for the ordering of property relationships. Here, property ownership was synonymous with personal freedom, and individual freedom was the exclusive birthright of white men and women. Defined as 'real estate' by an Act of 1668, enslaved Africans were themselves regarded as property, and as such were devoid of rights of ownership, their very bodies owned and controlled by their masters and mistresses. Some enslaved who managed to procure their freedoms held limited property rights, as did members of the free coloured community that emerged in the eighteenth century. The rights of these two liminal groups to own property was never secure, however, and was contested throughout the long colonial era.

Though their race secured their inalienable rights to freedom, white women did not enjoy equitable property rights with white males. The patriarchal culture of English society that demanded women's subordination to men was firmly implanted in Barbadian society, as early settlers saw little reason to wholly abandon English traditions and cultural mores (though they were not above discarding those cultural remnants that seemed particularly redundant or inappropriate). In some instances Barbadians displayed somewhat more liberal behaviours and attitudes than might be encountered at home – visitors to the island rarely failed to mention, for instance, the seemingly unrestrained conspicuous consumption displayed by the island's wealthiest and most successful planters. In the absence of the repressive puritanical influences of mid-seventeenth century England, elite white Barbadians revelled in displaying their phenomenal wealth, and the most visible manifestation of that wealth was undoubtedly property – either in land or in slaves. This was, after all, a society founded primarily for the purpose of rapid wealth creation.

There is still much debate among historians over the extent to which English gender relations were transplanted from the old world to the new. Some feminist historians have argued that white women experienced a radical enhancement in status during the early colonial period. Other historians have disputed this 'golden age' paradigm, but there can be little doubt that white women's relationship to property did undergo a marked transformation, much to women's benefit, in Barbadian colonial society. This is not to suggest that colonial property laws ceded greater property rights to women than those enjoyed by their counterparts in England. The specific circumstances of colonial life, particularly the peculiar demographic characteristics of a new society, engendered new possibilities for women's participation within the economic sphere. In short, life in the slave-based colonial plantation colonies offered white women a range of opportunities and privileges within a power structure ordinarily reserved for white males.[2]

White women's structural position as members of the property-owning class positioned them within the dominant, white ruling class. As Beckles has observed, although their lives were constrained by patriarchal ideology and practices, white women nevertheless defended the pro-slavery ideology of the plantocracy precisely because it served to further their own racial and class interests.[3] The participation of white women within the slave economy can therefore be seen as a furtherance of this interest. While the gender relations of Barbadian plantation society suborned white women to male patriarchal authority they were nevertheless legally free beings and were accorded a modicum of legal rights, albeit restricted.

This chapter examines some aspects of the socio-economic experiences of white colonial women in Barbados during the seventeenth and eighteenth centuries. Through analysis of a range of property records – probated wills, property deeds, marriage contracts, and household inventories, I argue that the nature and extent of white female economic participation in Barbadian plantation society was far more complex than has been previously understood. This assertion challenges existing Caribbean historiographies, which give primacy to the economic activities of male actors and, in the process, consign white women to the margins of the economic and social processes of slave societies.[4] An analysis of property records reveals the social agency of white women within the Barbadian property market, to an extent not previously recognised or understood. White women in Barbadian slave plantation society were social agents whose active participation in the Barbadian economy made them significant actors.

White women in the Barbadian economy

The property relations of any society constitute an important indicator of the state of gender relations in that society. Janet Momsen has pointed out that those who hold legitimate property rights may exert control and influence over those institutions that affect ideologies.[5] John Locke established the relationship of the control of property to independence, but as Leonore Davidoff and Catherine Hall have noted, he was unable to clarify how women's control of property and their subordination within the family could be reconciled.[6] Through law and custom, women's right to property has generally been constrained by historically specific ideologies of gender, race and class. In Barbadian plantation society, all white people had legitimate access to property, although women's property rights were largely determined by their marital status.

Several factors contributed to the emergence of white female property owners and entrepreneurs in Barbados, but this, I argue, was largely due to the specific demographic structure of the plantation society that facilitated white women's participation in the market, on a scale perhaps unprecedented elsewhere in the Caribbean.

Whether they arrived in the New World as indentured servants or as free migrants, the colonies offered white women opportunities to enhance their material conditions. The pursuit of wealth was not, in the minds of many women, the sole prerogative of adventurous males, and numerous Englishwomen viewed emigration to the colonies as a rational strategy through which they could fulfil ambitions to improve their own economic circumstances. For some women, ensnaring and marrying a wealthy planter represented the limits of their aspirations, but others viewed the colonies as a space within which they might create new identities as independent women. For enterprising women, the colonies represented a plethora of possibilities not to be squandered. Richard Ligon, one of the earliest chroniclers of Barbadian history, was suitably impressed by the enterprising spirit displayed by women passengers on his Barbados-bound ship, who generated income by hiring their services as laundrywomen to sailors on board.[7] Undoubtedly the long transatlantic voyage afforded shrewd women scope to deploy their 'special' feminine skills, either as cooks, nurses, or prostitutes.

Most white women on Barbados in the early days of settlement arrived as indentured servants. Indentureship required a servant to be bonded to an employer for a specified number of years, after which they regained their freedom. Most female servants were employed in agricultural and domestic labour, but it is highly likely that many also held trade and occupational skills that could be employed to good profit in the long term. Customs records reveal little data about the occupations and trades of white female passengers who disembarked on Barbados, but it would not be stretching speculation too far to suggest that among their numbers were many farm labourers, beer and ale makers, craftswomen, dressmakers, midwives, governesses, milliners, and small and petty traders.

Though the integration of white women into the political economy of Barbadian society has rarely been acknowledged, this does not necessarily imply that they were excluded from economic productivity. Rather, it suggests that women's economic participation was so common as to be taken for granted. Contemporary accounts offer tantalising though fragmentary glimpses of female economic activity. In what appears to be the earliest documented reference to a white Barbadian businesswoman, Ligon fondly recalled Joan Fuller, proprietor of The Bridge Tavern, much patronised by hungry planters when they had 'a mind to feast themselves with fish'. (Ligon, who considered himself something of a gourmet, introduced Joan Fuller and other tavern keepers to the new exotic ingredients and cooking methods of Barbados, and prided himself on having improved their recipes.)[8]

Joan Fuller was certainly not an isolated instance of enterprising womanhood; occasionally, the necessity to survive threw women into conflict with the authorities, thereby earning themselves a place in the public records. In 1681, Joyce Franklin and Alice Archer, described as 'the wives of butchers', appeared before the Council of Assembly to answer accusations of overcharging customers. This was in fact, the second time Franklin had been summonsed on the same charge. Undeterred however, Franklin had blithely continued the deceit, 'demanding 'three shillings sterling for six pounds of pork, which was a penny more than the said order'. On the same day the Council also dealt with Alice Archer, also accused of overcharging two customers. Archer compounded her offence by 'openly declaring in the market that she did not value the Governor's order of a farthing'. Along with Joyce Franklin, she was charged with contempt and committed to stand trial at the forthcoming Quarter Sessions.[9]

That these women engaged in economic activity was not a matter of public concern, but their alleged dishonesty was. Certainly, as male settlers acknowledged, there could be no place for idlers of *any* gender in a new society, and the contribution of every available able-bodied person, male or female, was necessary to the process of colony-building. Notwithstanding prevailing discourses of natural gender inequality, Barbadian society could, and did, accommodate white female economic activity in the early period of settlement. Granted, some economic activities remained largely the preserve of white males, but where opportunity presented itself, women seized the chance to integrate themselves into the economy. Few would have doubted that their economic activities were equally vital components to the process of colony-building.

Mary Butler has argued against representations of white Barbadian women as economically unproductive actors. Basing her evidence on an analysis of Jamaican and Barbadian property deeds and mortgage records, Butler contended that white women played a vital role in the economic life of the colonies throughout the colonial era, suggesting that their economic activities as mortgagees, as sellers and buyers of property, and as suppliers of credit made them important players in the economy.[10] Hence, persistent representations of white colonial women as an unproductive, marginal category cannot be sustained when subjected to critical scrutiny.

Reconstructing the extent and nature of white female economic participation presents a difficult challenge, for their activities and presence were seldom recorded. However, contemporary records, both public and private, reveal glimpses of white women operating as autonomous or semi-autonomous market actors. The patriarchal ethos of the day placed limits on the socio-economic activities of those women who were most closely allied to the plantocracy. However, the stark material realities of near or actual poverty forced other women into the marketplace. In any case, as historians acknowledge, patriarchal practice does not always follow the patriarchal ideal, and in the nascent society that was Barbados, both male and female settlers recognised that the exigencies of colonial life demanded flexibility in patriarchal norms. This was certainly the case where property rights were concerned.

Some women certainly had little interest in property ownership, possibly accepting the widely held beliefs among males (and some women) that women did not have the necessary financial acumen to manage or maintain property. But a substantial number of women could not and did not accept that property ownership should remain the prerogative of males, and actively resisted and challenged the legal restrictions that sought to limit their rights to property. Existing deeds of sale provide significant evidence of white women's agency within the plantation economy from the earliest phase of settlement. A 1638 census of property owners having possession of ten acres or more includes one woman, Dorothy Simmonds (her marital status is unknown). Although Dorothy Simmonds appears as the sole female landholder, it is entirely possible that more women were joint owners of land listed as belonging to males.[11]

Barbadian property deeds of the plantation era are replete with examples of property transactions carried out by single, married, and widowed women. Their high levels of involvement in the purchase and sale of property attest to their willingness to challenge prevailing ideologies that stressed their economic dependence on white males. As Erickson has warned, however, the fact that many white women of the seventeenth and eighteenth centuries owned property does not change the fact of their subordination to men – it merely points to inconsistencies between patriarchal theory and practice.[12] These contradictions were always prevalent in the New World, as its settlers endeavoured to construct a new society.

Gender and property rights

Even though white women are not generally considered as active economic participants, i.e. as actively pursuing entrepreneurial market strategies, the extent of white Barbadian women's interests in the property markets nevertheless gives them a hitherto unacknowledged significance in the economic activities of their society. In discussing women's relationships to their property, it is necessary to distinguish between married women and single women, whether widowed, separated or unmarried. These categories of women were treated differently before the law, for their access to property was largely determined by their marital status.

Barbadian property law, as it related to women's rights, was closely modelled on English law. The fragmentary state of records makes it extremely difficult to say with certainty how far English law regarding women's property rights was applied once transplanted to the colonies. Clearly there were modifications. Settlers to North America, for instance, also adopted English common law as the basis of their legal system, but modified it in crucial areas to meet the exigencies of the new colonies. The Barbadian legal system during the slave plantation era exhibited many deviations in its application, not least because the Barbadian legislature was often hostile to English law, and persistently sought to resist the imposition of many legislative aspects of Crown Rule. Roger Thompson noted that in the New World colonies, legal practices tended to become simplified, flexible and equitable, enabling women to reap considerable advantages.[13]

In common law, two traditional principles governed women's status and access to property: the first of these, governing women's access to property, was that of *femme sole*, which conferred on single women – either unmarried or widowed – the same property rights as men. The second principle, that of *femme covert*, defined the legal status of a married woman, and implied the virtual economic dependence of wives upon husbands. As a *femme covert*, the married woman's legal identity was conflated with that of her husband.[14] As Linda De Pauw observes:

> coverture is what happened to a woman when she married. Marriage made one person of two, and the person remaining after this operation was always male. The woman's legal existence disappeared. Her property rights, down to ownership of her petticoats, passed to her husband.[15]

Married women

Marriage effectively reduced women's status to that of a minor; once married, women were stripped of their independent identity, as well as their political, economic and social status. Unlike males and single women, they could not independently enter into contracts or negotiations, could neither sue or be sued in court, or obtain credit in their own name, and hence their ability to function as independent economic actors was severely curtailed, thus securing their economic dependence on men.

Yet, legal fetters did not wholly prevent married women's participation in the economic life of their society. Many participated with minimal constraints in a range of economic activities as traders, financiers, and investors in both land and slaves. When confronted with legal barriers, the more determined among them sought and found ways to circumvent the law. Many formed partnerships with husbands, male relatives, or friends who were empowered to sign contracts or sue for outstanding debts. Such an arrangementdid not confer complete autonomy, however. A discontented husband might withdraw his approval and support and refuse to sign a contract, effectively making it impossible for his wife to conduct her business. Thus, in 1658, before she could sell her Barbadian plantation of fifty-eight acres,

Elizabeth Barnes had first to obtain the consent of her husband Herman, who agreeably furnished his wife with a signed letter of attorney empowering her to effect the transaction.[16] An Act of 1672 makes clear that married women could sometimes be designated as *femme sole* for trading purposes. The Act, which sought to prevent Barbadians from leaving the island without clearing their debts, insisted that those intending to depart the island, first post notice to do so. The only exceptions to this requirement being, 'women-covert and children under the age of 14 [except] such women-covert that trade, use or exercise any trade as a sole or femme merchant within this island.'[17]

Common law recognised that some married women did have independent business interests and the extension of *femme sole* status to those married women must be read as efforts to accommodate them. Moreover, legal provision had to be made for occasions when husbands could not attend to their businesses, either through poor health, or during a period of temporary absence from the island. While many planters and merchants appointed managers or attorneys to oversee their business operations in their absence, others preferred to entrust temporary managerial power to their wife. Before leaving Barbados, Gabriel Goodman appointed his wife Ann as his 'lawful and undoubted deputy attorney', empowering her to 'ask, demand and recover and receive all [sums] of goods, debts and demands whatsoever either in sugar indigo, cotton, tobacco, fustic, ginger or whatsoever commodities due and payable unto me, from any person or persons whatsoever in this island'. As Gabriel's 'sole manager and director and disposer of plantation servants . . . whether English or negro . . . stock, cattle', Ann was empowered to 'sue, implead, prosecute or arrest in prison, to order to deliver by compensation or otherwise' any defaulters, and to direct the family business howsoever she saw fit.[18] In placing his entire affairs into her hands, Gabriel signalled his absolute confidence in his wife's ability to manage his business in his absence. He, like many other husbands, recognised and appreciated the advantages of an economically and financially astute wife. Indeed, few men expected that their wives remain ignorant about their business affairs, and many absentee planter-husbands heavily relied on their wives' operational knowledge of the plantation to ensure the smooth running of the estate in their absence.

In some instances, other men appear to have actively encouraged and assisted wives (and other female relatives or friends) in their quests to become independent economic actors. Katherine Adams bought and sold slaves with the full support of her husband, Captain Robert Adams, whose frequent voyages left him dependent on Katherine to oversee his Barbadian business operations.[19] When Abigail Tompkins's husband's business interests forced his temporary departure from the island, he made her responsible for the collection of rents from his tenants. One tenant, John Page, attempted to take advantage of Giles Tompkins's absence and refused to pay the agreed rents. Not to be thwarted, Abigail brought a complaint against Page, who was ordered to repay the outstanding debts to her.[20] Clearly then, as far as married women's relations to property was concerned, of necessity, Barbadian property law *had* to be elastic in its application.

Marriage placed restrictions on women's ownership of property, denying most the right to own or manage property independently of their husbands. Any property a wife brought to her marriage became that of her husband, and she could not expect to regain possession of that property even if her husband predeceased her. The alienation of married women from property rights was rooted in and reinforced by the prevailing ideology of female economic dependence on men. But many wives found to their cost that husbands could, and did, embezzle or ravage family property through mismanagement, financial ineptitude or through sheer wastefulness, leaving their wives and children vulnerable. Hence, courts recognised the disjuncture between theory and reality, and extended to married women a degree of protection over their property, making provision for women who wished to retain a measure of control over their property. Premarital contracts enabled some women to maintain at least a share of the marital property as a sole and separate estate during the course of their marriage. Not surprisingly, numerous white Barbadian women attempted to safeguard their futures by exercising their right to retain separate estates. Before marrying John Coyle of St Andrew parish in 1655, Susan Hodges forced him to sign a contract transferring to her half of his estate of 128 acres of land, and promising that he would not at any future time dispose of any of her separate estate without Susan's consent.[21] Edmund Cole also agreed to settle on his prospective bride Jane Gibbes and their future children, 'a sure and firm estate' of land amounting to over fifty acres for her own usage, and half of his own plantation estate of 160 acres of land.[22]

By implication, the principle of coverture defined women as subordinate beings, dependent on their husbands for economic and material security. Depriving married women of autonomy over marital property served to secure patriarchal authority in the domestic space; without independent means, many wives had little choice but to rely on their husbands for their economic security. It is not surprising then that those women who were able, sought to protect their future through a marriage settlement.

Pre-marriage contracts could help prevent the entire dissolution of family property, but even without this safeguard, courts recognised the right of married women to a share of the marital property – even if she did not receive it until after her husband's death. The provision of dower, generally a third share of the family property, was crucial in safeguarding women's future economic security, providing a measure of insurance against the wastefulness of a spendthrift or financially inept husband. When in 1667 heavily indebted Jonathan Bannister attempted to sell twenty-one negro slaves given to his wife Elizabeth as a present, she immediately appealed to the Barbadian Council to prevent the sale. The Council ordered that 'three of the best of the twenty-one negroes and their wages and produce ... be solely for the benefit and advantage of [Elizabeth, the couple's daughter]'. The Council further decreed that Jonathan establish with his various creditors the level of his current debts, and that he reveal the full extent of his outstanding debts to his wife. Only then would he be permitted to offer the remaining negro slaves for sale, and they could only be sold at the best possible market rates. Only then could he satisfy his impatient creditor's demands. At each stage, Elizabeth was to be kept properly appraised; Jonathan was to obtain Elizabeth's 'true consent and knowledge' to each individual sale, and no sale could be concluded unless Elizabeth agreed to accept the offer prices. Once the debts had been paid, Jonathan was to sell the remaining negroes, and the proceeds put in trust to be used for the maintenance of Elizabeth and her daughter.[23] In this instance, it is clear that Elizabeth, probably aware of her husband's profligate nature, intervened in his attempts to dispose of the slaves without her permission. Perhaps she feared that, left to his own devices, Jonathan would dispose of the slaves at prices below their market value, or might well fritter away the proceeds before settling his debts. Another wife, Mary Hallam, was also forced to ask the Council to intervene to prevent her husband's wastage of her daughter Elizabeth's inheritance. In September 1669, unable to stand idly by while her husband and 'Mr William Roberson [presumably his business partner]', laid waste to her daughter's property, Mary petitioned the Council to prevent further devastation of Elizabeth's inheritance. The Deputy Governor ruled that William Hallam 'forbear all further waste on the said land, upon pain of imprisonment for such this contempt'.[24] It is clear that the unscrupulous behaviour of some husbands was of concern, for in 1670 the Assembly enacted legislation establishing the precedent that where a husband wished to sell his wife's property, he was first required to certify her 'voluntary and free consent' to the sale.[25] Of course, without safeguards there could be no way of ascertaining the extent to which this supposed 'voluntary and free consent' had been secured under duress.

Thus, for many women, marriage represented not only a loss of individual identity and personal liberty, but it could also be a precursor to economic insecurity.

Physical and sexual abuse of wives was not uncommon, and the Barbadian Assembly was often called on to arbitrate in such matters. When wives petitioned for separation, or more rarely divorce, on these grounds, consideration had to be given to the division of family property. In 1668, Elisabeth Boswell finally tired of her husband Anthony's 'ill-usage' of her, and petitioned the Assembly for protection. The Assembly took a dim view of Anthony Boswell's domestic violence, and agreed that the couple be separated. The errant husband was ordered to provide his estranged wife and children with five acres of land and 'two negroes ... Pickanniny and Diego, [and] housing convenient for her use', a half-share of all household goods and stock. To ensure Anthony Boswell's compliance with their order, the Assembly appointed three attorneys to oversee the transfer of property.[26]

When marriages broke down, most wives had little choice but to remain within an unhappy marriage. Divorce was extremely rare, remaining a prerogative of the elite until well into the twentieth century, and the majority of unhappily married couples tried to get along as best they could under the circumstances. Annulments could be obtained on limited grounds – for non-consummation, where it could be proven that the marriage had been involuntarily contracted, or where the marriage had taken place before the bride had reached the age of consent. In 1670, twelve-year-old Mary Ditty petitioned the Assembly to annul her marriage to Thomas Higham. Mary argued that at the age of ten, she had been ordered to marry Thomas, 'by those her duty taught her to obey'. However, by the time she was twelve Mary had come to the realisation that she did not and could not bear any affection for her husband, and sought an end to the marriage. Thomas consented to the petition, testifying that he had 'never carnally known her as a wife'. The court ruled that as Mary had not yet reached the age of consent when the marriage was contracted, and as the marriage had not been consummated, that their union be declared null, 'and the said parties to be separated as if not married, and that the said Higham leave her free, and claim no more the said Mary Ditty as his wife'.[27]

At times, animosity between couples could bring the marriage to a tragic conclusion, as happened in 1672 when James Farwell was murdered by his wife. Farwell's estate was sold, the proceeds going towards the upkeep of his children.[28] To be sure, few wives ended their marriages in such an extreme manner, and it was more usual for unhappy marriages to be brought to an end by an act of desertion.

Most estranged husbands accepted their economic responsibilities towards their wives and children, providing them with a dwelling, and a share of the family's household goods, stock, negro slaves and/or land. Not all wives could be certain of this continued support once the husband had left the marital home; a husband might simply abscond from the island, refuse to pay alimony, or make only erratic financial contributions, leaving his wife and children to face the prospects of destitution. The Barbadian authorities – perhaps influenced by the fiscal burdens that the upkeep of deserted wives and children imposed on their limited resources – supported women's rights to alimony, but they could not always force the errant husband to meet his responsibilities. Such was the case in 1668 when Dorothy Bradbourne and her husband were formally separated. Dorothy successfully petitioned for alimony of £100 sterling annually, but Edward's reluctance or inability to comply with the Assembly's order forced Dorothy back to the courts on successive occasions over many years. When pressure was brought to bear on him to maintain his family, Edward instead went into hiding, from where he sent angry missives to the court complaining of injustices done to him. Despite being charged with contempt of court for refusing to answer summonses, and threatened with a prison term, Edward remained unrelenting in his refusal to admit financial responsibility for his estranged wife. Dorothy continued to pursue her claim for alimony through the courts, but by the winter of 1672/3, Edward had still not complied with the court order.[29]

Though husbands were the more frequent deserters, the Assembly had also on occasion to respond to petitions brought by husbands whose wives had abandoned their families and homes. Katherine Gibbons 'did abscond herself' from her husband, and despite a summons to the Council to explain her desertion, she refused to appear in court. A warrant was issued for her arrest, and the Provost Marshall conducted a protracted search for the absent wife, but Katherine remained missing. The Deputy Governor ordered that once apprehended Katherine be brought before the Council to answer 'as well [as] the complaint of her said husband, as the contempt she has shewn unto this Board'.[30]

In a society where property rights and relations were inherently intertwined with race status, white women could not be left entirely devoid of access to property. Certainly, it was taken for granted by the Assembly that even in instances where there was little family land or other household goods to be shared out, wives held a right to a share of any enslaved property belonging to the family. In the cases examined, in every instance the wife-petitioner received a share of the household's enslaved.

At the other end of the social spectrum, the wives and children of poorer men fared less well when a marriage foundered. Few among the labouring poor owned property of any worth, and without resources a deserted wife's options were limited. Most poor women had little choice but to seek assistance from the Poor Relief Board. Mindful of the severe strain that deserted wives and children could place on the already limited resources of the Poor Relief Boards, the Assembly sought with varying degrees of success to force errant husbands to maintain financial responsibility towards their families. In any case, the Poor Relief Boards did not look too kindly on poorer women considered sufficiently able-bodied to support themselves and family, and their response was commonly to bind out the children of poor women into apprenticeships. Moreover, relief was often limited to a specific period of time, making it imperative for poor women to find a way to become economically self-sufficient. In the precarious labour market of seventeenth-century Barbados, most poor women found their opportunities for employment limited. Without property or capital that might enable them to invest in the markets or establish their own small-scale undertaking, many faced the prospect of absolute poverty.

Marriage, then, could offer women increased economic security, but the uncertainties of life meant that even the most happily married wife had to be prepared for the premature death of a beloved spouse. Indeed, many marriages were short lived, especially in the early years of settlement. The humid tropical climate and various epidemics took a heavy toll on the white male population, who were renowned for their dissolute and depraved lifestyles. Fondness for excessive sporting and alcohol helped carry off many a husband to an early grave, and in an age when sea-voyages were still a perilous undertaking, many other husbands were lost at sea. Few wives could expect to remain married to the same partner for the duration of their lifetime. Many suddenly found themselves left alone to untangle a deceased husband's complex business affairs, while at the same time having to secure a livelihood to ensure their own and their children's survival.

Widowed women

Following the death of her husband, a married woman's legal status altered significantly, reverting back to that of a single woman, or *femme sole*. As a *femme sole*, a widow received a range of rights generally enjoyed only by men and unmarried women. She was now free of the legal constraints that circumscribed married women's lives. Yet widowhood marked an ambiguous state for women. On the one hand it reinstated their individual identity, enabling them to conduct business or invest in property as though they were single women. On the other hand, widowhood made most women economically vulnerable. How individual women would fare in this new period of their lives depended not only on their own innate resources and resilience, but to a great extent on their age and class position.

The death of a husband represented a traumatic transitional life-event for many women, as well as a deeply emotional one. At the same time as they struggled to summon the inner strength to cope with their own – and their children's – grief, they might be simultaneously forced to confront and address the financial implications stemming from the loss of the family's provider. For the majority of poor women, the death of a spouse inevitably exacerbated an already precarious economic situation. Few men of the poor classes could expect to amass sufficient property of any form to bequeath to their widows and children. Widowed women of the poor white class, then, faced stark choices: either seek early remarriage, attempt self-sufficiency, or throw themselves on the mercy of the Poor Relief Board. In contrast, most women of the elite and middling classes could ultimately expect that their economic futures would be taken care of through the provision of a dower.

Under common law, a widow was entitled to a dower for the remainder of her lifetime. Typically, the dower was equivalent to one-third of her husband's real estate and outright ownership of a third of his personal property.[31] With a substantial dower, a widow could be reasonably assured of long-term financial security for herself and her children. By careful investments in property markets, whether in land, dwelling, or slaves, elite widows could assure themselves of a relatively comfortable future. Others were less fortunate. Many newly widowed women only discovered the parlous state of the family finances after their husband's death. The grief of numerous middle-class widows was exacerbated by the unpleasant discovery that their spouses had died heavily indebted, with the estate liable to repay those debts. In such circumstances, the grieving widow had immediate and difficult choices to make. She could sell any family-owned property – which could include the family home/plantation, lands and/or slaves – in the hope that once the debts were cleared, sufficient funds would be left over to enable herself and children – if any – to begin anew. A second option was to remarry as quickly as possible (and preferably to a wealthy gentleman-planter), and a third was to throw herself on the mercy of her family and friends. Newly widowed Anne Evans had thought her family financially secure, but was devastated when it emerged that her deceased husband Robert had left her and her children without 'any other effects or estates', leaving Anne with no choice but to sell off the 'unspecified property of the deceased'. Moreover, although she had had little to do with the family's finances, Anne was now expected to take charge of her deceased husband's complex and muddled financial affairs.[32]

As wives, the principle of coverture defined women as legal incompetents, but the abrupt transition to widowhood thrust on women, literally overnight, responsibility for the complicated legalities of estate administration, and the expectation that they handle these matters with proficiency and competence. Estate administration could be an especially complicated and thorny business – especially when husbands died intestate – requiring the widow to negotiate the settlement of any debts and taxes, resolve crucial decisions about the management of her dower, determine the futures of any family-owned slaves, and make provision for their children's education. These responsibilities must have been particularly challenging to women who had previously been shielded from knowledge of their husbands' financial and business affairs.

Lacking intimate knowledge of their deceased husband's business or financial matters, widows such as Anne Evans could find themselves at considerable disadvantage in their negotiations with male creditors, particularly in the absence of trusted and legally competent male relatives or friends to act on their behalf. Ellinor Biddle discovered just how vulnerable widowed women could be in their dealings with unscrupulous men. Ellinor was forced to issue a complaint to the Assembly after falling victim to a fraud perpetrated by 'one Thomas Applethwaite, Gentleman'. It took the unfortunate Ellinor several attempts to have her case heard, but eventually the Assembly appointed an attorney to intercede on her behalf.[33]

While most widows within the sample studied accepted responsibilities as executors and administrators of estates, others appeared less confident of their ability to deal with the complex legalities of estate administration, choosing instead to appoint attorneys or agents to act on their behalf. They looked to well-regarded male relatives and friends to untangle complicated legal and financial matters, to pursue debts owing to their deceased husbands, or to arrange an estate sale on their behalf. Such was the course taken by Elizabeth Brown, who in July 1650 appointed her 'well-beloved friend Ancient John Jackson', as chief guardian and overseer of her estate.[34] Similarly, feeling unable to meet the challenges posed by the forced sale of her deceased husband's estate, Dorothy Cranfield appointed Adam Barwell as her attorney, empowering him to oversee the sale of her landed property. But the reliability or legal competence of attorneys could not always be assured, and other women adopted more shrewd measures.[35] When

Dorothy Hobbart's husband died, he bequeathed to his widow a portion of land. However, as he had died owing money to creditors, the land was seized and sold to clear the outstanding debts. Dorothy soon remarried a gentleman of means, and successfully persuaded her new husband to clear the debts, thereby enabling her to reclaim her property. Having regained the land, Dorothy then sold it to her father, presumably to place it beyond the reach of both her new husband and any potential creditors.[36]

Throughout the colonies, male life expectancy was shorter than that of women, and a woman might therefore find herself widowed not once but twice. In such a climate of uncertainty, the necessity of procuring an independent means of financial security must have prompted many widows to invest in property and, once in possession of that property, to maintain independent control over it. The widowed Joan Minor inherited thirty-six acres of land, including houses and other dwellings, from her deceased husband. In 1666, now contemplating remarriage to Richard Spenswick, Joan insisted on the drafting of a premarital contract. According to the contract, she resolved ('for reasons known only to herself', the exasperated groom stated), to retain lifelong ownership and control over her property. Joan's property holdings included nine adult male negroes, seven adult female negroes, five boy negroes, one girl negro, one bay stone horse, three bay mares, one brown cow, and two stills. The possession of twenty-three negro slaves indicates Joan's wealth and status as a propertied woman of some substance by seventeenth-century colonial standards. Joan was not content with securing her rights to maintain a separate estate, however. Anxious to remove any possibility that her future husband might get his hands on her property, Joan went one step further. She leased her plantation to James Couwens, on the condition that he vacate it on demand, especially in the event that the intended marriage did not take place. Finally she insisted to her prospective tenant Couwens that she retain lifelong rights to 'at all times hold rights of occupancy, use and benefits of any profits at her pleasure, without any let, hindrance or interruption from the said James Couwens'. To the prospective bridegroom, Joan also set out her terms. Once married, she insisted Spenswick could neither sell, lease or mortgage her property without her full knowledge and consent. Furthermore, she insisted that she be allowed to draw up her own will at any time during her married life, and through the provisions of that will, be empowered to dispose of her property however and to whosoever she saw fit.[37] Joan's endeavours to protect her property from both her future husband and James Couwens, suggests an independent-minded, financially astute individual who clearly attached significant meaning to her identity as an owner of property. Evidently harbouring doubts about her future husband, Joan went to great lengths to ensure that her property remained in her hands and under her control, safe from the potential deprecations of a man whom she feared might at sometime in the future waste or, dispose of her property. That she managed to persuade James Couwens to accept the terms of the contract (which he does not appear to have benefited from) indicates that he was either a trusted close relative or good friend.

The marriage settlements discussed in this chapter are among six such documents I have uncovered, although it is possible that many more survive in Barbadian archives. The existence of marriage contracts does not in itself prove conclusively that the women who devised them were in practice able to control or dispose of their property as they clearly intended to. The difficulty lies in knowing how far, or to what extent, marriage contracts were legally binding. Did women such as Joan Minor freely devise these contracts themselves, or were they induced to do so by male relatives – especially fathers – seeking to retain property within the family? Joan Minor's settlement certainly suggests that some women, either through a simple desire to control their own property, or with an eye to the vulnerability that often accompanied widowhood, were prime instigators in writing and negotiating these contracts.

Women responded to widowhood in diverse ways. Unwilling or unable to remain in Barbados, some elected to return to their former homes in the metropolis, or sought new lives elsewhere in the Americas. Emigration represented a new start in life, but it need not necessarily imply a decisive break with Barbados. Many who departed retained their property interests in Barbados, appointing attorneys and overseers to manage their interests on their behalf, and directed affairs from their new homes. In 1647 the widowed Bett Bravno, now residing in the City of London, appointed Floyd Evan as her agent and attorney, instructing him to sell her twenty acres of plantation land in Barbados in exchange for cotton, wool and tobacco.[38] Similarly, when Elizabeth Matthews' husband died, she emigrated to Antigua but retained a parcel of land in the parish of St Lucy. From Antigua, Elizabeth appointed her friend Samuel Johnson as her attorney, giving him full power to administer her property.[39] The numerous surviving letters in which widows now residing in England or elsewhere appointed male friends to oversee their property interests in Barbados suggests not only that a high proportion of wealthier widows chose to return to their place of origin following the death of their husbands, but also indicates the active participation of unknown numbers of women in England within the slave economy. Future studies of white women's roles within the colonial plantation economy must also examine their property interests both within and beyond the colonial space. Collectively, white women accounted for the minority of those among Barbadian propertied classes, *but* if we take in to account the proportion of non-resident women holding property interests in Barbados, the extent of female property ownership may well reveal a far more intricate pattern of female involvement.

Widowhood represented a period of anxiety and uncertainty for all women, irrespective of age or wealth. Elite wealthy women might take comfort in being financially well provided for, but they still had to make major decisions about the future management of their wealth and property. Widowed mothers of young children not only had to adjust to their new status, but also had to contemplate their children's futures. Without a substantial dower all women were vulnerable, but older women whose chances of remarriage were reduced were in an especially precarious position. The death of a husband not only deprived women of a loved partner, but also of his labour, a loss that carried significant implications for all women, though especially so for poorer class women and for women without wider family support. For all women, widowhood with its attendant new responsibilities represented a period beset by insecurity, vulnerability, anxiety, and uncertainty.

Yet, once over their initial grief, numerous widows came to regard this new stage of their lives as an opportunity to construct new self-identities as self-reliant, independent single women. For some women, widowhood presented the first moment in a lifetime that she was able to exercise autonomy over her life. Many rose to the challenge of independent womanhood, taking over single-handedly their deceased husband's business affairs, entering the waged labour market, establishing new ventures, and raising children as lone parents. Certainly, the most immediate business of widowhood for propertied women – establishing the terms of a husband's will and the amount of her dower, attending to the legal and financial administration of his estate – could inspire a newfound self-confidence in a widow's abilities as she negotiated with attorneys, administrators, lawyers, creditors, slave-traders, and a wide spectrum of people with whom she might hitherto have had only limited contact. Widowed mothers of minor children also found their responsibilities extended, not least because their children's education and future had to be mapped out and planned for. Where there were older children, plans and preparations had to be made for their future marriages. Other women might also find themselves taking on kinship responsibilities previously fulfilled by the deceased husband. Thus widowhood invariably imposed a whole new set of duties and interactions for widowed women.[40]

Widowhood signalled a period of economic insecurity for all but the wealthiest women, but for others, their newly independent status as *femme soles* opened up vistas that were possible only for a minority of *femme coverts*. Legally restored independence represented opportunities to participate in the public economy in diverse ways. It should not be surprising then that some widows entered this new phase of their lives intent on self-determination. Many bought property, slaves, land or dwelling houses, which they leased for rental income, other women went to trade, in some cases independently, but at other times in partnership, while some invested in business ventures. More intrepid women challenged the male domination of plantation ownership, purchasing working estates which they managed, either independently, or with the assistance of male friends, relatives, attorneys or an overseer. In 1654 Mary Cox, a widow of Bridgetown, purchased a 'piece of ground situated near the Church in the Indian Bridge Town' for the sum of 42,000 lb muscavado sugar. Additionally, Mary also bought 'all cattle stock, utensils and appurtenances, i.e. four cows, one bull, five breeding cows [...] four Negro slaves, one couch, three chairs, one iron pot, one baking stove, two broad houses, two narrow houses, three bells, three hatchets, one grinding stone, one bed and furnishings, two tables, two forms, one woman and one man'. The inclusion of cattle, four slaves and two indentured servants would suggest that Mary intended to work her land as a farm.[41]

Following the death of her husband, Margaret Sandifford evidently set out to accumulate substantial landholdings. In March 1670, Margaret acquired from Mary Jamie 'a plot or parcel of land in Speightstown... together with one boarded house... and all the profits and privileges whatsoever... for a lease of eighty-three years'. Margaret's new property came cheaply – 16 lb of muscavado sugar and 'one coffle of capons... as an acknowledgement, if they be lawfully demanded'.[42] The relatively low purchase price for this property suggests that Mary Jamie was either a close relative or a friend. One month later, Margaret was consolidating her property portfolio. On 14 April, she bought fourteen acres of land for which she exchanged 12,000 lb of muscavado sugar. Just four days later she resold the land to its original owner for 37,000 lb of muscavado sugar – triple the price she had paid and a tidy profit indeed.[43]

For many widows the ownership of real-estate property represented not only the most visible symbol of status, but a crucial means of guaranteeing present and future security. A study of Barbadian property deeds is particularly revealing of widows' efforts to acquire or extend property interests, both land and slaves. Landed property could serve several purposes. It could be leased to a tenant farmer for an annual rent and/or a share of the crop; it could be used to build a dwelling for the family, or leased as cattle grazing land. It could also be held against future hardships, to be sold when financial necessity demanded. Many widows also bought land that could be gifted to children on marriage. The 1654 deeds and inventory of Annie Barker, a widow of Christchurch, reveal a woman's ambitions in the plantation sector. Annie sold, and then re-mortgaged, a working plantation of eighty acres for the considerable sum of 135,000 lb of muscavado sugar. The attached inventory shows Annie to have been a woman of some wealth. The deed of sale and inventory included: a dwelling house, 200 sugar pots, four copper stills, one mill and frame house, two great cisterns and two great drinking tubs, cattle and fourteen servants (four women and ten men with periods of between four and no years of service still to be served).[44]

The prospects of infirmity and isolation in their later years weighed heavily on many widows, and surviving deeds of sale indicate that many sought to avoid this eventuality. Numerous widows bought and leased land for little more than a peppercorn rent, in return for an undertaking by the lessee that s/he provide for them in later life. Ann Spencer of Christchurch sold her son Hackett seventeen acres of land and buildings, in return for Ann's right to the 'use of one bedchamber', and an annuity of £10 sterling until her death. Hackett also agreed to provide his mother with sufficient food, drink, washing and lodging, and to care Ann's four cattle.[45] It is doubtful that Anne was a woman of economic substance, but she at least was fortunate to have a son to whom she could look to for her care as she approached old age. Elderly widows without children or other near relatives willing to care for them in later life could face a difficult old age. Anne Pomfrett, also of Christchurch, worried about the possibility of dying alone and penniless, and fretted that she might not receive a proper Christian burial. She resolved therefore to sell her plantation of five acres to Edward and Mary White for ten shillings, in return for their undertaking to maintain her for the rest of her life, and thereafter to provide a 'decent and Christian like internment after her decease'.[46] Twice-widowed Elizabeth Swan signed over the freehold of her plantation of ten acres and some dwelling houses to William Jones, in return for 'sufficient meat, drink, lodging and apparel' for the duration of her lifetime.[47] Numerous other property deeds stipulating similar arrangements for their care are suggestive of widowed women's strategies to achieve a level of economic security and care as they entered the final stages of their lives.

Women's economic participation extended beyond that of property investments. A significant aspect of women's independent economic activities was the supply of lines of credit and mortgages to planters, merchants and traders. Mary Butler's research reveals that in the twenty years between 1823 and 1843, women provided ten per cent of all credit to Barbadian planters.[48] Indeed, records indicate that from an early stage of settlement, considerable numbers of women were involved in money-lending. In 1649, the widowed Beatrice Oderane loaned David Bix the considerable amount of £150 sterling, for which he signed a promissory note to repay the sum of £350.[49] This arrangement represented only one of several of Beatrice's similar transactions. The participation of women in this sector of the financial market would appear to be a rational choice for many women, particularly for widows, for it enabled them to pursue economic interests without becoming embroiled in the demands that other forms of economic activity, e.g. plantation management, imposed on owners.

For the most part, however, few widows were apparently willing or able to trust their future security solely to the vicissitudes of the Barbadian market economy, and remarriage rates were high. Moreover, prevailing gender conventions emphasised women's 'natural' dependence on men; women's identity was closely merged with that of men, whether a husband or a father. Even the most financially secure of widows might view remarriage as a more attractive option than a solitary and lonely future.

Maintaining control over her property must have been a significant consideration for a widowed mother contemplating remarriage. There was little guarantee that a new husband would not seek to claim ownership of property that a woman might intend to bequeath to her children; or that in the event that she predecease him, a stepfather would feel a moral responsibility to ensure her children receive their rightful inheritances bequeathed to them by either of their parents. Indeed, in the mid-1650s, alarmed by the numerous court cases arising from the embezzlement and wastage of estates – especially by stepfathers – the Council moved to protect women and children's property rights by appointing committees in each parish to monitor estates and the conditions of orphaned children.[50] But still, some stepfathers found legal loopholes through which they could squander or waste their new wife's property, exposing her and her children to economic calamity. We should not therefore find it surprising that numerous widows took steps to ensure their continued control over the property they possessed.

The imperative to provide for themselves and their children propelled many widows into early remarriages, sometimes with disastrous consequences. When her husband Gabriel Wolfe died in 1652, his wife Anne subsequently remarried George Loome, who so violently ill-treated his wife that finally, in fear of her life, she was forced to apply to the Council of Assembly for protection.[51] Sometimes, remarriage threw up unexpected legal complications. In 1669 the Assembly was asked to decide on the distressing case of Sarah Payne who, believing herself to be widowed after her husband Richard disappeared at sea, took John Taylor as her new husband. Some time after this marriage Sarah learned that her first husband Richard was alive, and in Barbados. As if the shock of Richard's reappearance were not sufficient to throw Sarah into emotional turmoil, Richard opposed his wife's remarriage and appealed to the court to uphold his claim as Sarah's legal husband. After long debate, the Assembly decided in Richard's favour, ordering Sarah to henceforth 'live and cohabit with the said Richard Payne as her husband, and for the future, avoid the company of the said John Taylor'.[52] Frustratingly, we do not know how Sarah responded to the situation in which she had unwittingly found herself, but what this case does reveal are the complications of an ideology of marriage within which women are themselves defined as a species of property. Bigamous marriages – of which there appear to have been several in Barbados – could also disrupt women's married lives, for among the consequences faced by a woman unwittingly involved in such an illegitimate marriage was the loss of whatever economic security she had derived from her 'husband'.

Single women

Unmarried white Barbadian women's relationship to property differed significantly from that of married women. As *femmes soles* they could participate in the property market with few restrictions, sharing with white males the legal rights to freely and autonomously participate in the market economy. They bought and sold land, slaves, houses and other dwellings, purchased mortgages and leases, sold their labour as waged workers, entered into negotiations and contracts, sued for debts in court, devised their own wills, parented children alone, and managed their own households. At all times, though, they competed with white males – and later, free coloured women and men – for viable niches in the market economy. Beckles has made the point that their ventures were often confined to the less lucrative and illegal or informal sectors of the market; nevertheless, many were able to establish thriving businesses.[53]

Research has uncovered only fragmentary evidence of the economic activities of unmarried women of the wealthier classes, and the majority of documents analysed reflected the activities of widowed women of the propertied classes. Moreover, difficulties in untangling the marital status of some women does cloud the overall picture.

However, among the legal documents analysed, over fifty involved economic transactions by single women. In general, most of these transactions relate to the sale of small tracts of land, modest dwelling houses or a few slaves, such as the 1643 purchase by Anne Payce of 'two negro women ... Judith and Katherine'.[54] And in 1711, Katherine Squires acquired a mortgage on property previously owned by her parents, for the sum of £25 sterling.[55] The general pattern revealed in property deeds and wills, of women as holders of numerous small tracts of land, and as owners of few slaves, correlates with Beckles's assertions that white women were most likely to be in possession of smaller landholdings.[56]

For many unmarried women property ownership represented the most reliable insurance of future economic security, and property deeds reveal their vibrant activity in this economic sector, with women engaging in the sale and disposal of land, slaves and dwellings. These records must be read as an indication of the economic, social and cultural value that single women attached to property ownership. That numerous males also gifted or bequeathed property to women does suggest that despite cultural ideals of dependent womanhood, male Barbadians viewed single women's activities in the property market as commonplace. Unmarried women of the lower classes represented the most vulnerable group among the white Barbadian population. Marriage promised security for all women, and indeed was considered a necessity for their economic and social wellbeing. Yet the disproportionately high female–male ratio created a permanent pool of unmarried women, thereby undermining the reality. Some among these poor unmarried women were lone mothers and those who consciously chose spinsterhood and lone parenting over wifehood. Gendered expectations of women as the actual or potential dependants of males – whether father or husband – inevitably situated marriage and wifehood as the normative state, and women outside these institutions undoubtedly contradicted ideal expectations of dependent womanhood. In pursuing independent economic activities, single women challenged and contradicted prevailing ideals of passive and dependent womanhood.

Patterns of female property ownership

A survey of the Barbados census of 1680 by Brigitte Kossek estimated that white women owned between three and thirteen per cent of the total acres of land under cultivation in six Barbadian parishes; that they employed between three and sixteen per cent of indentured servants; and owned between four and eleven per cent of the total number of enslaved in the parishes surveyed.⁵⁷ Undoubtedly white males represented the majority of land and plantation owners. Richard Ford's 1769 map displaying the locations of the largest plantations, included only twenty-two women in possession of 100 or more acres of land. The largest of these female landowners were Madame Grace Silvester, with over 700 acres, and Lady Willoughby, who also appears to have also owned over 700 acres of land.⁵⁸

Bridgetown, the thriving capital city, offered many women opportunities for property investment, and documents reveal a significant degree of white female participation in the urban economy. Pedro Welch's research uncovered such women as Mary Lawrence, owner of several of the largest properties in Swan Street and Roebuck Street, two of the principal roads in Bridgetown. Another woman, Roberta Metcalfe, owned fifteen tenements in Reed Street, which we may safely assume were rented out for their incomes.⁵⁹ Records reveal little of these women and their business dealings, but their participation in the economic life of Bridgetown strongly suggests that whatever the constraining legalities and ideological practices, women's property interests represented a significant part of the urban economy. The high participation of women as economic actors in the city does not in itself suggest a departure from the patriarchal norms that structured Barbadian gender relations. What it does suggest is that white female participation in the property markets, particularly in Bridgetown, has implications for any analysis of their contributions to emerging class and cultural systems there.⁶⁰ How representative these entrepreneurial women were of white Barbadian women of their period is difficult to establish, but it is evident that they attached similar socio-economic and cultural value to property ownership as did white males. Property ownership for these women represented not merely a worthy form of investment, but signified their place in the race and class hierarchies.

It is clear that despite periods of dislocation when the largest planters were consolidating their landholdings – particularly as sugar production replaced tobacco production during the seventeenth century – white Barbadian women of all classes continued to participate in the property market in large numbers. Certainly, as Butler established, the years immediately prior to emancipation in 1838 saw an almost unprecedented involvement of women in estate purchases. Nevertheless, I believe that the evidence from this study, which predates Butler's study by up to 200 years, supports the general picture of the existence of white female agency in relation to property, prior to emancipation.

White Barbadian women acquired property through several routes. As *femmes soles*, they independently purchased tracts of land. When land prices escalated, as they periodically did, land could also be resold to realise profits. Women of substantial wealth such as Madam Grace Silvester and Lady Willoughby invested heavily in larger holdings on which they managed sugar plantations worked by hundreds of enslaved Africans. Few women, however, enjoyed significant independent wealth, and thus might find their aspirations limited. Undeterred, however, some went to great lengths to overcome their financial constraints. Many formed partnerships with relatives and friends of both sexes in order to join the class of landowners. In 1668 the widowed Joan Moody, too poor to afford the purchase price of £150 for 'a parcel of land containing 2,280 feet' joined forces with unnamed others in order to realise her ambitions.[61]

Other women, both single and married, gained a foothold in the property market as the result of gifts of land and real estate transferred to, or purchased specifically for, them by others. Mary Dobson received a gift of 7.5 acres of land, along with cattle, stock and household items, from John Cole, her husband's business partner. Cole transferred the gift 'freely, voluntarily and willingly' to Mary, for her lifetime, on the condition that she 'shall not sell, dispose of any part of the before mentioned estate during my lifetime unless it be for the paying of my debts or for my maintenance during my lifetime'.[62] In 1685, Anthony Anthony deeded to his friend Elizabeth Bishop twenty acres of land and six negroes.[63] And in 1791, although owning to some doubts over his paternity of their two children, Fortescu Beckles nevertheless gave to their unmarried mother Sarah Cunliffe a house on his land, 'in the same manner as in my life, a horse and saddle, and a boy to wait on her'.[64]

Gifts of land and other forms of real estate to female relatives and friends suggest that despite the patriarchal ethos and the legal restrictions that structured women's access to property, white Barbadian males generally recognised the symbolism and significance of property ownership for white women. Fathers commonly deeded gifts of land and/or slaves to married or spinster daughters. John Armstrong's gift of five acres of land to his unmarried daughter Rebecca represents just the tip of a pattern of male gifting to female relatives.[65] It is possible that the giving of land and other forms of real estate to daughters was intended to make them more marriageable, but it is also equally likely that parents gave their spinster daughters such gifts once it became clear that a daughter was likely to remain unmarried. This would have enabled these women to establish their own households separately from their parents.

At times, the circumstances under which some women acquired property bordered on the illicit. In 1727, Sarah Andrews, proprietor of the Russia Plantation, was charged with taking illegal possession of the estate and property of Wardell Andrews, her deceased brother. According to the terms of his will, Wardell had bequeathed his estate to William, his son. However, young William soon followed his father to the grave, and being a minor, had not made a will. The suit charged that Sarah somehow 'got into possession of the plantation and slaves and held them for many years. Through her Barbadian attorney she continued to receive the profits of the plantation until William Andrews discovered that he had an interest under the will of his cousin.'[66]

Undaunted by this challenge to her illegitimate ownership of the plantation, Sarah launched a successful appeal, and was granted legal ownership of the property. Whether Sarah acted alone is unclear. At the time of the suit she was living with her second husband, who may have played some part in the alleged deceit. But the fact that her husband was not named in the suit suggests that Sarah was the primary instigator. Possibly, Sarah's claim was upheld because the legitimate heir resided in England, and as far as could be established, had never visited Barbados. Moreover, she had turned a once-neglected plantation into a thriving and successful business, and was therefore in a strong position to defend her claim; in Sarah's case, possession was indeed nine-tenths of the law.

Sarah Andrews' manoeuvring to obtain her brother's property illustrates women's resistance to efforts to deprive them of property they considered rightfully theirs, and the complications that could arise from inheritance laws. Inheritance represented a major source of women's property ownership, and enabled unmarried single women, wives and widows to become 'first-time' property owners, or to extend or consolidate existing property holdings.

Land represented only one form of property transferred to women; gifts and bequests of slaves, jewellery, clothing, household furniture, cattle, livestock, bedsteads and cooking utensils regularly appear within wills and deeds of sale, and their value cannot be underestimated. Colonial Barbadians were highly dependent on the importation of costly consumer goods, and thus attached significant value to their possessions. A survey of household inventories and wills of both wealthy and poor white Barbadians is highly reflective of the material worth assigned to even the most everyday items. Finetta Abarbanell's carefully inventoried possessions, valued at £1,011 11s 3d sterling in 1796, included a board and shingled house, five slaves and a few acres of land, a small parcel of tin pots, kettles, a broken set of teacups, a scale beam and weight, stone jars and jugs, two chocolate stoves, two pillows, and a variety of bed linen.[67] Finetta's detailed inventory highlights the importance attributed to all forms of property, both real and personal. For the nominal sum of one piece of silver, Richard Vince deeded to his 'friend Mary Martin' all his 'goods, chattels, leases and debts due to him, ready money, plates, rings, household stuff, apparel, utensils, brass pewter, bedding and all my other substance whatever moveable' for her 'peaceable enjoyment'. What prompted Richard to present Mary with the entirety of his material goods is unclear.[68] The following section analyses wills probated in Barbadian courts to establish patterns of inheritance as they relate specifically to women.

Women and inheritance

A study of wills devised by male and female testators in plantation-era Barbados is not only highly revealing of the values that white Barbadians attached to property, but also enables us to comprehend better prevalent attitudes towards women as property holders. We have already determined that women's relationship to property was regulated by their marital status. Single women enjoyed the same rights as men to own and control property, but once married, forfeited their rights to independent property ownership. Without the provision of a separate estate, married women were precluded from exercising ownership or control over property. Not until the death of her husband was a woman's independence and legal rights restored to her. Widowhood therefore represented the restoration of individual identity and accompanying legal rights, enabling widows to become, once again, independent participants in the public and economic life of Barbadian society. Yet, although she was nominally an independent individual, the extent of a widow's freedom of will and action could be constrained by the nature and the terms of any inheritance received from her deceased husband's estate. Inheritance represented perhaps the most significant source of women's property, and a study of inheritance patterns derived from a survey of testators wills is vital to an understanding of women's relationship to property.

Inheritance laws dictated the extent and terms under which women owned and controlled property. As a *femme sole*, unmarried women freely decided the beneficiaries of their property. Widowed women however faced legal restraints in the ownership, control and disposal of inherited property, and many a widow came to understand that the rule of a deceased husband could extend beyond the grave. Widows could not freely choose their own heirs, especially where young children were involved, as it was usual for husbands to decide the distribution of the marital estate before death. In any case, the legal precept of primogeniture also dictated the distribution of inheritable real estate. The law did, however, safeguard a widow's rights, as embodied within a 1649 Act which countered attempts by husbands to exclude wives from inheriting property,

Widow's rights to dower ensured that an aggrieved or alienated husband could not deprive his wife of a share of the marital estate. The right of dower, however, offered women only limited security. Throughout the colonies, widows received their dower before the payment of estate debts, but they could not sell or dispose of property owned by their deceased husbands – including property that they themselves had brought to the marriage. Dower commonly amounted to one-third of the husband's total estate, and gave widows the right to a dwelling house, ordinarily the marital home. Where young children were present, the widow was likely to receive only a portion share of the dwelling house.[69] In addition to dower, widows might also receive a share of a husband's personal property, the rest being distributed among their children. Though any property that women brought to a marriage became that of her husband, any property that formed part of a pre-marriage settlement could not be attached for debt. This was an important provision, as it enabled women to maintain a separate estate that would provide for the future financial security of themselves and their children.

Among the wills surveyed, there was little evidence that male testators lacked a spirit of generosity in the provisions they made for their wife's widowhood. Some chose to give their wives more than her dower rights, and a few evidently bequeathed their wives the entirety of their property. Of thirty-two wills devised by married men, fourteen bequeathed the bulk of their estates to their wives, even where children were involved. John Phillips of Christchurch, bequeathed 'all my estate real and personal' to his wife Eliza, for her lifetime, stipulating only that she allow their children sufficient maintenance and education. Eliza was also to receive one of her deceased husband's two dwelling houses for use of herself and their children, while the rental income from the second dwelling house was to be put towards the children's maintenance and education.[70] Thomas Phillips of St Joseph also left all his real estate and personal effects to his wife Alice, but made provision for his mother-in-law to be accommodated in a dwelling house during her lifetime. Curiously, Phillips prioritised the needs of his wife and mother-in-law over and above those of his children, whom he insisted should receive their inheritances only after the death of their grandmother. Such was Phillips's esteem for his wife and mother-in-law that he appointed them – along with his friend John Hinkson – executors of his will.[71]

'It might be supposed considering the estate I am possessed of I might give larger legacies to my sons and daughters', ran the preamble to the will of wealthy Phillip Collyns of Christchurch, who evidently expected that questions would be raised over the relatively small legacies bequeathed to his children – £200 to each of his sons and £150 to each of his daughters, plus a negro slave and some silverware. Collyns had bequeathed the entirety of his substantial New England estates to his 'dear wife Alice'. She also held 'right and property on fifty acres of land wherein stands my mansion house, windmill and other buildings and several slaves'. Collyns, however, offered no explanation for his minor bequests to his children, although possibly he expected that Alice, appointed executor of his will and guardian of his children, would make provision for them in her will.[72] And Joseph Lee, a jeweller of Christchurch, bequeathed to his children all his slaves, while leaving to his wife the rest of his real and personal property, including his jewellery business.[73] Generally, however, where there were children, male testators tended to follow common law and practice, leaving their wives at least a third share of their estate, and distributing the remainder of the property between their children. Childless widows could expect to receive a greater share of their husband's estate.

Of the eight wills devised by apparently childless married men, six wives received the entirety of their husband's estates; two other wives received the bulk of the estate, with smaller bequests going to other relatives and friends. Thus the presence or absence of children was perhaps the most important determinant of the size of a wife's legacy. The state of a couple's marital relationship could also shape the amount of a wife's legacy. Some husbands elected to leave their wives a larger share than the customary 'third', but an unhappy husband might leave his wife only the minimum to which she was entitled. William Phillips of St Phillip made it clear that he was leaving his wife the third share demanded by law, and nothing more. His wife however, was more fortunate than his estranged son, deliberately excluded from his father's will, on the grounds of his being 'no more than a stranger'. Phillips' nephew received the bulk of his estate.[74]

Not all unhappily married men penalised their wives in this manner. Prefacing his 1672 will with a diatribe against his wife Millisaint, John Jennings, made public the source of his misery:

> Notwithstanding my most miserable life, through my most unfortunate match, and a more cruel and masculine and treacherous wife whom none (but God alone) can know in that sense . . . I hereby give to Millisaint Jennings my wife the management, use and income of all my lands for

her life, and desire my estate to be kept entire as it is now, for better satisfaction of all my debts which have been principally contracted by my wife's occasion, and the enabling my said wife *to serve her own desires during her life*.[75] (my emphasis)

Although heartsore and angered by the behaviour of his 'masculine' wife Millisaint, Jennings nevertheless placed no restrictions on her inheritance, except a fervent plea that the estate be left intact, and gave Millisaint only lifetime ownership of his property. Though claiming that his debts were the result of his wife's profligate habits, he nevertheless appointed her co-executor of his will. That Jennings appointed a co-executor suggests he was not confident of Millisaint's ability to properly manage his estate.

Unlike John Jennings, other Barbadian husbands did seek to control their property, and their wife's lives, even after death. Numerous husbands bequeathed the bulk or entirety of their estates to their wives, but attached caveats that altered the widow's fortune should she remarry, or fail to carry out to the letter their instructions for the care, education and maintenance of their children. John Leacock of St Lucy made several bequests of money and slaves to his children, but his wife Alice was to receive the bulk of his estate. Should Alice remarry, however, or attempt to take her dower out of his estate, then all of that part of his estate intended to pass to her children John and Ann, would instead descend by equal proportions to Elizabeth and Margaret, his biological daughters from a previous marriage.[76] Why Leacock should seek to disinherit John and Ann in the event of their mother's remarriage is unclear. It is possible that he was in fact their stepfather; if this were the case, it suggests that he perhaps experienced some apprehension that any future husband his widow might marry might not feel morally responsible for Elizabeth and Margaret. Thus, by 'threatening' to remove Ann and John's legacy, Leacock attempted to safeguard his own daughters' futures. Similarly, John Atkins of St Phillip also bequeathed to his wife Jean his entire estate 'for the duration of her life and her widowhood' with the proviso that 'if she should alter her name by taking another husband', she was to receive only a third share of his estate.[77] John Worrell of St Thomas left his wife an annuity of £100 sterling per year, 'and her living' on his estate, but was unequivocal in his desire that 'in case she marries or claim her dower, then she is to get off the estate'.[78]

Not all men sought, however, to prevent their widow's remarriage. John Phillips of Christchurch apparently had no qualms about such an eventuality. He granted his wife all his entire estate, real and personal, for the duration of her life, with the understanding that she provide for the maintenance and education of his children. He did worry, however, that a new stepfather might ill-treat his children. As a safeguard, Phillips stipulated that in such circumstances, his children should have possession of his plantation house.[79]

Notwithstanding these attempts to posthumously control the threat to their property posed by their wife's remarriage, Barbadian husbands commonly bequeathed the bulk of their estates to their widows. These findings do, however, stand in stark contrast with the conclusions reached by Trevor Burnard in his study of Jamaican wills. Burnard concluded that Jamaican men appeared to have little confidence in their wives' financial and management abilities, especially where the couple had children, and particularly where adult sons were involved.[80] However, the results of the Barbadian sample bear out the conclusions of a comparable study of seventeenth-century Maryland wills. Lorena Walsh and Lois Carr concluded that in conditions of high mortality, relatively short marriages, high patterns of widowhood and serial polyandry – demographic circumstances characteristic of Barbadian society in the seventeenth to nineteenth centuries – women enjoyed greater economic and social authority than did women in the Old World societies.[81]

Patterns of property distribution in women's wills
Unlike widows and single women, married women could not freely devise their own wills without first obtaining the consent of their husband. In law and custom, all marital property was assumed to belong to the husband, and in his person resided the right to manage or dispose of that property as he saw fit. Consequently, the majority of women's wills included in this study were devised by spinsters or widows. Notwithstanding the legal and customary restraints on women's rights to own and dispose of property, some more egalitarian husbands empowered their wives to devise their own wills. In 1734, Maud Beckles, wife of the Hon. Thomas Beckles, devised her own last will and testament in which she directed that her slaves be shared out among her daughters. Thomas signalled his approval of this arrangement with the addition of a memorandum confirming his consent to the will.[82] Elizabeth Macey, who also devised her own will, bequeathed to her husband the bulk of her estate 'excepting one negro boy', which she bequeathed to her son Nathaniel. Elizabeth also asked that her husband purchase a negro boy for another son, John, when he in turn reached his majority. Both sons were also to receive a gold mourning ring.[83] The rarity of wills devised by married women indicates the extent to which women's rights to dispose of property were constrained. But their very existence does suggest that when empowered

to do so, women appreciated the opportunity to control the disposal of their property in whatever ways they saw fit.

Some aspects of women's attitudes towards their property are attested to in the patterns of distribution, as indicated in their surviving wills. Amy Erickson's claim that women testators exhibited a distinct awareness of the economic vulnerability of their female relatives and friends is supported by this study's findings.[84] Women were far more likely than men to bequeath their property to a much wider circle of family and friends. Male testators generally favoured their sons with a larger share of the estate than their daughters, but widowed mothers proved slightly more likely to distribute their property equally between daughters and sons.[85] Women's more equitable distribution of property to their children might be read as an awareness of their daughters' economic vulnerability, and, therefore, as an attempt to provide against their daughters' future impoverishment. As most husbands chose to disadvantage their daughters by leaving their sons the larger part of their estates, it is likely that women believed their sons to be adequately provided for under the terms of their father's wills, and this is reflected in their efforts to increase the financial and material wellbeing of their daughters. Sarah Andrews' will reflects a degree of unease about her son-in-law's treatment of her daughter Amy. Although Amy was to inherit all her mother's property, Sarah worried that Amy's future security might be threatened, and therefore included in her will the caveat that should Amy's husband prove 'unkind' to her, the executors of the will were to ensure that Amy receive 'all necessary sustenance ... and something privately towards her maintenance'.[86] Women were also less likely to place restrictions on the use of property they bequeathed, except where the property involved slaves. Most female slaveowners left detailed instructions for the disposal and subsequent care of their slaves.

That women valued their property, and their ability to control and dispose of that property, is clear from an analysis of the patterns of distribution by female testators. Compared to male testators, women's wills are far more detailed both in terms of the description of their property, and of kin relationships, and are therefore extremely revealing of women's personal and emotional attachments to their property, their friends and families. Property in all its forms was to be valued, for women appreciated that property ownership represented the surest route to financial security and social status.

Wills constitute public documents, and in his weary description of his spouse as 'treacherous', 'cruel and masculine', John Jennings subjected his wife to public humiliation. Evidently, he regarded Millisaint's behaviour as a clear breech of seventeenth-century gendered ideals of submissive and modest womanhood. Certainly theirs was not a match made in heaven, and Jennings rued his unfortunate marriage to a wife who seemed to have little regard for the normative conventions of white womanhood. Yet, despite Jennings's very public defamation of his unfeeling wife, Millisaint's own will, written in 1685, reveals great affection towards a wide circle of family and friends. She bequeathed to her son Francis Cleaver all her sugar and cane crops on her Barbadian plantation, all but three of her slaves, all her cattle, and £200 sterling. To her daughter-in-law she bequeathed twenty shillings to purchase a ring.[87] Each grandchild received at least £50, and 5,000 lb of muscavado sugar. Other bequests were made to friends Elizabeth Millworth (£25 and one negro), Mr and Mrs Conrad Adams (twenty shillings to purchase rings), and their married daughter Priscilla, who received £10. Two more friends, Mary Powell and Priscilla Franklin, both also received twenty shillings, again to purchase rings, and other friends received bequests ranging from £5 to £50. Even two slaves, Ann Mapleton and Black Jack, were to benefit from Millisaint's generosity – both were to be manumitted immediately after her death.[88]

Mothers and fathers both bequeathed property to unmarried daughters. Property could ensure a young woman's financial security, but it could also enhance a daughter's marriage prospects. Sometimes, though, parents attached unreasonable conditions to their children's inheritances. Alice Richards, a widow, bequeathed all her property to her spinster daughter Sarah, but with the curious proviso that 'it shall not be delivered to her until it has pleased God to bless her with the gift of speech or utterance which she has not had at any time since her birth'. Just how Sarah, a deaf mute, was to survive should God fail to deliver to her the power of speech, is not considered.[89] Other daughters inherited property with less stringent provisos. In 1647, James Ashford bequeathed his entire estate to his daughter Elizabeth, his only stipulation being that she 'walk orderly in the face of the Lord and take the advice of friends'.[90]

Unmarried daughters were not the only single women to benefit from inheritances. Annie Brewerton, whose parents Richard and Elizabeth Brewerton were servants to planter Stephen Mott, inherited Mott's entire stock of hogs and their increase. Mott stipulated that income from the hogs be used solely 'for the livelihood of the said Annie, Elizabeth her mother, and Mary and John, her brother and sister'. When Annie reached the age of fourteen, she would then also inherit all of Mott's chattel goods, and any debts due to him. Finally, Mott ended his will with the request that Annie 'should be released from her indentureship, that she shall be freed from service of any kind... and her indenture to be cancelled immediately after my death'.[91] Again the records are frustrating for what is left unsaid: what considerations motivated Mott to leave his worldly goods to Annie, the child of his servants? Why did he exclude Annie's father from a share of the income derived from his hogs?

Women without land or slaves also made wills, but in the absence of real estate, bequeathed personal items to relatives and friends. This tendency further highlights the importance of all forms of property, both real and personal, to women. In a society where most household goods had to be imported, the capital worth of such items as furniture, clothing, jewellery, and even cooking implements was highly significant. Anne Borden bequeathed to her son Nathaniel her tenement house and all its appurtenances. Her married daughter Johanna received 'all the furniture in the chamber, my large copper pan, my chocolate stove, my oval table in the dining room and all my cloth and other things to be found in my large red leather trunk'. Ann, her granddaughter inherited '[her] newest bed with the feathered mattress, two pillows and other things being in the chamber called the cutlery chamber, a side chest of drawers, and a quart silver tankard'.[92]

Even items of clothing were regarded as valuable property. The widowed Elizabeth Badmadge left her two unmarried daughters her house and grounds, but her married daughter Elizabeth received '£10, a kettle, a stuffed vest, a crepe vest and a white calico coat'.[93] Similarly, Mary Calvin left her niece Ann Turpin 'one negro girl and all my wearing apparel and £20'.[94] Certain items of clothing therfore had real economic significance, as a well-made dress or petticoat could be passed down to and worn by several generations of women. But women's clothing and dress held other symbolism for the women who bequeathed and inherited these items. In her study of women's clothing in colonial plantation societies, Glory Robertson has suggested that women's clothing performed an important function by marking out the social distinctions between black and white women, and between white women of varying classes. Property ownership – even of apparel – could be a critical means through which 'whiteness' was signified and practised.

Patently, the distribution of women's property was shaped not simply by consideration of the beneficiary's economic status, but also by sentiment, as evidenced by the large numbers of gold mourning rings bequeathed to daughters, sisters, nieces and other female kin and friends. In any case, even for those women with modest real estate, the stimulus to making a will was prompted by a desire to ensure that however humble their property, it should pass to those they loved.

One aspect of inheritance that occurred regularly within women's wills should not go unmentioned. Eleven women in the sample bequeathed sums of money to vestries and charitable institutions for poor relief. It is not possible to know whether the benefactors were in the habit of making regular contributions to charitable causes during their lifetimes, but evidence suggests that many women viewed the welfare of the poor as the responsibility of the wealthier members of society. After making provision for her children and grandchildren, Margaret Ball asked that £10 go to St. Peter's Parish Church, and the remainder of her estate distributed among the poor.[95] Sarah Jelfe also bequeathed '40 shillings to be distributed among the poor by the minister as he sees fit'.[96] Ellenor Allamby's bequests included £20 and 'one piece of plate for the communion table' of St Thomas' Parish Church.[97] One factor that emerges clearly is the far greater number of charitable bequests made by women than by men. Indeed, none of the wills devised by males contained charitable bequests, but this does not mean that men did not contribute to charitable causes, as the Minute Books of the parochial vestries show.

Why did women feel the need to make charitable bequests of this nature? Perhaps, as was the practice in Europe, bequests to the poor represented an individual woman's spiritual reckoning with God; an attempt to secure a place in Heaven. Erickson comments on the propensity of women to leave bequests to the poor in their wills, that many women may also have been 'encouraged' in to making these last donations by the clergy and members of the vestry, who relied heavily on the goodwill of their parishioners.[98] Given the limited financial resources of Poor Relief Boards, bequests by charitable parishioners must have been a welcome source of income.

Although these documents can only provide fragmentary evidence, they do indicate that white women were active participants in the plantation economy, and helped sustain slavery in diverse ways that have hitherto gone unnoticed. Property relations have generally been analysed in terms of male relationships with and to property, but it is clear that property ownership was also imbued with economic, cultural and symbolic meanings for white colonial women. The ownership of property was a crucial signifier of social class and social status, particularly as it marked out the distinction between the free and the unfree. More importantly perhaps, property ownership defined an individual woman specifically as a white person. Their legal rights to property clearly distinguished white women from black women, who were themselves most often the property of white women.

Though in some circumstances constrained by law, white women nevertheless enjoyed legitimate access to property. It was as free, white persons that they held and owned property, engaged in property transactions – buying, leasing and selling land, slaves and other real estate, managed plantations, farmed land and provided credit to male and female borrowers. In general, women were not owners of large plantations, but there were notable exceptions. In the towns, white women also owned significant amounts of property and other investments. Although white women's access to property was determined primarily by their marital status, many married women nevertheless sought to retain control over property they regarded as rightfully theirs. And when their rights were threatened, they took legal action to protect their interests.

This chapter has attempted to outline the nature of female agency in the plantation economy, but in the process it has raised numerous questions. How far was the letter of the law adhered to in respect of women's property rights? At what stage did women enter the plantation economy? What occupations or trades could poor white women pursue once the plantations turned to slave labour? Finally, how representative were Barbadian women of other colonial women at the same historical moment? Historians of Caribbean plantation societies have only recently turned their attention to gendered analyses of these economic systems, but further research into the specificity of the white female experience will undoubtedly reveal new dimensions in the complex New World plantation societies.

Elite white women struggled to assert their rights to property, while poor women struggled merely to be accepted as legitimate members of the hegemonic white society. What they *did* commonly share across their social differences was their social significance in maintaining or breaching the boundaries of whiteness, through sexual agency. They also shared the possibility of economic participation in the plantation and new industrial economy. As in Barbados, for many white women in the American South, the acquisition of property – either land or slaves – represented the most viable means of securing an independent livelihood, and it is this aspect of white female agency in North Carolina that the next chapter explores.

Notes

1 Trevor Burnard, 'Family Continuity and Female Independence in Jamaica, 1655-1734', *Continuity and Change* 7:2 (1992), pp. 181-198.
2 John F. Campbell, 'Seeing "She" Across the Sea: Reassessing notions of womanhood in the eighteenth-century plantation world'. Working Paper No. 98-06, International Seminar on the History of the Atlantic World, 1500-1800, Harvard University (1998).
3 Hilary Beckles, 'White Women and Slavery in the Caribbean', *History Workshop Journal* 36 (1993), pp. 66-82.
4 Lucille Mair, 'An Historical Study of Women in Jamaica from 1655-1844'. Unpublished PhD thesis, University of the West Indies: Kingston, Jamaica, 1974.

5 Janet Momsen, 'Gender Ideology and Land', in Christine Barrow (ed.), *Caribbean Portraits: Essays on gender ideologies and identities* (Kingston: Ian Randle Publishers, 1998).
6 Leonore Davidoff and Catherine Hall, *Family Fortunes: Men and women of the English middle class, 1780–1850* (London: Hutchinson, 1987).
7 Richard Ligon, *A True and Exact History of the Island of Barbados* (London: Frank Cass: 1970).
8 Ibid., p. 35.
9 *Council of Assembly Minutes*, 1667–1682, Barbados Museum and Historical Society (hereafter BMHS).
10 Kathleen Mary Butler, 'White Women and Property in Early Nineteenth Century Barbados', Paper presented at the Symposium *Engendering History: Current Directions in the Study of Women*, University of the West Indies, Kingston, Jamaica (1993).
11 *Barbados Property Records* (Property Deeds), RB3/Vol.2/789/91 (Barbados Archives hereafter BA).
12 Amy L. Erickson, *Women and Property in Early Modern England* (London: Routledge, 1993), p. 20.
13 Roger Thompson, *Women in Stuart England and America* (London: Routledge, 1978).
14 Erickson, *Women and Property*, p. 24.
15 Linda G. De Pauw, 'Women and the Law: The Colonial Period', *Human Rights* 6:2 (Winter 1977), pp. 107–113.
16 *Barbados Property Records* (Property Deeds) RB3/Vol. 5/917, BA.
17 Richard Hall, 'An Act Concerning Persons Intended to Depart this Island, 1672', *Laws Passed in the Island of Barbados* (London, 1764).
18 *Barbados Property Records* (Property Deeds), RB3/Vol. 3/728, BA.
19 *Barbados Property Records* (Deeds), RB3/3/Vol. 2/271, BA.
20 *Council of Assembly Minutes*, 1667–1682, BMHS.
21 *Barbados Property Records*, RB3/3, Vol. 2/804, BA.
22 *Barbados Property Records* (Deeds) RB3/Vol. 8/185, BA.
23 *Council of Assembly Minutes*, 1667–1682, BMHS.
24 *Council of Assembly Minutes*, 1667–1682, BMHS.
25 Richard Hall, 'An Act Concerning the Conveyance of Estates' (1640); 'An Addition to the Act Concerning the Conveyance of Estates' (1670), *Acts Passed in the Island of Barbados, 1643–1762* (London, 1764).
26 *Council of Assembly Minutes*, 1667–1682, BMHS.
27 *Council of Assembly Minutes*, 1667–1682, BMHS.
28 *Council of Assembly Minutes*, 1667–1682, BMHS.
29 *Council of Assembly Minutes*, 1667–1682, BMHS.
30 *Council of Assembly Minutes*, 1667–1682, BMHS.
31 Trevor Burnard, 'Inheritance and Dependence: Women's status in early colonial Jamaica', *William and Mary Quarterly* 3rd Ser., 48:1 (January 1991), pp. 93–114.
32 *Barbados Property Records* (Property Deeds), RB3/Vol. 6/226, BA [Barbadians commonly classified as an orphan any child who had suffered the loss of at least one parent, most usually their father].
33 *Council of Assembly Minutes*, 1667–1682, BMHS.
34 *Barbados Property Records*, RB3/Vol. 3/780, BA.
35 *Barbados Property Records*, RB3/Vol. 3/272, BA.
36 *Barbados Property Records* (Property Deeds), RB3/Vol. 5/765, BA.
37 *Barbados Property Records* (Property Deeds), RB3/Vol. 6/223, BA.
38 *Barbados Property Records* (Deeds), RB3/3/Vol. 2/112, BA.
39 *Barbados Property Records* (Deeds), RB3/Vol. 4/698, BA.
40 Kirsten Wood, *Masterful Women: Slaveholding widows from the American Revolution through the Civil War, 1790–1860* (Chapel Hill: University of North Carolina Press, 2004).
41 *Barbados Property Records* (Deeds), RB3/Vol. 5/100, BA.

42 *Barbados Property Records* (Deeds) RB3/Vol. 8/37, BA.
43 *Barbados Property Records* (Property Deeds) RB3/Vol. 8/40–41, BA.
44 *Barbados Property Records* (Deeds), RB3/3/Vol. 2/789/91, BA.
45 *Barbados Property Records* (Property Deeds), RB3/Vol. 36/427, BA.
46 *Barbados Property Records* (Property Deeds), RB3/Vol. 4/542, BA.
47 *Barbados Property Records* (Property Deeds), RB3/Vol. 8/145, BA.
48 Kathleen Mary Butler, *Economics of Emancipation: Jamaica and Barbados, 1823–1843* (Chapel Hill: University of North Carolina Press, 1995), p. 107.
49 *Barbados Property Records* (Property Deeds), RB3/Vol. 5/765, BA.
50 Ibid., p. 173.
51 Council of Assembly Minutes, 1654–1658 cited in Larry Gragg, *Englishmen Transplanted: The English colonization of Barbados 1627–1660* (Oxford: Oxford University Press, 2004), p. 173.
52 *Council of Assembly Minutes, 1667–1682*, BMHS.
53 Hilary Beckles, 'White Women and Slavery', *History Workshop Journal* 36 (1993), p. 80.
54 *Barbados Property Records* (Deeds) RB3/Vol. 1/666, BA.
55 *Barbados Property Records* (Deeds), RB4,Vol. 2/102, BA.
56 Beckles, 'White Women and Slavery', pp. 69–70.
57 Brigitte Kossek, 'Representing Self/Otherness and "White" Women Slave-Owners in the English Speaking Caribbean, 1790–1830'. Unpublished paper presented at the Institute of Commonwealth Studies, London, 2000.
58 A copy of this map is reproduced in Peter F. Campbell, *Some Early Barbadian History* (Barbados: Caribbean Graphics, 1993).
59 Pedro Welch, 'Urban Context of the Slave Plantation System: A framework for the study of Bridgetown, 1680–1834'. Seminar Paper No. 5, Department of History, University of the West Indies, Cave Hill, Barbados, 1988.
60 Ibid., p. 15.
61 *Barbados Property Records* (Property Deeds) RB3/Vol. 6/567, BA.
62 *Barbados Property Records* (Deeds of Gifts) RB3/Vol. 8/172, BA. Given the conditions attached to Mary Dobson's acceptance of these gifts, it is possible that in transferring his property, Cole and his business partner, Mary's husband, were in fact seeking to avoid payment of tax and other duties.
63 *Barbados Property Records* (Deeds of Gifts), RB3/Vol. 4/205, BA.
64 *E.M. Shilstone Notebooks*, Vol. 18/19/443, BMHS.
65 *Barbados Property Records* (Deeds of Gifts), RB3-4/Vol. 2/424, BA.
66 *E.M. Shilstone Notebooks*, Vol. 1/2/96, BMHS.
67 *Barbados Property Records* (Inventories, 1764–1888), BA.
68 *Barbados Property Records* (Deeds of Gifts) RB3/Vol. 8/36, BA.
69 Wood, *Masterful Women*, p. 17.
70 *E.M. Shilstone Notebooks*, 30/486, Vol. 9, p. 379, 1762, BMHS.
71 *E.M. Shilstone Notebooks*, 33/355, Vol. 9, p. 110, 1778, BMHS.
72 *E.M. Shilstone Notebooks*, 18/105, Vol. 11, 1706, BMHS.
73 *E.M. Shilstone Notebooks* 26/196, Vol. 18, BMHS.
74 *E.M. Shilstone Notebooks* Vol. 9, 15/391, p. 15, 1665, BMHS.
75 *E.M. Shilstone Notebooks*, No. 2/8/402, BMHS.
76 *E.M. Shilstone Notebooks*, No. 3B, p. 18, BMHS; it is possible that Ann and Hambie were John Leacock's stepchildren, which would explain why he might attempt to disinherit them.
77 *E.M. Shilstone Notebooks*, No. 5/23/219, BMHS.
78 *E.M. Shilstone Notebooks*, No. 7/28/428, BMHS.
79 *E.M. Shilstone Notebooks*, No. 9/30/46, BMHS.
80 Burnard, 'Inheritance and Independence', p. 101.
81 Lois Carr and Lorena Walsh, 'The Planter's Wife', *William and Mary Quarterly* 3rd Ser., 3 (1977), pp. 542–571.
82 *E.M. Shilstone Notebooks*, Vol. 18/24/279, BMHS.
83 *Barbados Property Records* (Wills), RB3/Vol. 43/184, BA.

84 Erickson, *Women and Property*, p. 19.
85 Larry Gragg's 2004 study of the formative years of Barbadian settlement (1627–1660) suggests that, other than the very rich, who usually favoured their oldest sons, fathers commonly treated their children equally in the distribution of bequests, leaving equal amounts of property to each child regardless of gender. This assertion is not borne out by my own findings, though this difference may be accounted for by the differential sample sizes.
86 *Barbados Property Records* (Wills), RB6/Vol. 40/296, BA.
87 Barbadians commonly left friends and relatives sums of money to enable them to buy mourning rings.
88 *E.M. Shilstone Notebooks*, No. 2/10/427, BMHS.
89 *E.M. Shilstone Notebooks*, No. 20/3/499, BMHS.
90 *E.M. Shilstone Notebooks*, 11/40/381, BMHS.
91 *E.M. Shilstone Notebooks*, No. 24/11/534, BMHS.
92 *Barbados Property Records* (Wills), RB3/Vol. 6/103, BA.
93 *Barbados Property Records* (Wills), RB6/Vol. 44/293, BA.
94 *Barbados Property Records* (Wills), RB5/Vol. 21/397, BA.
95 *Barbados Property Records* (Wills), RB3–4/Vol. 43/172, BA.
96 *Barbados Property Records* (Wills), RB3–4/Vol. 43/172, BA.
97 *Barbados Property Records* (Wills), RB3–4/Vol. 43/160, BA.
98 Erickson, *Women and Property*, p. 211.

CHAPTER FOUR

'There may be my sphere of usefulness...'[1]: the making of a North Carolinian plantation mistress

In the late summer of 1853, Sarah Hicks Williams, the newly married bride of Benjamin Franklin Williams, left her family home in New York to begin a new life thousands of miles away in the Southern slaveholding state of North Carolina. Though excited about embarking on this new phase of her life, Sarah's parting from her close-knit, devoutly religious family was particularly tinged with sadness and distress, for she and her family understood that her marriage to Benjamin represented not merely her absence from the immediate family circle in New York, but an uncomfortable accommodation with the institution of slavery. As Benjamin's wife, Sarah was poised to become mistress of her husband's Clifton Grove plantation in Greene County, North Carolina. For most young brides of Sarah's generation, the prospects of managing their own households no doubt appeared a challenging though happy responsibility, but Sarah's marriage to a Southern planter thrust upon her additional responsibilities and anxieties. Brought up in a wealthy middle-class family employing a retinue of domestic servants had left her ignorant of housekeeping matters. Sarah nevertheless felt ready to accept this responsibility, and indeed looked forward to the challenge of building a comfortable home of her own. Yet as she began the journey southwards, Sarah could not stave off feelings of misgivings, for she was acutely conscious that as Mistress of Clifton Grove she would immediately become a member of the Southern slaveholding class. Though happy to embrace the duties and responsibilities expected of a wife, Sarah was rather more ambivalent about taking on the management of enslaved women, men and children. Becoming the mistress of a slaveholding plantation was certainly not a role that Sarah – the daughter of abolitionist parents – relished, for she shared their belief in the inherent immorality of the enslavement of Africans. Indeed, Sarah's anti-slavery convictions had for many years represented a major obstacle to her marriage to Benjamin Williams.

At twenty-six years of age, Sarah was considerably older than most first-time brides of her generation. This was, however, no sudden whirlwind marriage, for she and Benjamin had courted for eight long years. They first met in 1845 when both were students in New York; Sarah as a pupil at the Albany Female Academy, and Benjamin pursuing medical studies. They had been introduced by Mary and Harriet, the sister and niece of Benjamin, and Sarah's best friends at the Academy. All four shared lodgings at the same Albany boarding house, and it was almost certainly here that the romance between Sarah and Benjamin began. On the face of it, the couple should have made a suitable match. Both were young (he was seven years her senior), attractive, educated, and enjoyed a secure family background. Yet until 1853 Sarah hesitated to commit herself in marriage to Benjamin, for there were some seemingly irreconcilable differences in their respective backgrounds and world views that had to be overcome if the growing friendship could be allowed to develop to its logical conclusion. In a letter to her parents describing her life in Albany, Sarah revealed the unusual presence of a male lodger, Benjamin Williams, at her lodging house. She hastily reassured her parents that although it might appear unseemly for young unmarried men and women to share the same lodgings, Benjamin was a close relative of her best friends at the Academy. Moreover, he was held in high esteem by many of Albany's leading citizens, including his teacher and mentor, Dr James McNaughton, Professor of Theory and Practice of Medicine at the Albany Medical College. Benjamin was, she assured her parents, 'a very fine young gentleman, and Dr McNaughton, being one of our trustees, would not recommend him unless a fit moral young man'.

Though clearly smitten with the young medical student, Sarah's letter conveys a distinct sense of unease for, as she admitted to her parents, her friends Mary and Harriet were Southerners, the daughters of wealthy North Carolinian planters who owned over 300 slaves. She neglected, however, to mention Benjamin's own considerable slaveholdings, preferring instead to emphasise Benjamin's qualities. Torn between her growing feelings for Benjamin and her parents' certain disapproval of a slave-owner as their daughter's suitor, Sarah was reluctant to admit to her admiration for the young medical student. Sarah's parents might approve Dr McNaughton's assessment of Benjamin as 'a fit moral young man', but quite how to reconcile his status as an owner of human property with the staunch anti-slavery convictions of the Hicks family appeared an insurmountable problem.

Sarah's worries about the damage likely to be sustained by bringing a Southern slave-owner into the midst of her close, loving family circle were well-founded. A strong anti-slavery ethos united Sarah's immediate family members. Mrs Hicks's own anti-slavery sympathies were forged by a strong egalitarian Puritanism, and while Samuel, her politically active father, could not be considered a vocal opponent of slavery, he had nevertheless implicitly signalled his empathy with the anti-slavery movement by consenting to the marriage of Sarah's elder sister, Mary – an ardent abolitionist – to the Ohio-born businessman and politician James Monroe Brown. James was the son of Ephraim Brown, a well-known opponent of slavery and a prominent Ohio politician. By the 1850s James Brown had gained a reputation as an outspoken critic of slavery, and he counted among his friends some of the leading abolitionists of the day, including the prominent Ohio lawyer and abolitionist Joshua Giddings. James Brown's anti-slavery convictions went beyond mere political rhetoric, for it was widely believed that his Bloomfield, Ohio house was a way-station on the Underground Railroad[2] during the 1850s. The elder Hicks might have lacked the passionate conviction of his son-in-law, but he clearly liked and respected him, and valued his opinions, business acumen and political connections. By giving his blessing to a marriage between his daughter and a slave-owning Southerner, Samuel Hicks understood that he could potentially disrupt the mutually beneficial and respectful relationship he enjoyed with his son-in-law James. Moreover, neither Samuel nor his wife Sara were likely to encourage a match that would inevitably mean the departure of their daughter from the close-knit New York family circle. Both parents must surely have worried about the isolation Sarah would endure, far from family and friends, hundreds of miles away in North Carolina. They were no doubt aware of the hostility of Southerners towards 'interfering Northerners' whose increasingly vociferous attacks on slavery threatened to destroy the very foundation of the South's economy and culture. Both parents must have feared for their daughter's safety, for in North Carolina Sarah's Northern background would inevitably invite suspicion and distrust from her Southern neighbours.

At Sarah's insistence, then, theirs was a painfully protracted courtship, drawn out by her qualms about the possibility of familial and personal conflict that might follow in the wake of her marriage to Benjamin Williams. Sarah could have forgone parental consent and married Benjamin without waiting, in the hope that time and distance would heal any rift, and that her parents would eventually accept their youngest daughter and her husband back into the Hicks family circle. But marriage to Benjamin would involve relocation hundreds of miles distant from her family, and this physical and geographical separation would make hopes of a future reconciliation less certain. Moreover, Sarah was mature enough to know that the love of a good husband would be insufficient to sustain her; in the days and years to come, she would need the emotional support of her own family as she adjusted to her new life and role as Benjamin's wife and mistress of his plantation. Securing parental and familial approval of her choice of husband was therefore paramount. Twice Benjamin proposed, but each time Sarah refused, preferring to delay marriage until her family could be persuaded to accept Benjamin into their family. That the couple was forced to draw out their courtship for eight long years, far longer than the average engagement period of the time, testified to the profound wariness of the Hicks family in accepting this Southern planter into their family.

As their relationship progressed, the deep affection between the couple, and Benjamin's quiet respect for the family's anti-slavery beliefs, gradually eroded the Hicks family's misgivings about his suitability as a son-in-law. If they could not accept his pro-slavery politics, they were at least agreed that he possessed all the qualities they could wish for in a son-in-law. Long acquaintance confirmed Dr MacNaughton's opinion of Benjamin as a well-mannered and respectful, intelligent, hardworking and reliable gentleman. Samuel Hicks, at least, was undoubtedly swayed by Benjamin's acute business sense and his political connections. That the young Southerner had been willing to wait patiently for eight years for Sarah's hand provided further evidence of the strength of his love for Hicks's daughter, who was fast approaching an unmarriageable age. No doubt the prospect of spinsterhood also weighed heavily on Sarah's mind, for on 7 March 1853 – her 26th birthday – she wrote to her parents, enclosing a letter from Benjamin in which he proposed marriage for the third time. Reminding them of her two previous rejections of his proposals, Sarah pointed out Benjamin's steadfastness and commitment to her over the previous eight years, and hinted strongly that she intended to accept this time. '[I]f, as I do believe, his affection for me has outlived so many reverses I cannot but respect the man most highly. Eight years is a long time to test friendship and such fidelity is seldom met with in this world and is sufficient to cause me serious thought.'

While convinced of Benjamin's suitability as a husband, Sarah still had a couple of major reservations. In the letter she wrote to her parents signalling her intention to accept his hand in marriage she explained: 'There are but two things that I know of to dislike in the man. One is his owning slaves. I cannot make it seem right, and yet, *perhaps there may be my sphere of usefulness* [my emphasis]. The other is his not being a professing Christian.'

As an owner of human souls and a self-declared agnostic, Benjamin presented Sarah with profound moral and religious dilemmas to be resolved before pledging herself to him in marriage. Yet, paradoxically, these were the very character defects that would eventually enable Sarah to accept her suitor's hand. As Benjamin's wife, she reasoned, she believed that she could exert a positive moral and religious influence over her husband. In time, Benjamin might be persuaded to embrace both the anti-slavery cause and the word of God. In becoming Benjamin's wife and helpmeet, then, Sarah would also become the saviour of his soul. Thus could Sarah rationalise and justify her decision to accept Benjamin's marriage proposal. To bring Benjamin to a realisation of the wickedness of slavery, and to make of him a practising Christian was to be her own special 'sphere of usefulness'.

Sarah Hicks and Benjamin Williams were finally married on 20 September 1853, at the Hicks family's mansion. After honeymooning in Canada, the newlyweds enjoyed a leisurely journey southwards before finally arriving at Clifton Groves, Sarah's new home and the seat of Benjamin's plantation business, in Greene County, North Carolina. By the time of Sarah Hicks Williams's arrival in October 1853, the flat and fertile soil of Greene County had made the region one of the richest agricultural counties in the state. Located in the eastern central coastal region of North Carolina, Greene County was relatively small, with just under 700 white families. The total population in 1850 was probably equally divided between these whites and their slaves. Writing to her parents soon after her arrival, Sarah could not help but draw contrasts between this small sleepy rural backwater and her bustling hometown of New Hartford:

> Well mother, you like quiet. If you come and see me I'll promise you a plenty of it . . . if you call Long Island behind the times, I don't know what you would call North Carolina. It has been rightly termed Rip Van Winkle. I am a regular curiosity. You can imagine how thickly the county is settled when I tell you that in the whole of Greene County there are only about as many inhabitants as there are in the town of New Hartford, and more than half of these coloured. There are only two hundred voters in the county.

That the county's prosperity depended on a slave-based economy was evident; on the eve of the Civil War Greene County's enslaved population outnumbered whites. It was one of only sixteen North Carolinian counties where the enslaved population represented over half of the total population. Since the eighteenth century at least, the county's foremost source of revenue had been the production of naval stores and lumber products. By the time of Sarah's arrival in 1853, however, Greene County's farmers had began to turn their efforts to the cultivation of cotton, tobacco and sweet potatoes – agricultural products that would in a relatively short period eclipse the naval and lumber industries.

Sarah's residence in Greene County was to be fairly brief – the family resettled in Georgia in 1856 – but it was here that she experienced some of the most momentous changes in her life. In this isolated, rural Southern county, Sarah would be transformed from young, inexperienced bride to dutiful wife and mother. Embracing the dual identities of wife and mother occasionally caused Sarah much personal anguish, but perhaps never so much distress as the role of mistress of Clifton Grove. She had arrived at her plantation home convinced of the inequities of slavery, yet in Greene County Sarah's anti-slavery beliefs would be severely tested. By the time of the Civil War, Sarah, a Yankee born and raised, had been transformed into an ardent supporter of Southern culture and a proponent of African slavery.

Raised within a strong anti-slavery culture, the new mistress of Clifton Grove plantation determined to observe for herself the truth of abolitionist claims of Southern brutality towards their enslaved population. On her journey southwards she had carefully observed the conditions of the slaves she encountered. On her first night in the South, the couple broke their journey with an overnight stay at a hotel. There being no lock on the door to their chamber, the newlywed couple were denied privacy, and much to Sarah's bewilderment, curious slaves wandered in and out of their room at will: 'Twice before we were up, a waiting girl came into the room, and while I was dressing, in she came to look at me. She seemed perfectly at home, took up the locket with your miniatures in it, and wanted to know if it was a watch.'

Such over-familiarity on the part of the enslaved contrasted greatly with the relations between domestic servants and their employers in New York. At home, servants and employers maintained a respectful distance, but Southerners appeared to have a more relaxed attitude, treating their slaves with an apparently easy familiarity that would have been unacceptable in a well-ordered New York household. Sarah also could not help but remark on the very obvious physical presence of enslaved peoples – they were just everywhere; 'in the parlour, in your room, and all over', apparently aimlessly wandering unchecked in and out of guest rooms, seemingly bereft of any sense of propriety, unafraid to voice derogatory comments about the hotel guests, and generally getting underfoot.

Sarah's first experience with slaves as related here – the apparently easy amiability and interplay between planters and slaves – both mollified and puzzled her. Until that moment, Sarah's knowledge of Southern slavery had been largely informed by stark pictures painted by Northern abolitionists of the separate worlds inhabited by Southern whites and blacks. Yet, on her very first night below the Mason-Dixon line, the apparent informality and familiarity between blacks and whites caused Sarah to question abolitionist claims of the brutal character of Southern slavery. Instead of the expected sharply divided worlds of subjugated, demoralised and dehumanised blacks, and cruel and inhumane planters, these scenes of amiability cast doubt on abolitionist representations of the South as a world shaped by mastery and violence. Where were the unhappy slaves and the cruel planters of abolitionist literature? It seemed to Sarah on first impression that in many respects Southern slavery differed little from waged labour in the North. Indeed, the slaves she encountered at the boarding house seemed to enjoy a greater degree of freedom and lack of restraint than the domestic servants in her Northern house. With much relief, Sarah wrote to her New York family assuring them that although she had spent but a very short time in the South, 'I have seen no unkind treatment of servants'.

The sense of puzzlement pervades Sarah's early letters to her family in New York. Along the road to Clifton Grove the newlywed couple's progress was constantly interrupted by numerous apparently joyous plantation slaves eager to greet their master, and to welcome their new mistress. The apparent happiness with which the slaves greeted Benjamin, the easy banter and friendly gestures back and forth, served to underscore Sarah's initial impressions of the paternalism of Southern planters. 'All along the road we met them, and their salutation of "Howdy (meaning How do you) massa Benjamin," and they seemed so glad to see him that I felt assured that they were well treated.' Once at Clifton Grove plantation, her apprehensions were further relieved when their carriage was greeted by crowds of cheering slaves who, curious about their new mistress, turned out in welcome. Heartened by these scenes, Sarah confidently wrote to her parents a few days later that the horrific tales of the inhumanity of Southern slave-owners appeared to have little foundation: 'Indeed I think [the slaves] are treated with more familiarity than many Northern servants.' Even so, Sarah could not easily reconcile slavery with Christianity. Slavery, she reasoned to herself, represented a stain on humanity, and until Benjamin could be brought to see the error of his ways, it was her duty to ensure that the enslaved of Clifton Grove plantation were happy and contented. Their most immediate need, she believed, was spiritual salvation and guidance, a responsibility she resolved to undertake with all possible speed. As she had resolved to do her utmost to open Benjamin's heart and mind to the word of God, so too would she bring Christianity to her slaves. Therein, she now believed, was her sphere of usefulness.

So began this new, challenging but optimistic period of Sarah's life as a Southern plantation mistress. As was the custom among newly-weds, the first few weeks and months at Clifton Grove were an endless round of entertaining and visiting relatives and friends wishing to congratulate the couple. It was a very happy honeymoon period, made more so by renewed acquaintance with Sarah's friends from the Albany Female Academy, Mary and Harriet, themselves now married and raising their own families. Sarah was especially delighted to meet them because through her marriage to Benjamin she could rightfully claim them as her family. The only cloud on her horizon appeared in the guise of her mother-in-law, Mother Williams, who also lived at Clifton Grove. Mother Williams had initially appeared 'ready to extend a mother's welcome' to her new daughter-in-law, but to Sarah's distress, once the hearty congratulations were over, Mother Williams's demeanour towards her rapidly and inexplicably cooled, leaving Sarah feeling uncomfortable, awkward and an unwanted presence.

Mother Williams represented an awesome figure in the life of the plantation. Widowed since 1836, Mother Williams had taken up the reins of her late husband's plantation business, and despite the objections of her sons she still insisted on maintaining active involvement in plantation affairs. She decided which crops were to be planted, directed the work of the slaves, managed the household, and still found time and energy to intervene in the business and family affairs of her adult children. Accustomed to such autonomy, the widowed Mother Williams made clear her reluctance to give up the role of plantation mistress to her daughter-in-law. Eager to prove to Benjamin her capabilities as an efficient housekeeper, Sarah could not help giving way to feelings of dismay at being treated as little more than a guest (and, as it appeared to her, an unwanted one at that) in her own house. Friction between the two women soon became evident, and their strained relationship was to be the source of great unhappiness for Sarah as her mother-in-law continued to stifle her domestic ambitions.

Although determined to learn quickly and assume her new responsibilities as mistress of a household of seventeen slaves, Sarah found life at Clifton Grove an unsettling experience. 'I feel confused. Everything is so different that I do not know which way to stir for fear of making a blunder. I have determined to keep still and look on for a while, at any rate.' How much better it would have been, she reflected, had she and Benjamin 'gone to housekeeping straight away', even though to have done so would have meant deferring their marriage for a year. In this respect, Sarah's domestic arrangements were similar to many young Southern couples. Unless they were sufficiently wealthy, many young Southern newlyweds lived in the household of a close relative until they could afford their own home. Like Sarah, most couples strove for independence, but in the meantime accepted the temporary necessity of co-residence. In Sarah's case, a sympathetic mother-in-law might have done much to ease her difficulties, but Mother Williams seemed determined to rebuff Sarah's overtures of friendship. Unable to make her imprint on the household in any meaningful sense, Sarah could only grit her teeth and, as a dutiful daughter-in-law, determine to live amicably with the cantankerous and domineering old lady until she and Benjamin could establish their own household.

Sarah's unhappy start to married life could not be attributed to Benjamin's financial standing. Her husband, she discovered, was a planter of substantial means; as she informed her parents, 'Between you and me, my husband is better off than I ever dreamed of. I am glad I didn't know it before we were married. He owns 2,000 acres of land in this vicinity, but you must bear in mind that land here is not as valuable as with you.' Clifton Grove's landholdings, mostly planted with cotton, amounted to about '750 acres, worth from 12–15 dollars per acre', in addition to which Benjamin also owned the 1,400-acre turpentine plantation Sandy Run, seven miles from Clifton Grove. Besides these two main operations, there were another '73 acres at Snow Hill, of which we don't know the value'. Indeed, in the 1850 Greene County census Benjamin's real estate holdings were listed with a value of $12,000, a considerable sum, and one that had almost certainly increased considerably by 1853 as Sandy Run's turpentine business became profitable. The growing success of Sandy Run had convinced Benjamin to invest more of his time, energy and capital in building and extending his turpentine production business. Alongside his plantation business, Benjamin also continued to practise medicine, though over time he came to concentrate almost exclusively on his turpentine business.

Benjamin was, then, a planter of some considerable means, but as Sarah explained, their present housekeeping situation stemmed from the nature of his father's legacy, which placed Clifton Grove into his mother's hands. Benjamin would not come into his inheritance until after the death of Mother Williams, who in the meantime was determined to retain control over Clifton Grove's cotton operations. She had, however, conceded 250 acres of Clifton Grove's holdings to Benjamin for his immediate use, which he put to the cultivation of cotton, corn, yam, sweet potatoes and orchard fruit. The plantation house itself would one day belong to Benjamin and Sarah, but as long as Mother Williams was alive it was clear that she would not relinquish the title of Mistress to a Yankee interloper. Benjamin and Sarah would either have to bide their time and accommodate themselves to the situation, or buy or lease their own property elsewhere. This latter option might have been the most appealing to Sarah but, for all her assertions of autonomy, Mother Williams depended heavily on Benjamin's labour and presence at Clifton Grove, and Benjamin, ever the dutiful son (and perhaps mindful that Mother Williams might decide to bequeath the plantation house to his brother James), chose to make the best of an uncomfortable situation.

Benjamin's extensive plantation affairs took him away from home for weeks on end. In addition, his role as the elected Representative of Greene County made further demands on his time, and Sarah, like many other Southern wives, often found herself with only her truculent mother-in-law and the household slaves for company. Although nominally now mistress of Clifton Grove, Sarah's inexperience as a housekeeper and as a slave-owner forced her into Mother Williams's shadow. When an overseer employed by Benjamin to assist with operations in his absence struck one of the slaves, Mother Williams, outraged at this usurpation of her authority, discharged the incumbent without bothering to discuss the matter with her daughter-in-law.

As if her poor relationship with Mrs Williams were not enough, the domestic arrangements of the household caused Sarah some distress. As she complained to her parents, everything about her new home appeared strange. The plantation house itself was 'unassuming' and the furniture plain and 'of little consequence'. Despite the tales spread by abolitionists about the extravagant, lavishly furnished plantation houses of planters, it appeared that Southerners – certainly those of her acquaintance – cared little for sumptuous living, and were content to live in simple, unadorned rustic structures. Even her brother-in-law, James Williams, although 'a very wealthy man, lives in a brown wood house without lathing or plaster'. Clifton Grove plantation house was certainly a far cry from the mansion that was Sarah's New York family home. Built of hewn logs, it had just three ground floor rooms, and a further two bedchambers upstairs. After their marriage Benjamin extended the house, adding a separate kitchen structure and two more rooms. The couple shared a single chamber room so cramped that there was hardly space for the furniture Sarah had ordered from New York. Brother-in-law James's house might be rude and unfinished, but he at least could boast 'a handsome sofa [and] sideboards in his parlour', and Sarah could not help but notice how 'they contrast strangely with the unfinished state of the house. However, [Benjamin] proposes building soon. This, I might say is the common style of house, and ours, which is finished, the exception.'

The rude simplicity of Clifton Grove plantation house might have been better endured were the household efficiently managed but, looking about her, Sarah could discern no system. 'I do not pretend to know much of housekeeping, but I know I could improve on some things here in the way of order.' The household's slaves apparently had no fixed routines, instead they 'wash, bake or iron, just as the fit takes'. To Sarah's distress, although Mother Williams was herself a constant swirl of activity, the entire household appeared to be in a state of persistent disorder. 'The great fault lies in the want of system. Mother Williams works harder than any Northern farmer's wife I know. She sees to everything.' In a veiled criticism of Mother Williams's apparent inability to impose an efficient housekeeping system, Sarah could only lament to her mother, 'Mother Williams' ways are so entirely different from anything I have ever been used to that I some times feel disheartened and discouraged. She is very kind to me and I intend making my will bend to hers in every respect, but I assure you I miss the order and neatness which pervades a Northern home.'

Mother Williams found her daughter-in-law an irritation, but to the enslaved population on Clifton Grove, Sarah represented a curiosity. Mother Williams's determination to maintain authority over the household and its slaves meant that Sarah had little direct contact with the plantation labour force. On occasion, her daily walks around the plantation brought her into contact with slaves who viewed their new mistress with speculation and interest. Just a week after her arrival, she reported to her mother: 'I am quite the talk of the day, not only in the whole County but on the plantation. Yesterday, I was out in the yard and an old Negro woman came up to me. "Howdy, Miss Sara, are you the Lady that won my young master. Well I raised him". Her name was Chaney and she was the family nurse.' This meeting with Chaney apparently represented the first direct conversation with any member of Sarah's new slave 'family', yet strangely, Sarah's letter home omits her own response, and she said no more about the meeting. There is no doubt that she interpreted Chaney's forwardness as indicative of the paternalism of Southern slavery. Even after such a short acquaintance with the South, Sarah was already experiencing profound doubts about abolitionist claims about the ill-treatment of slaves. The chance meeting with Chaney undermined Sarah's confidence in abolitionist representations of planters as brutal and inhumane. Indeed, after this meeting, Sarah felt sufficiently able to rebut abolitionist claims, suggesting that perhaps Northern abolitionists were overly harsh in their judgement of Southern planters. 'I have seen enough to convince me that the ill-treatment of the slaves is exaggerated at the North, but I have not seen enough to make me like the institution.'

In her early letters from Clifton Grove, Sarah occasionally alluded to the institution of slavery, but she rarely mentioned Clifton Grove's individual slaves. This omission is striking, for besides Benjamin and Mother Williams, the household slaves were frequently the only other people around, especially after the whirl of visits by relatives, friends and neighbours that had marked the newlywed couple's arrival was over. It is difficult, therefore, to gauge Sarah's own feelings towards the slaves that passed into her hands on her marriage. In all the flow of correspondence to her New York family, she rarely troubled to identify individual slaves by name, though by contrast she carefully noted the names and details of all the white people, family, friends and respectable society she encountered. The limited references to the mere presence of slaves is also surprising, given Sarah's self-declared interest in determining for herself their 'true' conditions. Clifton Grove's enslaved population numbered around twenty 'full hands', and their number was often supplemented by hands from Ben's turpentine business. Perhaps it is possible to read into Sarah's silence on the issue of slavery an unwillingness to remind her abolitionist family of her own contentious role as a mistress of enslaved peoples, while at the same time enabling her to maintain a more comfortable psychological distance from the human property she owned.

Enslaved peoples were permanent, if unseen, figures on Sarah's landscape. They laboured long hours planting and harvesting cotton, corn, sweet potatoes and myriad other crops that sustained Clifton Grove's economy. In and around the house, female slaves laundered, cleaned, baked, cooked, polished, churned butter, raised poultry, milked cows, fed the pigs, and carried out a hundred and one other domestic tasks. They prepared the family meals, waited at table – one serving girl keeping a large broom 'in motion to keep off flies etc.', drew and hauled heavy casks of water long distances for Sarah's bath, helped with her toilet, carried messages and performed other errands. Yet for the most part, Clifton Grove's slaves and their labour remained invisible to Sarah's eyes.

Sarah's apparent lack of interest in the slaves is striking. Rarely in her letters home to New York did Sarah, in so many other ways a keen observer of Southern life, ever trouble to offer any reflections on their lives, their families, their conditions, their labour, attitudes, appearances or even, as noted before, their individual names. The brevity of her descriptions of slave life at Clifton Grove is notable. 'They have plots of ground they cultivate and have what they make from them. They can go to church (preaching, as they say) on the Sabbath. Indeed, a majority of the congregation is colored. On Sundays they dress up and many of them look very nice. They leave off work at sundown during the week.' Individual slaves who found their way into her letters are invariably represented as brazen or presumptuous, overly familiar and lacking in propriety. 'They are not diffident, either. One of the field hands asked me to fix a dress for her the other day. Another servant wanted to know if Massa Ben and I couldn't ride over to Snow Hill [the County seat] and get her a new dress.' Again, Sarah neglects to offer her response to such brazen solicitations. Of course, it is entirely possible that these two women were testing their new mistress's boundaries rather than harbouring real expectations. Sarah, however, interpreted their forwardness as emblematic of the humanity with which Clifton Grove's slaves were treated, rationalising that an intimidated labour force would hesitate to make such casual demands on their owners. As if further evidence were needed, she informed her parents that Clifton Grove's slaves were encouraged in their endeavours to amass savings [presumably to procure their manumission] through the sale of produce from their kitchen gardens and other labour. 'Dr has one man who will probably lay by fifty or sixty dollars this year. He attended the pine trees and Ben gave him a certain share & he told me the other day he would make that sum.' In these letters, Sarah represents her new husband as a humane slave-owner, ever mindful of the welfare of his enslaved labour force. Indeed, Benjamin's perceived humanity towards Clifton Grove's labour force played a large part in convincing Sarah of the weakness of abolitionists' claims. She had come to Clifton Grove determined to be critical of the institution of slavery; hopeful, perhaps, of convincing Benjamin of the inhumanity of maintaining individuals in bondage. Yet Sarah was soon harbouring misgivings about the basis of her own opposition to slavery. In the course of the following year, as she became more settled and integrated into Southern culture, Sarah would continue to reassure her parents of her opposition to slavery, but her letters home gradually came to reveal a less reflexive, more intolerant attitude towards the anti-slavery movement. Barely a year after taking up residence as Mistress of Clifton Grove, Sarah wrote to her parents denouncing the growing stridency of abolitionists. 'The recent discussions upon the slavery question have kindled the smouldering fires of animosity both in the North and the South. How I wish the Abolitionists of the North could see these things as I see them. If they knew what they were about they would act differently.' In Sarah's mind, it was not the institution of slavery *per se* that was the problem. Rather, she seems to suggest that the relentless attacks on the institution of slavery forced Southern slave-owners to adopt an even more spirited defence of slavery. As many Southerners argued, abolitionist agitation encouraged unrest and rebellion among the enslaved population, and

Southern planters had little choice but to respond to these challenges to their authority with brute force, thereby in Sarah's assessment 'tightening the bonds of the slave and putting farther off his emancipation'. The inflammatory anti-slavery rhetoric of those who knew nothing of the 'true' status of the slave's condition was, indeed, the cause of discontent among the slaves, who in Sarah's view were in need of spiritual salvation rather than physical emancipation.

How is it possible to understand the swift and radical shift in position of this Northern-born woman, who had once so worried about marrying a slave-owner that she had delayed her marriage for eight long years? Sarah herself does not offer an explanation for this volteface, but a close reading of her letters home to New York enables some tentative explanations. First, I make the argument that Sarah's growing awareness of the intertwining of her own welfare and security with Benjamin's successful business operations that relied on slave labour, was in some ways responsible for this sea-change in her opposition to slavery. Moreover, it is necessary to understand Sarah's increasing defence of Southern slavery as also closely interwoven with her own striving to become the epitome of a good Southern wife.

Before embarking on marriage to Benjamin, Sarah had worried incessantly about her suitor's ownership of human property. Once transplanted to Clifton Grove, however, Sarah had to confront the uncomfortable reality that her own welfare and security was dependent on slave labour. Quite simply, it was the unfree labour of enslaved black men and women that was responsible for Benjamin's steady accumulation of wealth. Though medically trained, Benjamin virtually abandoned his rural doctor's practice in favour of the greater profits to be derived from his expanding turpentine enterprise, and the family's entire welfare rested on the success of that operation. Sarah might oppose slavery, but she could not evade the fact that it was the revenues from Benjamin's slave-based operations on which the family's continued prosperity depended. In an earlier letter home, Sarah had mocked the Southerner's seeming obsession with land and negroes, informing her parents that 'ambition is satisfied here by numbering its thousands of dollars, acres of land and hundreds of negroes', but in a short time she too would come to share the Southerner's appreciation for land. The problem confronting this daughter of Northern abolitionists, however, was that the riches that land ownership promised could not be realised without a labour force to cultivate that land, and although initially holding reservations about slavery, Sarah came to accept that unfree labour represented the most satisfactory economic solution to the labour problem. To oppose slavery placed Sarah, therefore, in a contradictory position: she might concede it as immoral before God, but on the other hand, it was slavery and slaves that kept a roof over their heads, and literally put food on the table of Clifton Grove. But there may have been other explanations for Sarah's increasingly uncritical acceptance of the institution. Voicing opposition to slavery might possibly be interpreted as an implicit criticism of both Benjamin and the cantankerous Mother Williams. As a new wife, determined to maintain an uneasy peace with her mother-in-law and to transform herself into a wife worthy of Benjamin Williams, gentlemen planter and doctor, it was perhaps more prudent – at least initially – to hold her own counsel. To openly question the morality of slavery could well be perceived as an implicit challenge to Benjamin's patriarchal authority, a course of action likely to invoke deep disapproval from both husband and mother-in-law. In this respect, Sarah would probably have identified with numerous Southern white women who, for myriad reasons, privately disagreed with slavery, but whose allegiance to their husbands, families and the wider white society effectively secured public silence over the issue. A reading of the numerous journals and correspondence of Southern white women indicates there were more than a few who harboured serious doubts about slavery. Some objected on religious grounds, while others bemoaned the burdensome responsibilities that slaveholding thrust upon their shoulders. Few, however, were as outspoken as the sisters Angelina and Sarah Grimke of South Carolina, whose profound anti-slavery convictions would eventually force them to leave their Southern homeland to become prominent voices in the Northern abolitionist movement.[3] While many Southern women held deep misgivings about the continued existence of slavery, they knew that voicing their feelings would be tantamount to questioning the very foundation stone of Southern patriarchal culture.

Slaveholding and the Southern patriarchal tradition could not be easily disentangled. Indeed, the power of the largest landowners derived from their slave-owning interests, and male dominance was supported by state and religion. Slave-owning males wielded power and authority over their slaves, their rights to do so enshrined and upheld by legislation. Their authority extended beyond the slaves to every member of their white families, and their households became a crucial site of patriarchal male power. Free white women, younger men and children, and enslaved black peoples were subordinated to the authority of the patriarchal master who was to be accorded absolute obedience. The Southern ideal of womanhood – decorative and passive, submissive and serene, pious and cheerfully accepting of her roles of wife and mother – demanded women's increasing confinement to the private sphere of the plantation household. Indeed,

Sarah Hicks Williams's arrival in North Carolina coincided with the period when the Southern public space was increasingly being marked out as male terrain, and the private household as the proper place of Southern women. The 1850s also marked the moment when Northern white women's increased participation in public economic life was bringing them greater autonomy. Conversely, the patriarchal Southern male's control over Southern women was being strengthened. White women, no less than enslaved peoples, were deemed in need of the guidance and direction of males, and the Southern household represented the seat of white male exercise of power and authority. Of critical importance also, the 1850s marked a period when the country entered its greatest crisis, as passionate debates around the rights and wrongs of slavery assumed centre stage in Southern threats to secede from the Union. White Southerners closed ranks in defence of slavery, a move that at the same time required the intensification of white patriarchal male power within the household.[4] The voices of Southern white women were largely unheard in these debates, for to make public their grievances with slavery would be construed as a disloyal attack not only on Southern culture and the Southern way of life, but on the power of the very men they had been socialised into perceiving as their protectors – Southern male patriarchs.

To be a Yankee in the South was to incur immediate suspicion and hostility. Sarah Hicks Williams – 'a stranger in a strange land', striving to carve out her own Southern domestic haven – probably found it wisest to follow the example of anti-slavery Southern women, and keep quiet. She was no doubt also wary of bringing down local ire against her new family, who had long been prominent slave-owners in the region. No doubt many of Sarah's new Greene County neighbours felt a sense of unease at Benjamin's choice of a Northern bride, and for this Yankee wife to publicly express anti-slavery sentiments would create animosity and bad feelings between the Williamses and their Greene County neighbours.

All these factors made Sarah determined to remain, initially at least, an objective observer of the institution of slavery. She told her parents that 'It would be wrong, perhaps, for me to form or express an opinion in regards to the manners and customs of the people, after only two weeks' tarry among them. I shall not speak for or against, but will state things as I have seen them and you may form your own opinions.' Yet despite her intention to remain objective, in the space of a year Sarah's letters began to display an increasing antipathy: not towards slavery, but towards the enslaved. Moreover, it is evident that although she may have professed a 'dislike' of the institution, Sarah's actions do not reveal a woman averse to the appropriation of slave labour. Sarah's attitudes are contradictory, for while voicing doubts as to the morality of slavery, at no time did she question her right to appropriate the labour of enslaved men, women and children. Indeed, her struggles with Mother Williams stemmed partially from her own desire to assert her authority as Mistress over the enslaved. That she accepted as her right the ability to appropriate the labour of others is explained in some degree by her class position and upbringing, for Sarah had grown up in a middle-class New York household where free white servants did the domestic work. So it was not the appropriation of labour in itself that rested so uneasily with her, but the use of *unfree* labour that caused some initial discomfort. Once at Clifton Grove, though, Sarah accepted that the only household domestics she could call upon were enslaved women, for in North Carolina white women were generally excluded from domestic service. Sarah reconciled her doubts about slave labour by convincing herself that the slaves at Clifton Grove were well treated and underworked. 'The Negroes are certainly not overtasked on this plantation', she wrote to her parents, 'one house girl in the North will accomplish more than two here'. Sarah's sentiments regarding the laziness of the enslaved were echoed by many white Southerners – mistresses and masters alike. Though heavily dependent on enslaved labour for their wealth and comfort, slave-owning Southerners preferred to deny the centrality of slave labour to just about every aspect of their economic and material wellbeing.

Admiring the beauty of the pure white cotton bolls that weighed down the ripe plants, Sarah could not, as she mused in a letter home, help but think, rather naively, that the picking of such beautiful plants could be anything other but 'very light and pleasant work'.[5] That Sarah neglected to comment on the black hands whose task it was to pick the white cotton bolls is perhaps reflective of her unwillingness to acknowledge to her parents her dependence on enslaved labour. It also reveals her own inexperience of the demanding labour required in the cultivation of cotton. From the perspective of the enslaved who actually performed this labour, cotton-picking was anything but light and pleasant work; especially when done by hand, cotton-picking represented the most labour-intensive and physically demanding of plantation operations. During the summer cotton-picking season, Clinton Grove's slaves laboured from 'cain't see' to 'cain't see' under a hot broiling sun to pick the cotton from the four-or-five compartmented bolls containing the 'white gold'. Each labourer fastened around his or her neck a strap attached to one or two coarse cotton bags which reached almost to the ground. As they moved along the rows, the labourers dropped the picked cotton into the bags, which they dragged along behind them. Once one bag was filled the labourers then filled the second bag, and when both were full the contents were emptied into a large willow basket. When the day's work was finally done, the large basket containing the picked cotton would be weighed. Most planters expected that cotton pickers should be able to pick at least 150 to 200 pounds of cotton each day, though an experienced labourer might gather up to 500 lb a day. Cracked, sore, bleeding hands, and the endless bending down impeded the work, but there was little respite for any slave who failed to meet the required daily quotas, or whose baskets contained too much dirt or trash; they could expect a whipping from the overseer. Cotton-picking demanded the labour of every available slave, including women and children, who were especially valued by the planters for their nimble fingers and dexterity.[6]

Fortunately for Sarah, her naive belief that cotton-picking was easy work was never to be tested by herself, for cotton-picking was slave labour, and not suitable work for white women. While she frequently commented on the industriousness of white women around her, she rarely acknowledged the equally hard labour of the slaves. Mother Williams and her sister-in-law were, she believed, 'the busiest and smartest women she had ever met, as busy as any Northern farm-wife'. Her increasing antipathy towards the enslaved sharpened with experience and familiarity, as she gradually became more involved in the running of Clifton Grove's plantation household. December 1853, two months after her arrival, found Sarah engrossed in 'sewing a plenty ... for the servants'. Clifton Grove's enslaved population were provided with 'three suits of clothes a year and as much more in clothes and money as they choose to earn'. As Sarah's first Southern winter set in, Mother Williams turned her attention to outfitting Clifton Grove's enslaved with their winter clothing allowances. Each female slave had to be fitted out with 'a thick dress, chemise, shoes and blankets', while the men received 'pantaloons & jacket, shirt, blanket and shoes, besides caps and bonnets. The children too are clothed in the same materials.' Sewing the enslaveds' new clothing was a job normally performed by [poor white] seamstresses specially engaged for this purpose, but 'Mother Williams has always done it herself along with the assistance of her daughters when they were home'. In the absence of Sarah's sisters-in-law, each now ensconced in their own homes, Sarah volunteered to 'do [her] part', and proudly reported to her parents the results of her handiwork: 'I have made two pairs of pantaloons and we are now to work on the underclothes'. Such labour, however, was a Sisyphean task for almost as soon as the enslaved received their new clothing it was dirty and torn to shreds. As Sarah lamented, 'as a whole they are naturally filthy and it is discouraging to make for them, for it is soon in dirt and rags'. To be fair, however, she admitted that 'there are exceptions of course'. Referring to Harriet Beecher Stowe's *Uncle Tom's Cabin*, published just a year earlier in 1852, Sarah expressed a reluctance to even approach any of 'the little negroes' for, 'like [Miss Ophelia] I should wish a good application of soap and water, comb and clean clothes'. That the dirty, heavy demands of field and house labour might have accounted for the ragged state of Clifton Grove's enslaved population apparently did not occur to her.

In Sarah's imagination, the enslaved women and men in her midst rapidly came to represent a naturally dirty and lazy people, a view commonly shared by Southern whites. If the enslaved possessed a single redeeming feature, it was their ready and enthusiastic acceptance of Christianity. Indeed, as Sarah informed her parents, the enslaved exhibited a far superior knowledge of Christian teachings than could be said for their white owners. Wryly, Sarah noted that, 'As for religious privileges, they enjoy all their masters do. I should say more, for all the preaching I have heard has been more suited to the illiterate than to the educated.' In church one Sunday, her attention was drawn to the enslaved at worship. 'In the gallery were the colored (I should say slave population, for some are quite too light coloured to be Negroes) people and quite a large proportion of them found their places in the hymn books & joined the singing.' Such dedication to Christianity was to be encouraged. When a house-servant appealed to her for a copy of the Testament, 'I gave her one, and a tract. But the print of the former is too fine and I intend getting her a larger one. I told my husband and he approved my course.' Gaining the agnostic Benjamin's consent to distribute religious tracts to Clifton Grove's enslaved community represented a personal victory for Sarah, and indicated her growing influence over her husband's spiritual beliefs. Indeed, as she proudly related to her parents, she had even persuaded Benjamin to read with her the Northern theologian and prominent abolitionist Albert Barnes' *Inquiry into the Scriptural Views of Slavery* in which Barnes launched a stringent attack on the implicit role of the church in condoning and maintaining slavery.[7] Barnes's outspoken condemnation of Southern Presbyterianism did not, however, have much impact on Benjamin. As Sarah would discover, Benjamin's agnosticism and pro-slavery beliefs ran very deep, and she was soon forced to abandon her commitment to persuade her husband of the immorality of slavery. Nonetheless, she could at least fulfil the promise of guiding and advancing the religious development of the enslaved – though preferably at a distance.

With Mother Williams at the helm of plantation operations, steadfast in her refusal to hand over any significant household responsibilities to her daughter-in-law, maintaining a social distance between herself and Clifton Grove's enslaved population was relatively easy for Sarah. Nevertheless, she came to regard herself as a benevolent and kindly mistress, although her letters offer little evidence that she ever formed close relationships with Clifton Grove's enslaved community. She played no direct role in their management, displayed little curiosity about their lives and personal affairs, and apart from a concern for their spiritual welfare, evidenced scant consciousness or awareness of their presence, except in those instances when the slaves' circumstances impinged on her own life. Although she continued to experience overwhelming homesickness for the familiarity of her Northern home, she could not contemplate a move to the North, for as she piously explained to her parents, she was reluctant to sell her slaves for fear they might fall into the hands of less humane owners. But it was not solely concern for the slaves that prevented her return to the North. Benjamin would not countenance her intermittent suggestions that they invest the family's capital in non-slave markets, and he remained adamant in his refusal to give up the plantation businesses. Sarah therefore faced a stark choice: either leave Benjamin and return alone to New York, or accept the status quo. In the event, she chose the latter. As his wife, she was totally dependent on Benjamin for her welfare and survival, and thus was forced to submit to his authority.

As Sarah was to discover, it was the issue of slaves, or rather the fact that she owned none, that was the source of Mother Williams's antagonism towards her. Isolated from her New York family and friends, Sarah quickly came to rely on the respectable white women of the county for advice and guidance, and it was from these women that she learned why Mother Williams was so dissatisfied with her daughter-in-law. As she angrily explained to her mother, 'a Southern lady generally receives a number of servants as her marriage dower. I have no doubt that Mother had looked forward to her son marrying such a one and thus adding to the rather small number of hands ... Benjamin's marrying seems to have turned her against him.' Despite Sarah's respectable middle-class background, Mother Williams regarded her son's wife as a 'poor catch'. Four years previously, Benjamin's sister Mary had married and set up home some distance from Clifton Grove. She took with her a legacy from her father of twenty of the slaves then resident at Clifton Grove, and thus depleted the number of available hands on the plantation. At the time of Sarah's marriage the plantation slaves numbered twenty; far too few, according to Mother Williams, to meet the labour needs of the plantation. Clearly, Mother Williams had nursed the hope that Benjamin would marry a Southern belle who would bring with her a marriage portion of slaves sizable enough to significantly increase the plantation's slave population. Not only had

Benjamin committed the almost unpardonable sin of marrying a Northerner but he had compounded his actions by bringing home a bride without the longed-for additional slaves. As Sarah quickly learned, Southerners regarded land and slaves as black gold, and having brought neither land nor negroes to the marriage Sarah was, in the eyes of her mother-in-law, an unsuitable match for her son.

Despite Sarah's resolve to suffer her mother-in-law's rancour in silence, relations between them remained strained. For much of the next two years, Sarah's letters to her parents repeated her heartfelt desire for her own home, away from the domineering and critical gaze of Mother Williams. Benjamin would not contemplate setting up his own household while he was still needed at Clifton Grove, however. A year after Sarah's arrival at Clifton Grove, prompted perhaps by the unhappy state of relations between herself and her daughter-in-law, Mother Williams proposed a compromise. Benjamin would continue to work the plantation business for a year, then the profits would be divided between the family members, and each would henceforth attend to their own landholdings. Benjamin would immediately receive 250 acres, with further holdings to come to him on his mother's death. Sarah and Benjamin began to make plans to set up their own household at nearby Snow Hill. In the meantime, Sarah resolved to grit her teeth, and called on God to help her find the necessary patience until the day she and Benjamin could set up separate housekeeping, for as she candidly wrote to her mother, '[Mother Williams] would never forgive Benjamin for not marrying "niggers", never, ever, ever'. Brief respites came in the form of extended visits to friends and relatives, and a much longed-for visit to Clifton Grove by her parents. After this visit, relations between Mother Williams and Sarah improved markedly, but the truce was short-lived and Sarah determined more than ever to 'soon be in housekeeping'.

In the meantime, Sarah tried to hone her housekeeping skills. Mother Williams, stubborn as ever, refused to allow her daughter-in-law to take on any significant domestic responsibilities, but Sarah determined to take charge of some aspects of the plantation household's improvement. A new kitchen was built, 'a rough affair but better than none', and two new rooms were added to Clifton Grove's original structure of five rooms. A stove was ordered for the new kitchen, clothes were sewn for the plantation's enslaved population, for the white family, and for local poor whites, including 'seven dresses and a few jackets and pantaloon' for a poor white woman of the county. In 1854, Sarah and Benjamin welcomed the arrival of their daughter Sara Virginia, known as Lily, the first of their seven children. Motherhood added a new dimension to Sarah's life. Taking care of Lily's needs filled her days and consumed her attention. There were other sources of satisfaction, as well. She had started her own kitchen garden, a labour from which she derived immense fulfilment. In May 1855, she proudly informed her parents: 'I have just come from the garden. It is customary for the ladies here to attend the vegetable gardens. I am trying to learn and with Benjamin's assistance this season, I hope to be able to superintend it alone next year.' Motherhood, it appears, had given her more status. In Benjamin's absence, and with Mother Williams frequently confined her to her bed because of ill-health, Sarah had even begun to assume control of plantation affairs:

> Since [Benjamin] has been away, I see to his business. I am up before sunrise to give out the keys. He told me how to order and sometimes I steal mother's thunder. I watch and see what her hands are doing and then I order ours as if I knew it all. For instance, I set them to setting out sweet potato sprouts the other day ... now they are plowing and hoeing the corn. If Benjamin doesn't come this week I shall make them thin it out.

Later that month, Sarah again wrote of her vegetable garden,

> I have a vegetable garden, which I superintend. I have collards (most like cabbage) almost a foot high and leaves as big as the palm of your hand, peas that are running, Irish potatoes ..., cucumber[s] ... and mustard going to seed. We have had radishes a month or more. Another year, I'm going to see what I can do. If I live and am well, I am going to have the best garden in the county. I want some Shanghai chickens, and am going to try for a pair.

Sarah took great pride in these labours, as her own particular contribution to the household economy. She was learning the skills of an efficient Southern plantation mistress-cum-manager, a responsibility that would one day fall squarely on her shoulders.

Sarah's dream of setting up her own housekeeping was finally realised in 1856, as Benjamin consolidated his turpentine business. In 1854, Benjamin and his brother Richard had acquired an interest in a turpentine venture in Georgia. The following year, as a result of a contractor's losses during the economic recession, Benjamin acquired title to considerable turpentine and timber-lands in that state, significantly increasing his landholdings. Keen to develop his turpentine business there, Benjamin saw this as a good time to establish his own household, and relocated his family to Georgia. Preparations for the move began in 1855, and by January 1856 the family were finalising their plans for relocation. Early in the New Year Benjamin and Sarah took up residence in the village of Burnt Fort, on the Satilla River, Charlton County, Georgia. Benjamin's choice of Charlton County was an astute move. The undeveloped state of the turpentine industry in that region meant that there was little competition, and indeed in 1860 only five counties in Georgia were manufacturing turpentine. Moving to Georgia meant new beginnings for Sarah and her family.

It was here in Georgia that Sarah was to achieve the dream of her own home, though for several years the family lived in rough, temporary accommodation. Still, after the privations and stresses of living at Clifton Grove, the humble house seemed a haven. Sarah set about building a comfortable family home. Managing her own household made for greater happiness, but as she was to discover, the role of mistress brought with it considerable difficulties. Benjamin's political and business affairs took him away from the plantation for frequent and long absences, leaving Sarah isolated from other white people. A growing family of young children made visits to family and friends difficult, and with Benjamin away from home she could not leave the plantation. The demands of running a household left her little time for leisure. Without the assistance of Mother Williams, full responsibility for the household's smooth functioning fell solely on Sarah's shoulders, and she was overwhelmed by the sheer number of new roles and responsibilities that befell the mistress of a Southern slaveholding plantation household. In Greene County she had often bemoaned her enforced idleness, but now, 'My mind is so filled with eating and drinking and "wherewithal I shall be clothed" of our family of sixteen here, five up in Ware County and over thirty getting turpentine. Though these latter do not come to me for clothes and food, still they call this their home and several of them always are here Sundays.' Domestic slaves had to be instructed in the day's work, food and other supplies had to be provided for those slaves working away from the plantation, livestock to be cared for, vegetables to be planted, butter to be churned, pork to be cured, the silver to be polished, sick slaves to be cared for, clothes to be sewed and mended, cotton to be spun and woven, and her growing brood of infants needed mothering. The demands of the plantation were all-consuming, and there was little time or energy left for the busy round of socialising and letter writing that had filled her early days in North Carolina.

> I am going to attempt a letter, but whether it will ever be finished, will be known in the sequel. We are now planting and as usual, in such times, everything else must give in – washing, ironing and scouring, &c. The consequence is everything and everybody looks dirty and cross and sour. The Dr. has gone to Ware County much against his inclination and I look for him tomorrow. In the meantime, it's 'Miss Sarah' here and 'Miss Sarah' there and then little children must run to mama and the little black images will be around. I lie down at night tired enough to sleep

like a rock and yet I cannot tell what I have done but trot after the children, trot after the Negroes, trot after the chickens, eggs, and hens and turkeys and trot, trot, trot, all day. Then too, I have not the satisfaction of using my hands as I would like to do. This waiting other people's notion is not my will, but it is the Lord's will and I know I ought to be more submissive and more patient ... I have not been out of sight of the chimney nor inside a neighbours house since I entered this last October.

It was Sarah's responsibility for the enslaved that proved by far the greatest trial. Her own children were sorely in need of a teacher, and she worried constantly that she was neglecting them. Getting rid of this troublesome species of property, the slaves, would vastly relieve Sarah of this unwanted burden, and she once again attempted to persuade Benjamin to sell off the plantation slaves (in Sarah's view, the 'most unprofitable property a person can own'), and invest in non-slave property. But against her judgement and wishes, Benjamin continued to invest in slaves: 'Benjamin's self esteem is bigger than mine, so I yield'. But she did at least acknowledge the slaves' physical and capital value, albeit grudgingly.

> Benjamin hired a few more hands in addition to those of last year and bought Anarchy, Demps' wife (gave only a thousand dollars for her). She can cut out pantaloons, shirts &c & is a good sewer and can wash iron or cook and work out ... he also brought Lewis the distiller. Paid over $1200.00 for him, and a yellow boy about thirteen years old. I forgot what he cost – somewhere about a thousand I suppose. So, you see the Dr. believes in Negroes and pine land.

As a married woman dependent for her survival on her husband, Sarah was forced to defer to Benjamin who, while continuing to be a loving husband, nevertheless asserted his patriarchal authority over his wife. Theirs was clearly not an equal partnership, for Benjamin reserved to himself the privilege of making all the major decisions that would affect his family's life. His plans for his diverse business interests often collided with Sarah's own wishes for a permanent settled home. Rather than use his profits to build a family home, much to Sarah's chagrin Benjamin preferred to reinvest his capital in his numerous slave-dependent businesses. The family lived in a series of temporary homes, and Sarah's letters to her parents are filled with longing for a more permanent one. As she warned her parents, then contemplating a visit to Georgia, 'if you wait for us to get settled, I fear it will be long ere I see you again'.

In this letter to her father, Sarah reveals her growing acculturation as a Southerner. She might have resented slavery, believing it placed an onerous and unfair burden on her shoulders, but like many other

Southern plantation matrons she displayed an acute awareness of the monetary value of slaves. It is telling that Sarah blamed her difficulties not on her husband, not on the 'peculiar institution', but on the most disempowered, the slaves themselves. Managing a household of intractable slaves wore her down but, as a Christian, she could not forsake her duty to them. When Ann, a particularly unruly house-slave, became ill, Sarah nursed her throughout her final illness.

> The doctor told you Ann was dead. Poor thing, she suffered dreadfully. Demp's wife and Lizzie were with her night and day for two weeks and the Dr. employed counsel. Everything was done for her that could have been done for me. Well, she is gone and I feel that I did all for her I could. She expressed true sorrow for her sins and for two or three months appeared very differently from her former headstrong course.

The remaining slaves continued troublesome, especially Lizzie and Ann[8], persistent malingerers who wearied Sarah with their constant complaints. She deeply resented the demands of slave-ownership and domestic responsibilities, complaining that she could not devote as much time to her own children as she desired. Her children's learning was being neglected, she feared, for she had neither the time nor patience to read to or teach them. The best she could do was entrust them to the care of a nurse, Charity, who also doubled as a waiting girl. Even this arrangement was not particularly satisfactory, for the twelve-year-old Charity was little more than a child herself, and needed constant supervision. No wonder Sarah lamented to her mother, 'I do know what it is to be nervous and I wish from the bottom of my soul I did not know'.

Looming prospects of civil war added to Sarah's anxiety. Growing sectarian tensions from the 1850s onwards escalated as the debates about state sovereignty and slavery turned increasingly violent, spilling over into Congress itself. Southern passions, already aroused by what was perceived as federal government attempts to limit state rights, were further inflamed by Northern abolitionist's demands that the spread of slavery be limited. In 1857, the Supreme Court's decision in the Dred Scott case not only denied citizenship to slaves but also ruled that Congress could not prohibit slavery in the newly emerging western territories. The Missouri Compromise of 1820 had guaranteed that the new Midwestern territories would be free states, but the *Dred Scott* v. *Sandford* ruling declared that decision unconstitutional. This ruling fuelled abolitionist campaigns to limit the spread of American slavery, and Southerners responded with spirited defenses of slavery and the sovereign rights of states. The result was the further inflammation of both Northern and Southern passions. By 1859 it seemed increasingly unlikely that civil war could be avoided. In that year, Abraham Lincoln had begun his bid for the senate with the declaration that 'A House divided against itself cannot survive. I believe this government cannot endure permanently, half-slave, half-free.' To add to the political tensions, Southern slaveholding states were shaken daily by rumours of actual or attempted slave rebellions.[9] When, in October 1859, the abolitionist John Brown attempted to arouse Virginian slaves to insurrection, Sarah railed against this 'insane project ... one of the diabolical schemes of a set of fanatics, who if they had their way, would deluge the land in blood'. In the few moments of leisure she had, Sarah made it her business to keep abreast of political debates, anxiously reading both Northern and Southern newspapers for the latest developments in the North–South quarrel. Her letters reveal a clear grasp of the complex political issues that threatened to divide the Union. Attempts by abolitionists to provoke slave uprisings against their owners, she argued, actually worsened the conditions of the enslaved, as pro-slavery Southerners were left with no choice but to tighten their power and control over the South's black populations. And John Brown's foolhardy 'insane project' held personal implications for her.

> You ask, perhaps, what will be the result [of John Brown's failed actions]? I tell you what I think. Vigilance committees will be formed, every northerner, man or woman, will be closely watched and if heard advancing incendiary sentiment, let him or her be certain to take the first northbound express train. That is the great good the 'Philanthropists' have accomplished in addition to opening the African slave trade.

Despite having lived her entire married life in the South, Sarah had still to contend with the suspicions of her neighbours, who placed all non-Southerners under surveillance. Her prophesies about vigilante committees became a reality when a few months after John Brown's aborted uprising, Southern newspapers were reporting the formation of vigilance patrols throughout the South. 'What else could Southerners [be expected to] do?' she demanded of her parents. Northern abolitionists were infiltrating the South, inciting slaves to revolt with promises of eventual emancipation. Nowhere in the South was safe. In early December 1860, Sarah heard reports of one such aborted uprising:

> Yesterday we learned that a runaway was taken near here (who is now in the Waresboro jail) who says he was one of thirty others who were armed with guns. They were going east with two white men who promised them freedom. They travelled with them nights & he had left them and was trying to get back. You will see by the papers that Min-

utemen are forming companies all over the country. They are forming one at Waresboro.

In these uneasy times, Southerners regarded any Northerners in their midst as possible abolitionists and spies, intent on destabilising the South. Sarah worried constantly about hostility from her Southern neighbours. As she informed her parents, '[T]hey tell me the prejudice against Northerners is much stronger in the country than it is in the cities and towns of the South. I know that I have felt it ever since I was in the country, though marrying a slave-holder ought to free me from the charge of Abolitionism.' In truth, her neighbours need not have worried, for Sarah aligned herself firmly with the Southern cause, and sympathised with their strategic legislative efforts to defend their rights to retain state rights and the institution of slavery.

Just weeks after war broke out Sarah strongly defended the Confederacy in a letter to her parents:

> Before this reaches you, I expect to hear that Lincoln and his cabinet have found Washington too warm a place and have gone to Chicago. They have to contend with desperate men . . . who fight for their altars and their fires. I tell you now that Lincoln has played the aggressor. He will have to leave every inch of Southern soil. I need not tell you there is excitement. It is more than that, it is determination, it is the spirit of '76, the will to conquer or die.

Sarah's spirited defence of the Confederate Army was, however, tempered by the knowledge that her views would not be shared by her parents in New York. 'I suppose, Pa, you will favour the Union Party?' she asked of her father. However, she stopped short of declaring her allegiance to her adopted Southern homeland, still cherishing the hope that the Union might be preserved:

> I look to God alone to guide our ship of state over these tempestuous waves and angry billows into a haven of peace and safety. And I cannot but believe that this Union, founded as it was by men who feared God, prayed for by Washington, will be preserved and a man raised up to guide us, erring and sinful as we are, across these troubled seas of political turbulence . . . One who has ties in both sections can but regard it as a sacrilege.

While Sarah continued to assure her parents of her opposition to slavery, the reality was that residence in the South, and marriage into a slave-owning family, had left its indelible mark. By the eve of the Civil War, after less than a decade in the slaveholding South, Sarah's previously held beliefs of equality and liberty for all human beings had been severely undermined.

A few years earlier in North Carolina, Sarah had questioned the preacher James Sprunt's assertion that enslavement represented the natural state for negroes, but now, faced with the possibility of the enslaved's imminent emancipation, she could no longer envisage any other possible condition but slavery for negroes. In Sarah's estimation, slaves were too childlike to be left to their own devices, and required the steady guidance of superior white owners. Neither could she imagine that the slaves themselves might value their freedom. 'You will readily see how very anxious (I speak ironically) the slaves are to be liberated, when the few that joined Brown & Co. were compelled, and one who would not was deliberately shot. I wonder what his dying thoughts of "freedom" were.'

The prospect of war weighed heavily on Sarah, for besides the profound upheavals and loss of life war would bring, it was also likely to seriously disrupt her relations with her New York family. Postal services, erratic at the best of times, would be suspended, and visiting in either direction was out of the question. Benjamin's frequent absences and her own myriad responsibilities effectively tied Sarah to the plantation. Besides, she did not relish the prospects of embarking on the long journey north with four young children. In April 1861, barely two weeks into the conflict, Sarah was reluctantly forced to discourage a proposed much-longed for visit from the elderly Hicks, fearing that as northerners, 'in the present unsettled state of the country', they might be exposed to 'vexations and troubles'. Preoccupied with his diverse Georgia business operations, Benjamin refused to consider her pleas that the family relocate to the North, and a despondent Sarah was forced to accept the possibility that she might never again see her aging parents. 'I know not when I may see you again', she fearfully informed her mother and father, 'but may we not all strive by true repentance and faith in the Son of God to live here so that we may spend Eternity together'. Two years were to pass before Sarah had any prospects of communicating with her parents. Postal services between North and South were suspended almost from the outbreak of war, and continued so for the duration of the conflict. On a few occasions a temporary truce was declared, giving Sarah a rare opportunity to send or receive correspondence. Such chances were rare, however, and in any case the shortage of paper and postage stamps meant that Sarah could not often take advantage of the temporary postal services. Between April 1861 and 1864, the exchange of correspondence between the Hicks and Williams families slowed to a trickle, often reducing an already over-wrought Sarah to deep despair and anxiety as to her parents' fate.

THE MAKING OF A NORTH CAROLINIAN PLANTATION MISTRESS

Another concern for Sarah was the imminent prospect that she might soon be denied access to the labour of her slaves. Indeed, in 1860, Sarah found herself even more dependent than ever on the household servants. Benjamin's long-promised move to a new permanent home finally materialised, but the sheer logistics of organising the household's relocation to Sunny Side, their new home in Ware County, left Sarah depleted. Benjamin had gone on ahead to oversee the final building works to Sunny Side, taking with him some of the household servants from Burnt Fort, and leaving Sarah with insufficient household labour.

> I have to pack the six mule wagon, & these hands with Fan's help had the packing and boxing to do. Ann, Demp's wife, went with the wagon, so once more I tried Lizzie for cook, who you know is sick often. She gave out last Tuesday, the day the Dr left and has been sick since. Today Jin was sent home from the [turpentine] still half sick, so now I have two to take care of. The prospect of a two or four horse wagon coming to load in the course of a few weeks adds to my cares, but Fan and I can do it. I tell you, I'm sick of servants. After all, Fan and Lett [two household slaves] are my main dependence.

Troublesome property they might be, but in reality Sarah relied heavily on the labour of enslaved women and men. In truth, mistress and slaves depended on each other, but Sarah appeared blind to the possibility that her slaves might themselves resent their enforced state of dependence on those who held them in perpetual bondage.

As a young married woman, Sarah had once worried that selling her slaves might be an act of unkindness to them, and could thereby justify her resolve not to rid herself of her 'troublesome property'. In any case, this was never going to be a decision made by Sarah alone, for Benjamin's various business enterprises relied heavily on unfree labour, and he continued to regard slaveholding as a profitable investment. Curiously, as the prospects of war loomed, Sarah's letters reveal little about her attitudes towards the likely emancipation of the slaves, and scant, if any, concern for their post-emancipation welfare. Perhaps she continued to hope that war might be averted, and that a peaceful compromise could yet be reached. Given her often-repeated pleas to be free of her 'troublesome property', it is possible that, like many other Southern plantation mistresses, Sarah heaved private sighs of relief at the prospect of the emancipation of the South's slaves.

The suspension of postal services meant that few letters passed between Sarah and her family during the war years, consequently depriving historians of a rich and valuable source of data about the

Civil War experiences of this transplanted northern woman. Sarah's few hastily written letters dating from this time were brief, for the most part merely conveying hurried assurances about her family's welfare, and expressions of desire to be reunited once more with her Northern family. We can only imagine the depths of despair and anxiety of both families as their only means of communication were disrupted. For much of the Civil War, Sarah could not even be certain that her parents were still alive.

Few families on either side of the North–Side divide remained untouched by the conflict and the Williams family did not escape unscathed. Southern agricultural production and trade were among the first casualties of war, and Benjamin's turpentine operations, probably depleted of slave labourers, sustained severe financial losses. Sarah's few letters written during the war years convey little sense of the destruction and havoc that the conflict wreaked on the South. Fortunately, however, the volumes of journals, letters and other writings detailing the wartime experiences of Southern women and men have contributed to a rich Civil War historiography. These personal writings detail the fall from power of the once hegemonic slave-owning class, but they also relate the intense suffering faced by many Southerners, white and black alike.[10] Livestock and agricultural crops were appropriated by the Union Army as it marched through the South, and thousands of white Southerners experienced severe hunger and starvation for the first time. Drought and Union blockades contributed to food shortages throughout the South, fuelling dramatic price rises and, in some states, food riots. Thousands of Southern women, left behind while their men went off to fight the Confederate cause, turned to kitchen gardens, though few had either the money or seeds needed to cultivate new crops. Material for clothing could be bought only at overinflated prices, and little fuel could be found for cooking stoves and hearth-fires. For many white Southerners the most devastating consequence of the war was the loss of their slaves, many of whom had fled the plantations at the earliest opportunity. Without their field hands, crops could not be cultivated or harvested, and were left to rot in the fields. Those planters who for some reason were unable or unwilling to join the Confederate Army now found themselves performing labour previously defined as 'negro work'. In the absence of their menfolk, either away at war or killed in action, thousands of wives and mothers across the South now had little choice but to turn their hands to work that had been defined as masculine labour, and many plantation mistresses were forced for the first time to take on the burden of plantation management and agricultural cultivation. Some fortunate mistresses could rely on help from whatever loyal slaves they were able to retain, but for thousands, the task of wresting a living from often depleted soil had to be accomplished without slave labour. Mistresses now found themselves labouring for long hours in corn or cotton fields, performing work from which they would have been exempt in pre-war days by virtue of their gender, race and class. Narratives of many ex-slave women recall their satisfaction at seeing plantation mistresses toiling away at the same 'unfeminine' labour that black women had previously been forced to perform. To some extent the Civil War was certainly a great leveller, as former antebellum sexual and racial divisions of labour were necessarily abandoned – albeit temporarily.

The loss of the Williams family's primary means of economic survival added to Sarah's already considerable burden. Life had been hard before the war, but the conflict took her hardships to new dimensions. There was scarcely a free moment to be had, either for Sarah or her remaining slaves: 'We pass no idle moments. We all wear clothes made upon the place. Ann and Lizzie do the spinning and weaving, I do the teaching, knitting and sewing. Charity is nurse and waiting girl. Virginia [her eldest daughter] can spin real well and sew and knits a little. Fan and March do the cooking, washing, ironing and cleaning. Henry [her eight-year-old son] makes the chicken coops.' All available hands, including her children's, had to be put to work, but the persistent daily struggle for the family's survival was achieved largely through the labour of slaves, who continued to serve the family. Lizzie and Ann, whose poor health and suspected malingering had previously driven Sarah to distraction, remained with the Williams household, as did Charity, Fannie and Let, three other enslaved women. In pre-war days, these enslaved women had represented the chief source of Sarah's troubles, and she had frequently expressed deep resentment at what she perceived as their intolerable dependence on her. Now, in wartime, Sarah was no doubt made conscious of the extent to which her family's survival depended on these women. Had Charity, Fannie or Let followed the example of thousands of enslaved people across the South and fled their former plantation homes, Sarah's arduous domestic responsibilities would have been greatly increased. She could not have failed to realise the irony of her position now; a Union victory would inevitably herald the demise of Southern slavery, an outcome that would deprive Sarah of the very property that she had for so long expressed fervent desires to be rid of. Free from the cares of slave-owning she might be, but without their labour power her own responsibilities would increase three-fold.

When, on 9 April 1965 Confederate General Robert E. Lee surrendered to the Union Army at Appomattox Station, Virginia, there could have been few Southerners who were not relieved at the war's end. The conflict had taken a heavy toll on the South: thousands of lives were lost, families had been torn apart, plantation houses lay in ruins, their fields razed and crops devastated. And slavery, the cornerstone of Southern economy, was in tatters. Thousands of emancipated Black Americans deserted their former plantations, with but one aim in mind – to put as much distance as possible between them and their enslaved past. Many thousands remained in the South, perhaps believing that they could be full participants in the restructuring of the post-war South. The once-mighty class of Southern slave-owners had been brought to its knees, but the Southern economy and infrastructure would need rebuilding.

Even before the war's end, the question of securing an adequate and willing labour force to rebuild the plantation economy lay heavily on the minds of Southerners. Plantation owners had only to look to the example of the larger West Indies colonies, where slaves had deserted their plantations *en masse* after their 1838 emancipation. To fill the labour vacuum left by the blacks, planters on some of the larger islands looked outwards to India and China for new sources of plantation labour. In time, their labour needs would eventually be met by successive waves of Indian indentured labourers.[11] Southern planters, however, had neither the means nor enticements necessary to lure sizable numbers of either foreign or domestic labourers to the rural South. Though their economy was in dire straits, few Southern whites were willing to fill the labour gap left by the freed blacks. Southerners gradually concluded that their economy could be rebuilt only through free, waged, black labour. The post-war relations between black and white Southerners would, however, require redefinition as emancipated blacks asserted their rights as free citizens. The traditional relationships – white as superior master, black as inferior slave – that had girded the antebellum Southern society and economy, would not withstand the aspirations of the newly emancipated.

Like many other Southern mistresses in the post-war economy, Sarah Hicks Williams turned to hiring waged labour for domestic help. But this arrangement proved unsatisfactory, for many emancipated African-Americans quickly left the South in search of new opportunities in the North. Domestic labour no doubt evoked memories of their recent enslavement, and to Sarah's frustration the household servants came and went with regularity, and it was difficult to find and keep reliable domestics. Emancipated black women contested their former mistresses' rights to their labour power, even under a free, waged labour system. Few were willing to return to *any* form of plantation labour, field or domestic, preferring instead to take their chances as free marketers. Others refused *all* forms of paid labour, asserting that as white men protected and provided for their wives, so they too expected to be provided for by their husbands. Thousands of freed black women, however, had little choice but to look to the plantations for their survival, and many were forced to hire out their labour to their former owners. When the opportunity presented itself, however, black women found new means of survival, and expressed their new-found independence by literally walking off the job, much to the despair and anger of their employers.[12] That they should blithely 'abscond' from their employers enraged Sarah, and it confirmed her beliefs in black inferiority and ingratitude. 'Three have run away during the last few months that we had clothed up to be decent. They came to us all but naked. They are an ungrateful race', she complained. As in pre-war days, whites complained of the natural indolence and laziness of blacks who, without the controlling regimes established by the slave system, would simply refuse to work. In her condemnation of these 'ungrateful' people, Sarah Hicks Williams revealed her acceptance of a Southern race ideology that defined blacks as lazy, workshy beings, even while inadvertently bemoaning her dependence on them. By the end of the Civil War, time, experience and exposure to racist Southern ideologies of black inferiority had conspired to transform this inexperienced Northern bride into the quintessential Southern slave-owning plantation mistress.

The letters of Sarah Hicks Williams to her family in New York reveal far more than merely the reflections of an educated Northern woman gradually coming to terms with the alien customs of the South. A critical reading provides some insight to the ways in which the intersections of gender, class and race played out in the antebellum South. Throughout the Southern states, gender identity was always intersected by race and class. Moreover, for non-black women such as Sarah, her gendered identity could not be extricated from her racial identity as a white woman. Women were then not simply gendered beings, but racialised bodies also. When Sarah viewed her world, she did so from the perspective of a white self. When she scathingly condemned the 'natural' inferiority of her 'unprofitable property', she did so from her standpoint as a member of the ruling white group, wrapped in the security of her own racial superiority. She never questioned the essentialist assumptions on which her world-view of race was based, but, in common with other Southern white women, accepted and embraced her whiteness as a signifier of civility and superiority. Although Sarah viewed slave-owning as a burden, slave ownership permitted her a privileged status that conferred the right to appropriate enslaved human labour, the right to status as a lady, the right to exercise power, and the right to be protected by her husband. The privileges she enjoyed were derived not merely from her gender (for being a woman was not enough to procure these privileges) or class (for class position also determined the allocation of privilege and status), but on her white identity also. In this sense, the fact of whiteness, or white identity shaped her gendered identity, differentiating her from all non-white women. With the exception of some trangressive women, i.e. women who engaged in sexual relations with black men, or engaged in the illicit sex trade, Southern white women from all parts of the class spectrum were accorded a social status that derived from the fact of their whiteness. Yet we know little of how 'whiteness' *per se* shaped the contours of white women's lives.

When white Southern women such as Sarah Hicks Williams penned their thoughts on race, they rarely, if ever, addressed their subjective whiteness, or questioned the content or stability of that whiteness, or their rights to the privileges obtained. In their journals and correspondence, while Southern women often commented on the perceived inferiority of negroes, they rarely reflected on, or drew attention to, their own whiteness. In Sarah Hicks Williams's letters, the race of non-white individuals is nearly always clearly stated, while the race identity of her white relations, friends and neighbours is never alluded to. By making these clear distinctions between those who are black and those who are white, Sarah brings a sense of order to her world.

In Sarah's mind, whiteness represented the given; the norm. It was the natural state against which all 'others' were defined. When she alludes to the race of those non-whites she encounters, she unconsciously points to the normativity of whiteness, forcefully captured by Richard Dyer: 'Other people are raced, we [whites] are just people'.[13] While many white women railed against the patriarchal gender structures that constrained their lives, few perceived the interplay of the relationship between the patriarchal order and the crucial ways in which their own whiteness made them a critical element in the reproduction of that order. Even the abolitionist sisters Angeline and Sarah Grimke, whose abhorrence of slavery led them to leave the South, were unable to perceive clearly the way that whiteness was manipulated and pulled into the service of white control. As Frankenberg has stated, the privileged position that white women have occupied renders them unable to see the effects of racism (in this case, whiteness, white privilege) on their own lives.[14] Thus when Sarah Hicks Williams bemoaned the difficulties of managing unruly and unwilling slaves, she blamed not slavery, or the patriarchal order that sanctioned white male power and slave-owning authority, but the enslaved themselves. And when, after the Civil War, she found it difficult to get domestics, again it was the 'ungrateful' blacks on whom she vented her anger and frustration. It was the slaves/servants who wore her down, the slaves/servants whom she castigated – those with the least social power.

Southern women did not all experience whiteness/white identity in the same manner, for modes of whiteness were shaped not solely by gender, but also by class relations. The social structure of North Carolina displayed a variety of different white social strata ranging from the elite slave-owning planters to an impoverished, landless tenantry, with numerous social divisions in between. Slavery and the imperatives of a white supremacist patriarchy impacted on white women of all classes in different ways. While the majority of white Southern women derived social advantages by virtue of their 'whiteness', elite plantation women derived status and privileges above and beyond those of non-slaveholding women, and in particular, of poor, landless white women. Kate Davy has stated:

> some white women have more mobility than others; it is at the intersection of class privilege that whiteness is fully mobilised. The symbology of white womanhood is not that of the fallen, disenfranchised white woman, but that of the respectable white woman.[15]

Richard Dyer has also pointed to the inclusive/exclusive nature of whiteness: not all white people are securely white. The poor white non-elites of Southern societies were never, unlike their elite neighbours, indisputably white. And just who can be counted as white or non-white is always subject to political and historical change.[16]

In the South, poor white women represented a threat to white supremacist power structures, through their potential slippage from their positions of white privilege into the 'white trash' category, and throughout the colonies, poor white women in particular were made the subjects of state control. In a return to Barbados, in the next chapter, I address the place of race formation and social class differences in their intersections with gender that shaped the material experiences of poor white women. I will then continue by addressing these same issues as they pertained to their apparent counterparts of North Carolina.

Notes

1 Sarah Hicks Williams letter to her parents, 7 March 1853. All extracts and quotations from the correspondence of Sarah Hicks Williams are derived from a collection edited by James C. Bonner, 'Plantation Experiences of a New York Woman', *North Carolina Historical Review*, 33: 2&3 (July and October 1956), pp. 384–412 and pp. 529–586.

2 'The Underground Railroad (occasionally referred to as the 'Underground Railway') was a loose network of abolitionists, sympathetic whites and free Blacks who organised clandestine routes by which nineteenth-century enslaved African-Americans attempted to escape slavery. Escape routes stretched from the Southern slave states into the free North and on to Canada, and sometimes even overseas. From 1810 to 1850, between 30,000 and 100,000 people are thought to have escaped enslavement via the Underground Railroad.
3 Gerder Lerner, *The Grimke Sisters from South Carolina* (Oxford: Oxford University Press, 1998).
4 On the secession crisis see: William H. Freeling, *The Road to Disunion* (New York: Oxford University Press, 1999).
5 Thanks to the anonymous reviewer of this manuscript who astutely pointed out the similarities between Sarah's admiration of the abstract beauty of the cotton bolls which replicates Richard Ligon's similar admiration of the beauty of plantains carried on the heads of 'hansome Negroes, men and women, with every one a grassegreen bunch of these fruits on their heads ... the black and green so well becoming one another' (see Richard Ligon, *A True and Exact History of the Island of Barbados* (London, Frank Cass & Co., 1970).
6 Jeffrey J. Crow, *A History of African-Americans in North Carolina* (Raleigh: North Carolina Division of Archives and History, 1992), p. 55.
7 Albert Barnes, *An Inquiry into the Scriptural Views of Slavery* (Philadelphia, 1846).
8 This Ann may have been a field slave who was brought into the Big House to take the place of the deceased Ann.
9 On the Dredd Scott decision, see: Paul Finkelman, *Dredd Scott v. Sandford: A brief history with documents* (Bedford: St Martins, 1997).
10 See for instance: Catherine Clinton, *Tara Revisited: Women, war and the plantation legend* (New York: Abbeyville Press, 1995); Virginia Barr (ed.), *The Secret Eye: The Journal of Ella Gertrude Clanton Thomas* (Chapel Hill: University of North Carolina Press, 1990); Beth Crabtree and James M. Patton (eds), *Journal of a Secesh Lady: The Diary of Catherine Ann Devereux Edmonston, 1860–1866* (Raleigh: North Carolina Division of Archives and History, 1979).
11 See Verene Shepherd, *Women of the Caribbean: The British colonised territories* (Kingston: Ian Randle Publishers, 1999).
12 On black women's lives in the Civil War South, see for instance, Noralee Frankel, *Freedom's Women: Black women and families in Civil War era Mississippi* (Bloomington: Indiana University Press, 1999).
13 Richard Dyer, *Whiteness* (London: Routledge, 1997), p. 1.
14 Ruth Frankenberg, *White Women, Race Matters: The social construction of whiteness* (London: Routledge, 1993).
15 Kate Davy, 'Outing Whiteness: A Feminist/Lesbian Project', in Mike Hill (ed.), *Whiteness: A critical reader* (New York: New York University Press, 1997), pp. 204–25.
16 Dyer, *Whiteness*, p. 12.

CHAPTER FIVE

White lives, black bodies: Barbadian women and slaveholding

In 1778, Anne Phillips, a widow of St Michael parish, sat down with her eighteen-year-old daughter Eleanor and carefully drafted what was to be her last will and testament. Anne Phillips's probated will is the only surviving trace of her existence, and hence we know very little about the life and experiences of this white Barbadian woman. Nor do we know for certain the situation or motivations that prompted Anne to devise her last will, but it is entirely within the realms of speculation that Anne approached this morbid task in the sure knowledge of her impending death. My concern here, however, lies not with the immediate circumstances that led to the writing of the will. Rather, the focus is on Anne as the owner and Mistress of a specific form of property, and on the nature of that property. As Chapter 3 showed, Barbadian property law conferred upon widows the power to dispose of their personal property as they saw fit, and the ways in which Anne Phillips chose to exercise this privilege are of interest.

That Anne Phillips was vested with the authority to devise her own will, and to decide autonomously the post-mortem disposal and distribution of her property, is revealing of her social status – as a widow of property and some wealth, but above all as a free white person. In 1774, when Anne put pen to paper, few non-white people in Barbados could legitimately own property, and the few property-owning non-whites – the majority of whom were free(d) coloured persons – suffered legal constraints in the disposal of their property, particularly when that property was human. Foremost among Anne's concerns was the future welfare and security of an enslaved woman, Kate, whose body and labour power Anne had possessed, appropriated and exploited for some years. Again, the silences within the will do not reveal the motivations guiding her decisions, and we can only speculate that Anne's concern for Kate's future wellbeing was driven by her desire to repay Kate for her many years of service within the Phillips household. That the two women, one a free white of European origins, the other an enslaved woman of African ancestry, shared a close and intimate relationship that bordered on a friendship is certain, and Anne's final testament was certainly devised with that closeness in mind. Perhaps unwilling to entrust another member of her circle of family and friends to carry out her final wishes, Anne appointed her daughter Eleanor executrix of her estate. According to the terms of the will, Anne's last wish was that Kate be:

> given the free use of the house in the yard where she now lives with the liberty of a free passage to and from the same in the same manner as in my lifetime until my daughter Eleanor shall hire or provide a proper house for her to live in at the rate of £6.00 per annum to be paid ... also Kate shall not be put to any labour or slavery for or by any person but is to be allowed free liberty the same as if she had been freed, and I also order that Judy, Kate's sister be and remain with Kate in the capacity of a slave to Kate during her life, and be in no way ordered and controlled by any person except Kate.[1]

What are we, from our perspectives at the dawn of the twenty-first century, to make of this eighteenth-century document? What, if anything, can a reading of this last will and testament left behind by a Barbadian mistress of enslaved people reveal about the significance of whiteness and gender in the colonial space? What, if anything, does it tell us about the human body as simultaneously the site of both power and oppression? And what can it say about the discursive practices that construct particular racialised bodies as legitimate free human subjects while other bodies are deemed fit only for enslavement, denied agency, denied legal protection, denied the right and ability to exercise control over their own lives?

An initial superficial reading of Anne Phillips's will reveals little beyond the evident determination of an apparently benevolent mistress to safeguard the welfare of Kate, her elderly and apparently much favoured slave. Clearly Anne intended that the faithful Kate should, for the rest of her life, be exempted from the rigours of slave labour, evident in her directive that Eleanor provide Kate with an annuity of £6, and a secure dwelling house. I am suggesting, however, that another interpretation of the last will and testament of this white Barbadian widow will open up critical spaces through which we might think about whiteness as a position of structural advantage, with this as just one instance of how white women were implicated within colonial relations of dominance. It might also enable a clearer understanding of the complexities of gender and race (specifically whiteness) as they informed each other in colonial societies. The persistent representation of white colonial women as mere victims of patriarchal white male authority becomes severely disrupted.

We cannot simply read Anne Phillips's will without regard to the racialised subjectivities of the principal characters. For it is Anne's *whiteness* that legitimates her status as the owner of black Kate's body. It is also her status as a white woman that enables Anne to consign Judy, Kate's sister, to a lifetime of slavery (and thus perhaps undermining initial assumptions of her benevolence). In 'giving' Judy into the perpetual service of her own sister, Kate, Anne literally renders Judy's status as that of slave of a slave. Again, the silences of Anne Phillips's will tell us nothing about how the sisters Kate and Judy viewed this extraordinary arrangement. What the silence *can* reveal is the powerlessness of enslaved women, while highlighting the relative power of Anne, their owner and mistress. Kate and Judy may well have been favoured or well-cared for domestic slaves, but as enslaved persons, their legal status was that of real estate property, and neither woman could lay legal claim to their own bodies, nor to any property, let alone devise their own wills. Anne Phillips may well have been motivated by good intentions – perhaps she wanted to ensure that the sisters remained together, rather than endure the pain of separation that a future sale would undoubtedly bring. But ultimately, the fortunes of each sister rested in Anne's hands, for in the physical act of penning her will she charted their respective futures.

Barbadian property laws of the eighteenth century restricted white women's access to property, but economic considerations notwithstanding, all white women enjoyed the right to own or at least access the bodies and labour power of enslaved women and men. Even poor white women could access slave labour through the system of 'hiring out' of slaves, a common economic enterprise that provided many white women with a source of income. Indeed, as noted, the right of white women to own slaves was recognised by Barbadian courts, as is evident from the successful petitions of separated and divorced white women who claimed custody and ownership of a proportion of slaves considered to be joint marital property. The expectation that white Barbadian women should also be allowed access to slave labour was possibly the decisive factor in the Council's adjudication of the suit instigated by Sarah Andrews (discussed in Chapter 3). A judicial judgement against Sarah may possibly have left her without slaves or estates, not only depriving Sarah of valuable property, but at the same time reducing her social status as a white woman.

It is also their whiteness that legitimises the status of Anne Phillips and her daughter Eleanor as free citizens, albeit second-class citizens by virtue of their gender. In Barbadian slave society, only free white citizens were legally empowered to own and dispose of property without constraints. A careful reading of Anne's will reveals the inherent power, social privileges and structural advantages that whiteness conferred on white colonial women.[2] Although patriarchal ideologies and practices constructed white women as dependent individuals subordinated to male authority and in need of the protection of white males, paradoxically, white women in colonial Barbados were themselves able to wield power over the bodies of African men and women.

This paradox raises questions about the body and social power. Feminists have argued that white women have rarely held agency over their own bodies. Yet the social and race relations of colonialism enabled white women who could not exercise autonomy over their own bodies to exercise the power of life and death over enslaved black peoples. It is important to note that Anne Phillips chose *not* to emancipate Kate but instead, as her will indicates, directed that Kate be allowed to live '*as if she had been freed*' [my emphasis]. Anne wanted Kate to 'enjoy the right of free passage', but this is clearly not the same thing as being free. Thus, a reading of Anne's will forces us to think also about the body as the site of both power and oppression, and moreover about the centrality of the body within the colonialist project.

The enslavement of African peoples rested on European justifications of black bodily and intellectual inferiority. In many ways, European discourses on race resonated with parallel debates on the nature of European womanhood. Enlightenment philosophers such as John Locke and Jean-Jacques Rousseau described white women in terms that were not unlike those used to describe Africans – childlike, in need of white male guidance and protection, closer to nature in their lack of reason, but possessed of a potentially dangerous sexuality, and therefore in need of control.[3] Feminist theorists since Mary Wollstonecraft have equated the subordination of (white) women with the enslavement of Africans but this metaphorical association misses and obscures some fundamental truths: that white women were not and could not be enslaved, and further, that white women were themselves deeply implicated within, and derived specific advantages and benefits from, colonialism. Anne Phillips's ownership of enslaved people, their bodies and their labour power, and her ability to define the limits of their individual lives and freedoms, indicates only one mode of power that white women derived from their position as members of the dominant ruling-class white group. White males simultaneously feared and revered white womanhood because white women were regarded as the potential source of disruption of an imagined white purity, while at the same time being the standard-bearers of virtuous, passive and dependent femininity. Though they were regarded as suspect creatures, the right of white women to live as free citizens was never threatened. Anne Phillips's whiteness shielded her from the possibility of enslavement, for in colonial slave societies, to be non-black meant to be non-enslaved, to enjoy an unquestionable and inalienable right to liberty.[4] Even though the nascent plantocracy frequently complained about the intractability of white indentured servants who constituted the primary labour force on Barbadian plantations before the advent of large-scale slavery, there was at no time any suggestion that servants be enslaved, and indentureship was always time-limited.[5] On another level, Anne Phillips's will reveals the implicit relationship between black and white women in the formation of gendered and racialised subjectivities, a theme that is pursued later in this chapter.[6]

Anne Phillips's last will and testament also invites us to reflect on the role of white women in the reshaping of African women's gendered identities, under the slave mode of production. Hilary Beckles has argued that slavery involved a regendering of male and female roles among enslaved Africans, but suggests that this process found its most brutal expression in the gendering of African women's roles. Beckles notes that the imperatives of plantation slavery demanded the 'defeminisation' of African women whose value, in contrast to white women, was grounded in their perceived natural ability to withstand the arduous field labour demanded by sugar production.[7] European ideologies of white womanhood reified white women precisely because their reproductive capacities represented the future of the white race, and the continuance of white supremacy. While paying homage to white motherhood and maternity, white Barbadians consistently negated these same qualities in black women. White Barbadians, then, configured white women as mothers, and black women as breeders.

This discursive distinction between white women as mothers and black women as breeders is clearly revealed in Anne Phillips's will when she turns her attention to the disposal of her remaining slave property. She bequeaths to her grandson Thomas the 'negro girl' Betty, who was in the early stages of pregnancy at the moment when her mistress sat down to pen her will. It is clear that for Anne, Betty's value lies solely in her reproductive capacity: she advised her daughter Eleanor that, in the event that Betty should miscarry her unborn child, Eleanor should 'sell and dispose of the said Betty ... and make and agree a good sale, and the money arising should be used to purchase another negro for my grandson'.[8] Anne's patent disregard for Betty and her unborn child signals her complicity in the devaluation of black motherhood. Betty's value resides solely in her (re)productive capacity as a breeder of slaves. Anne's directions to Eleanor regarding Betty's future suggest that white Barbadian women probably perceived black women as breeders and labourers. If, as Beckles suggests, white Barbadian women shared the same ideological values as white males, then the expectation must be that they neither rejected nor challenged the dominant ideologies of African women's gendered identities that were closely tied to their reproductive and productive labour functions.[9]

Critical scrutiny of Anne Phillips's will highlights the interconnections of gender and whiteness, and shows how whiteness functioned as a position of structural advantage within plantation society. It also reveals the ways in which women who may be constructed as objects may, at the same time, be active subjects with the propensity to objectivise 'others' to whom they stand in relationships of dominance. Anne Phillips's instructions to her daughter Eleanor for the sale of pregnant Betty are not suggestive of the actions of a victim. Rather, Anne's directives reveal her to be an economically shrewd agent acting in a rational-market manner, and expose her pro-slavery commitment. For in denying the slave woman Kate the ultimate human status of freedom, Anne implicitly signals her support for, and complicity in, the reproduction of slavery as an institution.

The right to own property served as a critical line of demarcation, establishing the boundaries between free white women and enslaved black women. Except for married women, white Barbadian women were autonomous, independent, and free participants in the plantation economy, and their acquisition and disposal of real estate property made them important actors in the market. In an era when property ownership signalled not only freedom, but the route to social power, influence, wealth and status, those women who were in a position to take advantage of the property market could seize whatever opportunities presented themselves, even when their property rights were constrained by law and custom. It is their power to own human property that identifies white women in the slave colonies as a distinct group.

White women's social position as pro-slavery agents (as indicated by their investments in, and ownership of, slaves and their shared political, social and economic interests with white males), suggests their adherence to, and support of, the pro-slavery ideology and practices that constituted the basis of Barbadian social relations. It is when white women are revealed as independent or semi-autonomous owners of female and male slaves that the notions of shared womanhood or common ground between white and black women in patriarchal plantocracies disintegrates. What they share through their gender is differentiated by racial and social status. White and black women might have been subject to the authority of white males, but black women and black men were further subjected to the authority of white women who could utilise law and violence to enforce their own authority over the bodies of black women and men. Elizabeth Spelman makes the point that, while white planters' wives lacked the patriarchal power of white men, they nevertheless enjoyed a degree of power, however derivative it might be, situating them in significantly different positions from black women, who lacked the same power to appropriate white bodies, or to whip with impunity. Neither black nor white women enjoyed the same unrestricted power as white males, but they were not subject to the same abuses of his power, and neither were they equally powerless in relation to him.[10] Therefore, to explicate white female agency in Caribbean plantation society and the implications for relations between women, some critical analysis of their independent activities as slaveholders is imperative. I argue that through their ownership of slaves, white women themselves targeted and preyed upon black women and men in pursuit of their own social and economic interests.

Enslaved black women represented the majority of the slave labour force in Barbados as early as 1673. Their lower purchase price (estimated by Richard Ligon to have been between £2/£3 sterling), and their potential for natural increase through reproduction, would undoubtedly have made them a more attractive proposition to female purchasers, especially for women of the middle to lower classes in need of domestic or urban workers.[11] Barbadian planters tried as far as possible to operate a balanced sex-ratio labour policy, but by the end of the seventeenth century female slaves outnumbered male slaves.[12] Possibly the mortality rates of male field hands was higher; the female slave majority stemmed not just from the planters' desire to ensure stability among the slave community, but also because the relatively larger numbers of white women demanded higher numbers of women slaves to meet their demands, both in the domestic world and the public spheres of the Barbadian markets. As I shall later show, although white males were the predominant owners of slaves in the plantation sector, white women dominated the ranks of slave-owners in the urban sectors of Barbados.

The emphasis in existing literature on white women as plantation wives serves to locate white female agency firmly within the domestic sphere, as 'helpmates' on white male-owned plantations, on which white male planters, attorneys, managers and overseers owned, directed and controlled, brutalised and abused the bodies of black individuals. White women's participation in the markets – whether as autonomous or semi-autonomous actors – belies the enduring representations of white women as unproductive actors, marginal to the slave economy. This chapter therefore challenges conceptualisations of white women as passive bystanders in the slave society and economy. By highlighting their activities and their pursuits of their interests in this sector, it is possible even from fragmentary evidence to argue that white women were not powerless plantation mistresses, or unwitting victims of a patriarchal venture; they were also, potentially and in practice, active, rational, economic actors, whose participation was pivotal in the reproduction of slavery, in securing the boundaries of whiteness and the dominance of the white racial group.

In what follows, I explore the nature and extent of white women's participation in the economy as slave-owners; women's property rights as they related to slaveholding; the routes through which women became slaveholders; and patterns of women's distribution of slaves through deeds of gifts, sales, and wills. I will further analyse the nature of relationships between white women and their female slaves, while also indicating some contradictions of manumission.[13] The arguments put forward derive from an analysis of property deeds, deeds of gifts, and probated wills. Having previously indicated the difficulties of using these documents as sources of data in investigating women as owners of real estate, I will only add that the difficulties apply also to their ownership of the enslaved.

Women as slave-owners: the social and legal basis

Caribbean slavery afforded white women a range of social and economic opportunities that were perhaps beyond the reach of most women in Europe. While landed property represented the apex of women's property ownership in Europe – a property relationship that was always constrained by custom and law – slavery provided white Caribbean women with a further dimension of property ownership: human lives. Furthermore, white slaveholding women came to wield a larger degree of authority and power over their slaves than could be possible with landed property that was, in the final analysis, subject to the ultimate authority of male owners.

It is extremely difficult to establish the extent to which white women were direct participants in the importation of African slaves. Part of this difficulty arises from the fact that bills of sale tended to identify males as primary purchasers, a practice that effectively submerged the extent of women's participation. As there were no legal barriers to women's ownership of slaves, it is possible that wealthy women also invested directly in the slave trade. It would be illuminating to establish just what proportion of investors in the African trade were white women, or their total share of the capital invested in, or profits garnered, from New World slavery. Even though bills of sales for the enslaved generally identify males as the purchasers, much of the capital used for investment in the African trade would have been derived from jointly held marital capital. This does not necessarily mean that all wives were willing partners in these transactions, but it does not require too great a stretch of imagination to imagine that many were willing investors. Women were as likely as men to value the material and economic benefits of investing in human property.

As the Barbadian plantation system was consolidated, and the internal slave market established, it becomes easier to find evidence of white women's independent transactions. This is particularly the case where the purchasers of slaves in the Barbadian internal market were widowed or single women, as property deeds denote gender and marital status of purchasers. The deeds are less helpful, however, in revealing the sources of women's purchases of slaves – did white women tend to buy directly from slave merchants and traders, or were their purchases the results of transactions between existing Barbadian slave-owners? Purchasing Creole (Barbadian-born) slaves might have been a more rational choice for both male and female owners, for Creole slaves were more likely to accept their status than slaves newly imported from Africa, and were therefore less likely to rebel against their enslavement.

The right of white women to slave labour was recognised by the legislative authorities. In April 1668, the Barbados House of Assembly passed an act that established the status of slaves as real estate, rather than chattel property. As such, they were counted as fixtures and fittings of an estate, and were therefore subject to legislation that governed the disposal of other forms of real estate. In the preamble to the Act, the legislators acknowledged that 'the considerable part of the wealth of this island consists in our negro slaves, without whose labour and service we should be utterly unable to manage our plants here, thereby relieving our own wants, and bringing the considerable increase of revenue'. The Committee went on to clarify the rights of widows whose husbands had died intestate:

> And whereas some lawsuits have arisen, and other great inconveniences have followed, where diverse persons dying intestate, have left their right and interest of their negro slaves to be by law disputed between their heirs, executors and administrators... wherein the various judgements have some times found for the one, and at other times for the other... for a full remedy of these inconveniences, and to the intent that the heir and widow, who claims dower, may not have land without negroes to manure the same, and to all other ends and purposes whatsoever.[14]

This was an important amendment, for it clearly acknowledged and enshrined white women's reliance on slave labour. No white woman could be expected to farm land or manage a plantation without slave labour. The Act also clarified the disposal of slaves through inheritance. Where disputes occurred over the rightful heir to an estate's slaves, for instance where a husband had died intestate, the widow's right to the slaves superseded all other claims, especially when it appeared that slaves were likely to be removed from the estate.

As has been previously noted, any property a wife brought to her marriage became that of her husband, and this was as true of slaves as it was of any other form of property. But it is apparent that wives did retain the right to direct and manage household slaves as they saw fit, with a minimum of intervention from their husbands. This is not to make the claim that white women's ownership of slaves was entirely free from the legal interference of men, but rather that their rights to own slaves went unchallenged. In marital disputes over property, for instance, courts commonly upheld women's rights over jointly owned slaves. In petitions for divorce or separation, women were generally granted slaves as part of a settlement. Hence in 1667, in addressing Anne Longstaff's petition for maintenance from her estranged husband Thomas, the Barbados Council took the view that the wayward Thomas was unlikely to observe their order that he give his wife three negro slaves belonging to him. They therefore resolved that the slaves in question be taken into the custody of the Provost Marshall, who would then place them into the keeping of James Lee, Anne's father. Though the slaves were henceforth to pass to Anne Longstaff, in order to stave off future attempts by Thomas to regain control of them, James Lee was to 'have and hold' the slaves for the sole use of his daughter and grandchildren. In this instance Thomas Longstaff, perhaps not wishing to become embroiled in struggles with his father-in-law, consented to the arrangement, and Anne was able to enjoy use of her negroes.[15] When Elizabeth Boswell also sought a separation on the grounds of her husband's 'ill usage' of her, the Assembly ruled that along with a share of her husband's real and personal estate, Elizabeth was also to receive 'two negroes by names Pickaninny and Diego'.[16] The evidence that courts defended white women's ownership of slaves points to a general recognition that the status of white 'ladies' derived in large part from slave ownership. To deprive white women of slaves was to erode the boundaries of whiteness, for it was in their ability to access slave labour that the racial and gender distance from black women was established. No black woman, even though free, could own a white woman, no matter how poor. But the reverse was always true. No matter how poor a white woman, she at least had the legitimate right to own, or gain access to, the labour of black women, men and children.

Property deeds relating to slave purchases are useful in indicating the marital status of single and widowed women. They are less helpful in untangling the slave purchases of married women, making it difficult to establish with certainty the extent of married women's independent purchases of slaves. As property law circumscribed married women's independent operations – with a few exceptions – slave purchases made by married women were generally joint transactions undertaken with their husbands. We do not know how far such purchases were instigated by married women, rather than by their husbands, and their independent transactions are therefore submerged. Katherine Adam's purchase of seven negro slaves in 1647 remains the sole instance in the numerous property deeds surveyed of independent purchases of slaves made by a married women.[17] Whether this represented a one-off purchase by Katherine, and why it was Katherine rather than her husband who made the sale is not known. But it provides tangible evidence that married women did buy slaves when empowered to do so. Hester Gascoigne, wife of Stephen Gascoigne, one of two agents of the Royal African Company of Traders in Barbados at the end of the seventeenth century, was identified from the deeds as a substantial planter. After her husband's death, Hester continued to make major investments in both land and slaves. That Hester's business activities only begin to appear in property deeds after her husband's death raises the question of whether she had, in fact, been an active partner in Stephen's trading activities.[18]

White women depended on slave labour not only because it freed them from the drudgery of domestic work, but also because slave labour was the means by which white women could secure a livelihood. Their dependence on slave labour was not confined to the plantation domestic sphere, either. Within the grand houses of the planters, the appropriation of slave labour enabled some wealthier white women to lead the leisured, pampered lives so witheringly described by Maria Nugent.[19] An apocryphal tale aptly illustrates the level of dependency of white women on their retinue of female house slaves. In the heat of a Barbadian afternoon, Mistress Anne sat down beside a closed window, fanning herself. As the room became unbearably hot and stuffy, the languid mistress called her servant Mary to tell 'Sukie to tell Quasheba to come open the window'. Or, as another example: the tale of Miss Ann, who while one day sewing some muslin handkerchiefs, dropped her needle. 'Polly', she called to her waiting maid, 'go tell Nancy to tell Judy to come pick up my needle!' Endless variations on the same theme are told and retold in the Caribbean, even today.

But we do not need to rely on such tales to establish the extent of women's dependency on slave labour. Property deeds and wills reveal that women bought, sold, inherited and hired slaves. Although deeds do not generally supply the motivations behind the purchase, it is clear that white women regarded slave labour as necessary to fulfilling their domestic responsibilities, and necessary also in the pursuit of independent economic ventures. When they perceived their proprietary rights over their enslaved to be threatened, they were willing to go to the law to protect their interests. In 1667, Avenina Bannatine petitioned the Barbados Assembly for assistance to help her recover ownership rights to Locust Hall plantation, together with 'negroes, cattle and stock' worth £20,000 sterling. Avenina complained to the Assembly that three years previously she had been 'most illegally dispossessed by order of Lord Willoughby who for the sum of £2,400 . . . sold the same, to one Edward Pye'.[20]

White Barbadian women's proprietary rights as slave-owners were upheld in the law courts, and even the poorest slaveholding white women could take recourse to the law to protect their property. Margaret Dwelling, 'an indigent minor', appeared before the Barbadian Assembly in 1672/3 to request that the court assign her a guardian so that she might pursue a claim against one Colonel George Thornborough who had 'detained' her negro boy Robin. Pleading poverty, Margaret successfully requested the services of court-appointed counsels to assist her suit against Colonel Thornborough.[21] Other women slave-owners fought for compensation when they lost their slaves. When a slave belonging to the widowed Ann Hawkins was executed on criminal charges, Ann successfully applied for an order of recompense to be paid. Accordingly, 'His excellency, taking the same into consideration, and it appearing the petitioner was very poor, declared with the consent of the Council, that he would issue a warrant for paying the petitioner the sum of £25 sterling for the loss of said negro'.[22] Without recourse to Robin's labour, Ann Hawkins would have been placed in a vulnerable economic position.

Within the ideological framework that legitimised white racial superiority, slave ownership signalled more than simply wealth – for even the poor could gain access to slave labour. Ownership of human property served both to demarcate racial identities and also to signal social status. The more slaves one owned, the higher one's status. The right to slave ownership secured white social status by legally marking the line between the free and the unfree. White women's access to land and other forms of real estate may have been restricted by law and custom, but their rights to enslaved bodies and their labour generally went unchallenged.

Women as slave-owners: social class and economic activity

How white women participated in slaveholding was determined primarily by their social class. At one end of the scale were elite women such as Lady Willoughby Yeamans and Madame Grace Silvester who, in 1679, each owned sugar plantations of over 700 acres; owning between them over 700 slaves. The extent of their property holdings placed them firmly among the ranks of the elite planters of their day. Barbados at the end of the seventeenth century was dominated politically and socially by 175 large planters. Only sixty-six of these planters did not hold political office, and of these, twenty-five were identified as women planters, minors or Quakers. Many more women were 'middling' planters, i.e. in possession of between thirty and 100 acres. It would have been extremely difficult to manage a plantation of 100 acres without the help of at least fifty slaves, for the general belief among Barbadian planters was that one slave was needed for every two acres of land in order to maximise production, although few but the wealthiest could afford the optimum number of slaves.[23]

For elite white women, slave ownership signified their wealth, social status and a measure of power. For poor white women such as Margaret Dwelling, the ownership of one or more slaves secured rather more than status as a member of the racially superior class. Slaveholding also provided a critical means of economic independence and security for poorer women. Beckles notes that the ownership of African slaves was a critical means of livelihood for white women of the middle to lower classes. Commonly, poorer women's economic activities were situated in the less lucrative sectors of the informal market economy that were generally shunned by white men. Property deeds reveal that collectively, white women comprised a significant proportion of Barbadian slave-owners. Beckles' assessment of white women's accumulationist strategies in Barbados suggests that their businesses were generally located within the periphery of the urban economy, particularly within the service industries that flourished in Bridgetown. So prominent was white women's participation in the slave economy of Barbados that by the early nineteenth century they were the foremost owners of slaves in the urban sector, especially in Bridgetown. Slave labour enabled white women to own and manage hotels and taverns, small shops and businesses. Beckles estimates that by the closing decades of slavery, white women owned fifty-four per cent of all those enslaved in Bridgetown.[24] In the rural areas, white women farmed smallholdings with the use of slave labour.[25]

An enslaved person bought at auction required an initial outlay of capital, but this could be recovered quickly through the common practice of 'hiring out'. White women who were either too poor to afford their own slaves, or who had insufficient slaves to meet their domestic or labour demands, commonly turned to hired labour. Enslaved people of both sexes were hired out to these households for a fee. Beckles has suggested that the hired slave market was a form of small business dominated by white women.[26] Women's participation in the slave hire businesses enabled white women to secure for themselves the domestic labour needed for their own houses, while at the same time providing them with an independent income. Slave labour underpinned many of the small-scale business enterprises operated by white women. In this way, white women who had been displaced from domestic labour on the plantations after the transition to slave labour were to some extent able to re-appropriate domestic labour through slave ownership. Pedro Welch argues that the mores of an ideological system built on racism bound even the poorest white women to the wealthy white elite. Even in the almshouses poor white women were allowed the laundry services of enslaved African women, paid for by the vestry.[27] Hence, slavery afforded even poor white women a dimension of power not attainable by their counterparts in non-slaveholding societies.

Although differentiated by social class, slave-owning offered all white women valuable social and economic opportunities. As the numerous surviving bills of sales, wills and other records bear testimony, white women of all social classes invested in the 'peculiar institution' that was New World slavery. Beckles has pointed out the specific demographic features of Barbadian society that produced a greater tendency for white women to participate in the market economy as autonomous agents, and to pursue independent accumulationist strategies based upon the ownership and possession of slaves.[28]

Routes to slave ownership

White women acquired slaves through a number of routes – by direct purchase at slave auctions, through private transactions with other individuals, through transfers of gifts, or through inheritance. For some women, marriage also provided the means to enter the ranks of the slave-owners, or to increase slaveholdings. In the following, we will take a closer look at these routes.

Deeds of sale

Mary Butler has noted that it was not unusual in plantation-era Barbados to witness white women fondling the genitals of male slaves on auction blocks before making a purchase.[29] There could have been few white women in Barbadian plantation society who did not understand the economic imperatives of slavery, and fewer still who were not apprised of current slave prices. Slavery brought social, economic and political benefits to investors, and the extent of white women's participation in the slave economy does not suggest that they were any less reluctant than males to invest in slave labour. Since a means of securing a livelihood was a critical issue for many white women, slave ownership, or the ability to access slave labour, was a vital means of procuring economic security and independence.

Women bought and sold slaves for a variety of reasons, although their motives for these transactions are not stated. It is not possible to know why individual women chose to sell slaves, and neither is it possible to know, in most cases, whether the vendor was disposing of some, rather than all, of her slaves. In February 1689 the widowed Sarah Almond paid £165 to John Belgrave for three slaves (two female and one male), a house, outbuildings and land. Why Sarah made the decision to move from rural St Lucy – where she had been living before her husband's death – to urban St Michael, is not known, but the purchase of the three slaves indicates that she may have been hoping to establish a small business venture, perhaps by hiring out the slaves, in that town.[30]

Many of the transactions in the deeds of sale occur during periods of economic depression. This suggests that many of those women may have been selling their entire possessions of slaves, land, and/or dwellings in order to join the exodus of disillusioned emigrants who left the island in search of better opportunities elsewhere. In 1685, Alice Baines of St Michael parish sold her plantation consisting of twenty-three negro slaves, together with houses, three coppers and two stills, cattle and stock, and various other items of real and personal property to John Boynton.[31] That she was selling her entire stock of slaves, along with land and houses, suggests that Alice intended to leave Barbados.

Conversely, the periodic crises that befell Barbados would have allowed other white women and men the opportunity to join the ranks of slaveholders as the value of land and slaves decreased. Many white women and men used these crises as an opportunity to increase their holdings, buying land and slaves from those leaving Barbados. Hester Gascoigne paid £210 for ten acres of land and four slaves, 'one negro man known and called by the name of Toby, and two negro women Nam and Amah and one female child called Young Amah with all the offspring of their several bodies'. A year later Hester purchased seventeen more slaves: men, women and children. That the majority of the slaves in Hester's purchases were male is highly suggestive of Hester's intention to operate a sizable plantation, if she was not already doing so.[32]

Widows were frequent participants in these transactions, suggesting that the death of a husband was often the spur to women's entry into the slave labour market, and moreover that women's independent acquisition of slaves was linked to their marital status. Of forty purchases involving white women, only six were the joint purchases of married couples. This does not mean that married women did not buy slaves, but that males were more likely to be identified as the main or sole purchaser, a practice that would hide the real extent of married women's participation in the slave market. But at the same time, unmarried women made fewer purchases than widows. Only seven purchasers were identified as spinsters. That spinsters were less likely to be purchasers indicates that they lived in family households where slaves were already present, and were likely to make independent purchases only when they lived alone. The relatively low number of slaves purchased by spinsters, generally no more than a single slave, might also indicate that these buyers were more likely to be from the poorer classes. Overall, the greater number of widowed women involved in the sale of slaves would suggest that inheritance from their deceased husbands placed widows on a surer financial footing, enabling them to invest in slaves, if only on a small scale.

Strikingly, few of the transactions involve the sale of slaves by white women; rather, the majority of deeds involving women record the *acquisition* of slaves. Of fifty deeds of sale examined, only eleven involved the sale of slaves by women, while thirty-nine recorded women's purchases of slaves. Two further trends are suggested by these data. First, the numbers of slaves involved in individual transactions were generally low. With one or two exceptions, the number of slaves in any one transaction did not amount to more than four. Second, the majority of slave purchases by women tended to be adult females and/or young girls. In the fifty property deeds analysed, a total of 105 slaves were transferred between owners. Of these, women and young girls constituted over half (sixty-five) of the total number of enslaved, while men and young boys accounted for another thirty-one; the gender of another nine slaves was not declared. Deeds of sale provide evidence of women's participation in the wider economy. Deeds of gifts, however, indicate the distribution of the enslaved, as property, between a relatively small circle of women and their relatives and friends.

Deeds of gifts

The extent of women's ownership of slaves was in part due to the widespread practice of conveying slaves as gifts. Parents frequently gave a daughter the gift of at least one slave on her marriage, or when she reached the age of majority, whichever came soonest. In a survey of twenty-one deeds in which women were the sole conveyors of slaves, a total of fourteen women acquired slaves from mothers, aunts, other female relatives or friends. Together, the deeds record the disposal of thirty-six slaves. The majority of slaves (twenty-seven) conveyed in these transfers were women or young girls. Only nine of the slaves in these transactions were male, and of this number six were described as boys or young males.[33] In 1685, Katherine Swinhoe gave to her married daughter, also called Katherine, 'for her own proper use and benefit and disposal one negroe man named Pumy and one negro woman named Wheeler and her increase'.[34] In 1690, the widow Ruth Bowen gave her daughter Elizabeth Alford the deeds to 'one negro woman Judith to have, hold, dispense of, to take and enjoy'[35] and, in 1728, Anne Chambers of St Thomas gave her daughter the deeds to eight slaves.[36]

Marriage also presented further opportunities for white women to acquire slaves. Prior to his 1690 marriage to the widowed Margey Lee, Thomas Hickock bestowed on his future wife a wedding present of four negroes, 'one negro man by name of Effe and Genefer who is the said Effe's wife and one negro girl by name Reato and one negro girl by name Rose'.[37] Thomas directed that his wife should have sole ownership of the slaves, but without access to her will, it is impossible to know whether he kept his promise. Of course, while marriage could be a route to slave ownership, it could also threaten women's ownership and control over any slaves they brought to the marriage. This knowledge compelled some women to devise premarital settlements, as examples in Chapter 3 revealed.

Male relatives and friends also benefited in the conveyance of slaves by deed of gift. For unspecified reasons, Sarah Almond gave John Bellgrave '10 negros, men, women and children'[38]. Though their relationship is not specified, it seems certain that the two were related. Five male relatives also presented female relatives and friends with a total of eleven slaves. Of this number, six were female slaves, two were described as boys or young males, and the gender of three others was not stated. Thomas Walker transferred the deed of ownership of 'one negro girl and all her issue' to his niece Mary Porter,[39] and Adam

Sinkler of St Lucy gave his married daughter Sarah three negro slaves, whose gender was not specified.[40] The remaining deeds of gifts documented the transfer of slaves from women donors to male recipients.

Beyond a general declaration of affection and consideration, deeds of gifts rarely stated the benefactor's motivation, although, overwhelmingly, the majority of these transfers of slaves were from mother to daughter, an indication of women's concern for their daughter's future security. That most of the transactions involve only a few slaves might indicate that the majority of the individuals involved were of the middling to poorer classes.

Wills

A similar pattern of gender bias is evident in the distribution of slaves in probated wills. Women were more likely to bequeath slaves to other women, and daughters in particular were the recipient of slaves through their mother's wills. Of a total of fifty-two wills devised by women, just over half (twenty-eight) contained bequests of slaves, land, money and other items of property, while the other wills contained bequests of land, and items of personal property, but no slaves. Nineteen of these testators were mothers. From these mothers, seventeen daughters and four granddaughters were the main beneficiaries of over thirty slaves. In the remaining wills, the slaves were either bequeathed to other relatives including mothers, sisters, aunts, grandsons, sons, and friends. In three cases, the slaves were either to be manumitted or sold off to pay estate debts.

An assessment of women's wills indicates the extent of slave ownership among women, and to some extent it enables us to grasp the meanings that slave-owning held for white women. Although the ability of married women to dispose of slaves belonging to the marital estate was constrained to some extent by law, some women probably viewed the ability to dispose of their slaves in a way that suited them as a measure of power, not only over the slaves they held, but also over those with expectations of inheriting. However, some women may have found their ambitions tempered by the terms of their husbands' wills that prevented them from selling or disposing of estate slaves. Alexander Bentley's will of 1681 bequeathed a plantation in Carolina, and the negroes on his Barbadian estate, to his wife Mary, but stipulated that the negroes on his Barbadian estate 'should not be sold or sent out of this island, but they may be hired out'.[41] Nathaniel Cave of Christchurch, however, gave his wife complete freedom to decide the fates of their jointly owned slaves after his death. In his 1779 will, Nathaniel left explicit instructions that his wife should have 'full power to dispose of my twelve negroes as she shall make choice at the time of her death or her remarriage'.[42] It is likely that the couple were childless, for in most cases, husbands tried to ensure that their estates remained intact for an heir. Other men tried to provide guidance for their wives in the future management of plantation estates. William Worrell of St Michael left his wife an annuity of £30 and her living on his estate, but 'only during her widowhood'. William further entreated his wife and daughter Susan to 'join together their strength of negroes together [on my plantation] and mutually work together, as I did in my lifetime. They are to be maintained on the place ... in order to enable them the sooner to pay my just debts and funeral expenses.'[43]

In terms of the distribution of slave ownership by gender, white women were more likely to own a greater number of female slaves than men. Pedro Welch provides a profile of the typical female slaveowner: urban-based, in possession of ten slaves or fewer, of whom most were female.[44] This typology is supported by the findings of my survey of wills. Of the fifty-two white women in the sample of probate wills, a majority (eighty-nine per cent), owned female slaves. These enslaved women would commonly be hired out to labour either in the households or fields, and performed a wide range of occupations – as wet-nurses, field hands, hairdressers, washerwomen, cooks, domestic servants, or in some instances, as prostitutes. Beckles argues that a significant number of black slaves were pushed into prostitution. A thriving sex industry located around the Barbadian ports also provided white women with a lucrative – if not respectable – market niche, as they came to dominate the less desirable markets of the Barbadian plantation economy[45].

By way of contrast, within the sample of ninety-six wills, male testators were more likely to leave landed property, i.e. plantations or land, to beneficiaries. This differential can possibly be accounted for by the fact that slaves, as real estate, were tied to the plantation and could not be easily removed. In any case, wives and children were more likely to be the recipients of slaves. Over half of the women within the sample bequeathed at least one slave to another individual. While many women distributed other forms of property (land, houses, jewellery, clothing, money), to their circle of kin and friends, they were more likely to leave slaves than any other form of property.

Thus inheritance was a critical route through which women were able to enter the ranks of the slave-owners, or to increase their holdings. In this way, Mary Stansford became the owner of 'one negro woman and her son, a mulatto boy' on the death of her friend Susannah Jones in 1750.[46] Mary Hunt's will of 1720 also left 'one negro and her increase' to her daughter and her grandchildren.[47] In the same year, Mary Calvin bequeathed two negro slaves to her niece Anne Turpin and her god-daughter Mary West.[48] Mary Hall left her married daughter Mary Bushall 'four negroes and my little white horse'. Another daughter, Frances, a spinster, was to receive six slaves, '4 female and 2 males, my great silver tankard, 9 silver spoons, one large spoon, the largest silver salver, a dozen silver teaspoons, a cedar chest of drawers, a large black hanging glass, all the china, a black walnut table, my chaise and a horse'. Presumably Mary's decision to leave her unmarried daughter the greater part of her estate reflects her desire that Frances should have a reasonable dowry, or at least a decent standard of living.[49]

Much as wills may tell us of their author's intentions, there is no way now of knowing with certainty how far their wishes were followed. For instance, although parents generally provided well for their children, the arrival of a new step-parent could threaten a child's inheritance, particularly when widowed mothers remarried. Fathers often took steps to ensure that their children's inheritance would be protected from a new stepfather, and the courts generally tried to protect children's inheritances. An example includes the 1681 lawsuit bought by Margaret Dickinson in which she appealed to the court to prevent her stepfather selling Young, a slave boy willed to her by her deceased father. While stepfathers posed the greater threat to a child's inheritance, stepmothers could present an equal threat, as Maud Beckles, wife of Thomas Beckles, recognised.

Writing her will in 1734 when she was terminally ill, Maud Beckles acknowledged Thomas's proprietorial rights and interest in the slaves she had brought to the marriage. However, she secured from Thomas his agreement that he would waive his interests in favour of their four daughters. When Maud died soon after, her thirteen slaves were shared out between the couple's four daughters. Thomas took a new wife, Margaret, relatively quickly, but took care to safeguard his daughters' inheritance left to them by their mother. In his will, also written in 1734 after his remarriage, he reiterated that he had relinquished all proprietary rights to the thirteen slaves, and confirmed that their ownership had now passed to Maud's four daughters. Anticipating that his son Robert might protest this arrangement, Thomas appealed to him to allow his sisters to hold the slaves without interference.[50]

Women's wills often exhibited a degree of financial acuity in the transfers of their slaves. For instance, many directed that specific slaves should be sold off to pay their 'just debts and funeral expenses'. Jean Hooper's will asked that her three gentlemen friends should look after and rent out her houses and other property, including seven slaves. The profits, she instructed, should go to her son, and on his death should pass to her three daughters. Jean also directed that her old slave Affiniah was to be hired out as a laundry woman, and her son George to receive the income from Affiniah's rental.[51] Elizabeth Phillips also viewed her slaves as a means of clearing her debts, directing in her will that 'my seven negroes be hired out at the best advantage ... all the money arising ... to be applied to the payment of my debts and funeral expenses'.[52]

Given the predominance of white women as owners of female slaves, it is important to consider some aspects of their relations with these slaves. American studies of Southern slavery have already documented the antagonism that existed between white and black women.[53] My intention here, then, is to explore two areas rarely addressed. Firstly, white women's appropriation of black female slave bodies, their reproductive capacities and labour, and secondly the role of white women as manumitters of slaves. I examine these relationships through an analysis of slave-owning women's wills.

Subordinated women and subordinating women

Given women's proportionately higher ownership of female slaves, it is not surprising that the majority of slaves mentioned in women's wills and other property transactions are female. Perhaps women's greater ownership of female slaves can be explained by reference to white women's greater difficulties in maintaining discipline over male slaves – although from the testimonies of slaveholding women such as Elizabeth Fenwick, female slaves often proved equally intractable. Elizabeth's account of her time as a slaveholder is a litany of complaints against her domestics, who time and again resisted her efforts at imposing discipline.[54] Female slaves were primarily valued by slaveholders for their reproductive capacity. As Deborah Gray White has argued, much of a young slave woman's worth rested in her ability to have children, and this is demonstrated in the reluctance of many slave-owners to purchase slaves known to be infertile, or past childbearing age.[55] The long-term value of fertile female slaves did not escape white women either. As slaveholders in a rational market economy, white women's participation in the slave economy conferred on them the rights over the reproductive labour of slave women. In numerous instances, the unborn children of female slaves were distributed among family and friends before they were even conceived. Thus, Catherine Searle's will, devised in 1765, expressed her desire that her mother Thomasina should receive her 'mulatto wench' Sarah. At the time the will was devised, Sarah was in the early stages of pregnancy. Catherine directed that Sarah's unborn child was to go to her brother Aron. Any future children Sarah bore were to go to 'each of my sons Isaac, Jacob and John... one apiece of her first three children'.[56]

To many white female slave owners, slaves represented no more than a commodity – albeit in human form – that could be bought, sold, exchanged, mortgaged, hired out or sold as the necessity arose. This is evident from the way in which women disposed of their slaves in their wills, often without regard for the welfare and future of individual slaves and their families. Some women clearly held genuine regard for slaves, and tried to ensure that slave families remained together, or were passed to a friend or relative who could be trusted to look after them. Other women used their wills as an instrument for conferring freedom on favoured slaves, but generally few women were willing to give even favoured slaves their freedom.

Anne Phillips's instructions for the disposal of her pregnant slave girl Betty reflect a rational market strategy pursued by male and female planters alike towards fertile female slaves. Patently, Anne Phillips's wishes for the distribution of Betty and her children were viewed not as a callous act of inhumanity towards Betty and her unborn child, but rather as the generous gesture of a loving grandmother towards her grandchild. It is unlikely that Betty would have been aware of her mistress's plans for her, but the prospect of being sold away from family and friends would no doubt have caused her great distress. From Anne's perspective, Betty's worth laid solely in her fertility.

It is precisely at this juncture that the limits of any shared bonds between mistresses and their female slaves are most evident. Enslaved women lived with the knowledge that a mistress, no matter how affectionate or kind, could at any time effect their separation from husbands, children, family and friends. In the final analysis, slaves were valuable items of property, with no rights to their own children. As Barbara Bush has suggested, the root source of the integral relations between white and black in the New World plantation societies was the exercise of power over the bodies of others.[57] Although excluded from the arena of political power in their society, white women's ownership of human bodies confirmed a specific form of power that has rarely been recognised. As mistress, Anne Phillips wielded power over the bodies and futures of her slaves. She could legitimately appropriate not only the physical, domestic labour of her females slaves, but literally, their bodies and reproductive capacity also. Her seemingly callous disregard for Betty, and for Betty's own feelings about the eventual fate of her unborn child, was merely an expression of that power.

Yet Anne did not perceive of all of her slaves as disposable objects of labour. The concern she displayed over the future welfare of Kate serves as a means of reflection on one of the most curious contradictions of the peculiar institution of slavery. Whatever the level of intimacy and affection between them, Kate remained a slave, albeit comfortably provided for. Even in the charitable eyes of her mistress, she would always remain a slave. As a white woman in a racially ordered society organised around the basis of unfree slave labour, Anne's unwillingness to manumit Kate signals a firm attachment to the pro-slavery ideology of the planter class. However, Anne's decision not to manumit Kate could, in one sense, be construed as a charitable act. As a free, elderly and possibly infirm woman, Kate would have had to fend for herself. Moreover, by assigning Judy as Kate's own slave, Anne's intentions might have been to keep the two sisters together, to prevent one or other of them being sold off. On the other hand, Kate might well have preferred to risk the uncertainties of freedom; but her voice, and that of her sister-slave Judy, is silenced within this narrative.

In the final event, Anne's actions were driven by economic motives. Should the young slave Betty suffer a miscarriage, then plainly she represented a capital liability, and as such, could be easily disposed of. In authorising Eleanor's disposal of Betty, Anne displays a shrewd grasp of the economic value of fertile female slaves, who were viewed first and foremost as reproducers of the next generation of slaves. Anne Phillips knew as surely as any male planter knew that a good 'breeder' was critical to augmenting the economic wealth of the planter's family. By authorising Betty's sale, Anne was merely acting in a market-rational manner. Despite the depths of intimacy that sometimes arose between mistress and slave, the racial ideology that framed their world view did not permit slaveholding women to regard even their most favoured slaves as anything other than their social and racial inferiors, who were bound to perpetual servitude.[58]

Anne Phillips's will represents a particularly interesting example of its kind, but is not an isolated example, although the lengths she went to in providing for Kate's welfare exceeded that of the normal mistress-slave relationship. There are several other examples. In her will, drafted in 1761, Margaret Phillips of Speightstown directed her daughter Prudence to 'provide a house for my negro woman Melly to live in, and that no hard labour be imposed on her, and that she be decently buried when she dies, at the charge of my estate'. Her will also stipulated that Melly was to receive an annuity of forty shillings for the rest of her life.[59] Elizabeth Greaves, a spinster of St Lucy, also directed that all her slaves should be freed and given land and money to help them establish themselves.[60] And Mary Hill, a widow, similarly directed that her slave Dick should 'be given his liberty and freedom' on her death.[61]

Sometimes, the testator's desires to manumit individual slaves conflicted with the beneficiary's own ambitions or wishes. When Elizabeth Reece, a spinster of St Michael, died, she intended that her mulatto slave Mary should pass to her sister Hester Reece, also a spinster. Should Hester die, Mary was to revert to the ownership of a relation, John Bascomb, 'in trust and in confidence that he will enable the said Mary to work for and obtain her freedom'.[62] However, it appears that Mary was destined to remain a slave, for when Hester died, her will directed that Mary be sold 'for the satisfaction of debt and funeral expenses'.[63] The question to be asked is why Elizabeth did not herself free Mary, if this was her ultimate intention?

Caribbean historians have argued that white women were less likely to be manumitters of their slaves. Pedro Welch claims that Barbadian records indicate that white males were more likely to manumit slaves, and the majority of these were more likely to be female slaves. However, as he points out, the reverse was true in Bridgetown, where white women were the principal manumitters of slaves.[64] To some extent, this is borne out in my own study of wills. Of fifty-two female testators, three made provision for the manumission of their slaves in their wills, while a further three made arrangements for other slaves to be 'pensioned off' to live out their lives in a state of quasi-freedom. Of forty-four wills devised by males, only one male testator manumitted or made provision for slaves.

Why did some women manumit their slaves? It is possible to read women's acts of manumission as a conscious rejection of the pro-slavery ideology of the society. Yet this is too simple an answer to a complex question, as underscored by the example of Anne Phillips. Women no doubt manumitted slaves for a variety of reasons, but it is clear that a critical factor in the decision to manumit was whether the testator had children or other close relatives who might expect to inherit. In three cases of manumission, one woman was listed as 'spinster', while the other two were widows. No children or other close relatives were mentioned in these wills, and it is possible therefore to conclude that these three women were childless and, having no direct heirs, were then free to manumit their slaves.

This chapter has outlined the general features of white female participation in the economy of Barbadian plantation society. Although the sample represents only a small proportion of documents, it does suggest definite trends in women's ownership of slaves. When the extent of their participation within the slave economy is analysed, it becomes clear that whatever the ideas and practices that constrained women's material conditions, women nevertheless resisted these limitations. Amy Louise Erickson has observed, 'the twin pillars of common law control over women's lives – primogeniture inheritance and coverture in marriage – were draconian in theory, but had less impact in practice.[65] White men may have dominated the rural plantation economy, but in the urban sector, white women dominated the ranks of urban slaveholders. Because the focus has been on males as the primary participants in the slave economy, the extent of white women's participation in Barbadian plantation economy has been underestimated. Butler's study of women's economic involvement concluded that at emancipation, white women in Barbados accounted for thirty-seven per cent of the total claims for compensation.[66] What Butler does not make clear, however, is whether these claims were submitted by single women (widowed or spinsters), or were the joint submissions of marital couples. If the former proves to be the case, then the actual extent of women's involvement may be somewhat higher.

In racially stratified Barbadian society, the right of white women to access property was critical to the stability of the white ruling class. To exclude white women from access to property, particularly to slaves, would clearly have severely undermined their positions as members of the superior white ruling class, and possibly alienated their support for the pro-slavery ideologies. Thus, property ownership served as a marker of whiteness, and women of all social classes acquired access to slave labour.

White women's structural position within the dominant white ruling class severely undermined considerations of shared gender identity, or a shared sisterhood, with enslaved (or free) black women. As Fox-Genovese has noted of Southern slavery, the mutual antagonisms that characterised relations between white and black women effectively precluded the possibility of a shared female consciousness. In this respect, 'gender counted for little'.[67] Ultimately, as pro-slavery agents, white women's interests lay not with enslaved women, but with the enslavers. An alliance with enslaved women would undermine their own precarious but privileged position, and would serve to threaten their own socio-economic and political interests. Some women might have expressed reservations about the system, but few were willing or able to relinquish the privileges that accrued from slavery.

Perhaps one reason that white women remain so invisible within Caribbean economic histories is the assumption that most white women were tied to plantations under the authority of males. Patently, the high ratio of unmarried or widowed women who lived in single households and pursued independent livelihoods forces a reconsideration of the extent and limits of male patriarchy. Although white women were clearly subordinated to white male authority, the social relations of Barbadian slave society throw into sharp relief the ways in which patriarchy as a system of female oppression intersected with other forms of domination – in this case, the matrix of race, class and gender served to create a complex web of social relations. Within this system, white women's property relations placed them in alliance with the pro-slavery, patriarchal elite. At one and the same time, white women were therefore both oppressed and oppressor, victim and victimiser.

This chapter has explored some elements of white women's relationships to enslaved property. Many more questions need to be asked. Little is known of the extent of white women's involvement in the Atlantic slave trade, and without further research, it is not possible to understand the full extent of their participation. Since white women were the primary sources of acculturation for many slaves, particularly of domestic slaves, how did white women's attitudes shape the gender identity of female slaves? How did white males and African slaves perceive white female slave-owners? How did white women view themselves as slave-holders? How did white women view their relationships with the slaves – female and male – that they owned? What alternatives presented themselves to women who could not, or would not join the ranks of the slave-owners? How far did white Barbadian women develop or share a sense of womanhood with female slaves? In a climate hostile to independent women, how did women manage successful plantations and business operations? And if property ownership served as a demarcation of whiteness, what were the mechanisms through which white women constructed an identity that was distinct from those coloured individuals who also gained the right to own property? Finally, it seems clear that the ability of white women to participate independently or otherwise in the slave markets was determined by locality also. How typical were Barbadian white women of their counterparts in other plantation societies of the same epoch? Exploring the lives of plantation mistresses in North Carolina in the next chapter, we may find some answers, but questions will remain; for example why, unlike women in the slaveholding states of the North American mainland, did white Barbadian women not emerge as part of the nascent feminist and anti-slavery movements? Social historians have only recently begun to address these and other questions, and there is still much room for an economic history that will lead to the recovery and understanding of the full extent and nature of white women's socio-economic and political participation in the life of plantation societies.

I have outlined previously some of the problems embedded within universalistic representations of the 'white colonial woman'. A common social positioning of women can only be claimed by leaving unexamined evidence of white women's agency in producing and reproducing the ideologies and practices of slave economy and society, and the significance of white identity in elevating white women above all other women; the simultaneous significance of social class in dividing and diversifying them, despite their commonalties of gender and whiteness. Representations of white colonial women as victims of patriarchy can illuminate white male power over white feminine identities, bodies and sexualities, but do little to further understanding of the ways in which gender is mediated by race, nor the ways in which those who are constructed as social objects may seek to challenge their defined status in their quests for 'subjecthood'.

Notes

1 Will of Anne Phillips, E.M. Shilstone Notebooks, No. 9/23/16, Barbados Museum and Historical Society (Hereafter BMHS).
2 This is not to suggest that white women shared the same relationship to property as white males. Until late in the nineteenth century, only widowed and single women were empowered to devise their own wills. Married women could do so only with the consent of their husbands. The point I am making, however, is that their legally defined status as property meant that enslaved African women and men could not freely decide the disposal of any property they possessed, for property cannot own property.
3 As Anderson and Zinsser have commented, 'there was no Renaissance or Scientific Revolution for women, in the sense that the goals and ideals of those movements were applicable to men, so there was no Enlightenment for women'. Of course, there was no Enlightenment for black people, either men or women, as the ideals of this movement were applicable only to white European males. For a discussion of the Enlightenment *philosophes'* attitudes towards European women, see Bonnie Anderson and Judith Zinsser, *A History of their Own: Women in Europe from prehistory to the present*, Vol. 2 (Harmondsworth: Penguin Books, 1990).
4 Ruth Frankenberg (ed.), *Displacing Whiteness: Essays in social and cultural criticism* (Durham: Duke University Press, 1997), p. 10.
5 For discussions of planter treatment of and attitudes towards white indentured servants, see Jill Sheppard, *The 'Redlegs' of Barbados: Their origin and history* (New York: KTO Press, 1977); Richard Ligon, *A True and Exact History of the Island of Barbados* (London: Frank Cass, 1970).
6 There is an extensive body of scholarship on the relationship between black and white women and the formation of gendered and racialised identities during the era of plantation slavery. See for instance: Hilary Beckles, *Centering Woman: Gender discourses in Caribbean slave society* (London: James Currey, 1999); Verene Shepherd et al (eds), *Engendering Slavery: Caribbean women in historical perspective* (London: James Currey, 1995); Barbara Bush, *Slave Women in Caribbean Society 1650-1838* (London: James Currey, 1990); Barbara Bush, 'History, Memory, Myth: Reconstructing the history (or histories) of Black women in the African diaspora', in Stephanie Newell (ed.), *Images of African and Caribbean Women: Migration, displacement, diaspora*, Occasional Paper No. 4, Centre for Commonwealth Studies, University of Stirling (1996).
7 Hilary Beckles, 'Centering Women: The political economy of gender in West African and Caribbean slavery' in Christine Barrow (ed.), *Caribbean Portraits: Essays on gender ideologies and identities* (Kingston: Ian Randle Publishers, 1998), p. 95.

8   Will of Anne Phillips, *E.M. Shilstone Notebooks*, No. 9/23/16 BMHS.
9   Beckles, 'White Women and Freedom', in *Centering Women*, p. 61; see also Barbara Bush, 'Hard Labour: Women, childbirth and resistance in British Caribbean slave societies', in David Barry Gaspar and Darlene Clark Hine (eds), *More than Chattel: Black women and slavery in the Americas* (Bloomington: Indiana University Press, 1996).
10 Elizabeth Spelman, *Inessential Woman: Problems of exclusion in feminist thought* (London: Women's Press, 1990).
11 Ligon, *A True and Exact History of Barbados*.
12 Hilary Beckles, *Natural Rebels: A social history of enslaved Black women in Barbados* (London: Zed Books, 1989).
13 Manumission was the legal instrument through which the enslaved could be freed by their owners.
14 'An Act Declaring the Negroes of this Island to be Real Estate', in Richard Hall, *Acts Passed in the Island of Barbados, 1643-1762* (Printed for Richard Hall: London, 1875).
15 *Council of Assembly Minutes, 1667-1682* (BMHS).
16 *Council of Assembly Minutes, 1667-1682* (BMHS).
17 *Barbados Property Records* (Deeds), RB3/Vol. 2/271, Barbados Archives (Hereafter, BA).
18 *Barbados Property Records* (Deeds of Sale) RB3/4/506 (BA).
19 See: Phillip Wright (ed.), *Lady Nugent's Journal of her Residence in Jamaica from 1801-1805* (Kingston: Institute of Jamaica, 1966).
20 *E.M. Shilstone Notebooks*, No. 59/442 (BMHS).
21 *Minutes of Council of Assembly, 1667-1682* (BMHS).
22 *Minutes of Council of Assembly, 1667-1682* (BMHS).
23 Richard Dunn, *Sugar and Slaves: The rise of the planter class in the English West Indies, 1624-1713* (New York: W.W. Norton, 1972), p. 98.
24 Hilary Beckles, 'White Women and Slavery in the Caribbean', *History Workshop Journal* 36 (1993), p. 70.
25 Ibid., p. 71.
26 Ibid. p. 71.
27 Pedro Welch, 'Urban Context of the Slave Plantation System: A framework for the study of Bridgetown, 1680-1834'. Seminar paper No. 5, Department of History, University of West Indies, Cave Hill, Barbados, 1988; see also: Welch, *Slave Society in the City: Bridgetown, Barbados 1680-1834* (Kingston: Ian Randle Publishers, 2003), p. 298.
28 Beckles, 'White Women and Slavery', p. 69.
29 Kathleen Mary Butler, cited in Hilary Beckles, 'Historicizing Slavery in West Indian Feminisms', in *Feminist Review* 59 (Summer 1998).
30 *Barbados Property Records* (Deeds of Sales), RB3/4/500 (BA).
31 *Barbados Property Records* (Deeds of Sale), RB3/4/151 (BA).
32 *Barbados Property Records* (Deeds of Sale) RB3/4/506, RB3/4/584, RB3/4/589 (BA).
33 Thirty deeds of gifts were examined. Some of these deeds included gifts of land and slaves, land only or slaves only. The deeds analysed here fall in to the latter category. That is, they convey slaves only.
34 *Barbados Property Records* (Deeds of Gifts), RB3/Vol. 4/189 (BA)
35 *Barbados Property Records* (Deeds of Gifts), RB3/Vol. 4/612 (BA).
36 *Barbados Property Records* (Deeds of Gifts), RB3/42/93 (BA).
37 *Barbados Property Records* (Deeds of Gifts), RB3/Vol. 5/264 (BA).
38 *Barbados Property Records* (Deeds of Gifts), RB3/Vol. 4/464 (BA).
39 *Barbados Property Records* (Deeds of Gifts), RB3/Vol. 36/342 (BA).
40 *Barbados Property Records* (Deeds of Gifts), RB3/Vol. 36/224 (BA).
41 Will of Alexander Bentley, *E.M. Shilstone Notebooks*, No. 3/17/289 (BMHS).
42 Will of Nathaniel Cave, *E.M. Shilstone Notebooks*, Vol. 5/23/219 (BMHS).
43 Will of William Worrell, *E.M. Shilstone Notebooks*, Vol. 7/28/498 (BMHS).
44 Welch, *Slave Society in the City*, p. 294.

45 Ibid., pp. 88–93.
46 *Barbados Property Records* (Wills), RB3/Vol. 21/438 (BA).
47 *Barbados Property Records* (Wills), RB3/ Vol. 6/65 (BA).
48 *Barbados Property Records* (Wills), RB3/Vol. 21/397 (BA).
49 *Barbados Property Records* (Wills), RB3/Vol. 21/318 (BA).
50 Will of Maud Beckles, *E.M. Shilstone Notebooks*, No.18/24/279 (BMHS).
51 Will of Jean Hooper, *E.M. Shilstone Notebooks*, Vol. 6/6/152 (BMHS).
52 Will of Elizabeth Phillips, *E.M. Shilstone Notebooks*, Vol. 9/22/156 (BMHS).
53 See for instance, Elizabeth Fox-Genovese, *Within the Plantation Household: Black and White women of the Old South* (Chapel Hill: University of North Carolina Press, 1988); Patricia Morton (ed.), *Discovering the Women in Slavery: Emancipating perspectives on the American past* (Athens: University of Georgia Press, 1996).
54 A.F. Fenwick (ed.), *The Fate of the Fenwicks: Letters to Mary Hays, 1798–1828* (London, 1927).
55 Deborah Gray White, *Ain't I A Woman: Female slaves in the plantation South* (New York: Norton and Norton, 1985).
56 Will of Catherine Searle, *E.M. Shilstone Notebooks*, Vol. 16/ 31/281 (BMHS).
57 Barbara Bush, 'White "Ladies", Coloured "Favourites", and Black "Wenches": Some considerations on sex, race and class factors in social relations in white Creole society in the British Caribbean', *Slavery and Abolition* 2:3 (December 1981), p. 246.
58 Fox-Genovese, *Within the Plantation Household*, pp. 134–135.
59 Will of Margaret Phillips, *E.M. Shilstone Notebooks*, Vol. 9/301/319 (BMHS).
60 Will of Elizabeth Greaves, *E.M. Shilstone Notebooks*, Vol. 16/66/206 (BMHS).
61 Will of Mary Hill, *E.M. Shilstone Notebooks*, Vol. 2/6/177 (BMHS).
62 Will of Elizabeth Reece, *E.M. Shilstone Notebooks*, Vol. 14/1/171 (BMHS).
63 Will of Hester Ann Reece, *E.M. Shilstone Notebooks*, Vol. 28/60/80 (BMHS).
64 Welch, *Slave Society in the City*, p. 134.
65 Amy Louise Erickson, *Women and Property in Early Modern England* (London: Routledge, 1978), p. 224.
66 Kathleen Mary Butler, *The Economics of Emancipation: Jamaica and Barbados 1823–1843* (Chapel Hill: University of North Carolina Press, 1995), p. 95.
67 Fox-Genovese, *Within the Plantation Household*, pp. 47–48, 326–327.

CHAPTER SIX

'She Would Labor Almost Night and Day': white women, property rights and slaveholding in North Carolina

When Alice Ward Loomis, a widowed plantation mistress, fell in love in 1822, she could not have imagined that her efforts to woo and win Harris Loomis, the object of her affections, would be placed at the centre of one of the bitterest and most intriguing court cases ever heard in antebellum North Carolina. Within a few years of her death in 1836, members of Alice's community in Onslow County, friends and neighbours, women and men, rich and poor alike, would be drawn into an acrimonious legal dispute. Before the case was concluded, relatives would be forced to take sides against each other, neighbours would be set against each other, and long-standing friendships would end. The origins of *Ward* v. *Dulaney*, the court case that would breed such antagonisms, lay in Alice's unrequited and perhaps unwise passion for a younger man to whom she was also related by marriage. Neither Alice nor Harris were present during the case, death having overtaken both long before the drama unfolded in North Carolina's Supreme Court. Alice's story, however, is not simply one of unrequited love. As the court would hear, the events that led to the suit embraced far wider issues that are of interest to contemporary gender historians of the antebellum south. Alice's story forces us to consider white Southern women and their relationship to property, women's management and control of that property, and the implications for white women in a society within which wealth and social status was grounded in property ownership. Alice Ward Loomis Dulaney was a woman of considerable substance, the wealthy owner of at least two plantations and an unknown number of slaves, and when she died intestate that property became the subject of legal dispute. This then, is the story of Alice, as it unfolded before the court.[1]

In June 1826, Alice Ward Loomis married Col. Daniel M. Dulaney. This was not the first marriage for either of this middle-aged couple. Alice had previously been married to a Dr Nathaniel Loomis, who died around 1814. Dulaney had also been previously married, though little is known of that first union. Unhappily, the marriage between Alice and Daniel Dulaney proved short-lived, for after only nine months the couple separated. Dulaney was not, it appears, an ungenerous man, for after their separation he built Alice a substantial house, and made adequate provision for her support, maintenance and comfort. Perhaps Dulaney hoped for a future reconciliation, for the two apparently enjoyed a strong and enduring friendship that ended only with Alice's death in the early autumn of 1836.

Despite two marriages Alice remained childless, and when she died intestate Dulaney became by law the sole inheritor of her substantial property interests – much to the chagrin of Alice's relatives. In 1852, 16 years after her death, Alice's nephew and nieces, the minor children of her deceased nephew Eli W. Ward, represented by their friend George W. Penn, instituted a bill in the Superior Court of Chancery, pleading that they, and not Dulaney, be recognised as Alice's rightful heirs. Moreover, the plaintiffs requested that Alice's marriage to Dulaney be retrospectively annulled on the grounds that Alice had been insane on the date of her marriage to Dulaney, and she could not therefore, have entered into the union wilfully and freely. The plaintiffs argued that Alice's insanity undermined her capacity to enter into a marriage contract. Dulaney, they insisted, had taken advantage of Alice, pressurised her into a marriage she did not want, and had by these unscrupulous means, come into ownership of her estate by fraud. Thus, the plaintiffs maintained that Alice's insanity at the time of her marriage should be sufficient cause for the marriage to be declared null and void. A judicial decision in their favour would establish the plaintiffs' rights as Alice's lawful heirs, and Dulaney would be forced to relinquish the property he had acquired by right of his marriage to Alice.

In law, an individual contracting a marriage conducted while insane had the legal right to petition for an annulment of the union within six years of the marriage. To be sure, Alice and Dulaney had separated, but she had not at any time sought an annulment of her marriage. Dulaney in turn contested the action, asserting that Alice had not been insane, but had willingly entered into marriage with him, and that he therefore had legal right to her property. Further, Dulaney argued that even if Alice was insane at the time of their marriage, she 'became [sane] afterwards, at a period ten years preceding her decease, and being so compos mentis, was capable of asserting and maintaining her own rights ... and recovering the property from him as she was sole and unmarried'.

Plaintiffs and defendant both called an array of witnesses in evidence, many of whom had known Alice since childhood. The conflicting nature of evidence presented must surely have bemused the learned judges whose task it was to sift and sort through the testimonies. Three questions were before them: (i) Was Alice insane on 8 June 1826, the date of the marriage? (ii) If so, did she become sane at any time during the six years before the suit was bought? (iii) If so, would the statute of limitations bar the right of the plaintiffs to recover in the suit? As the learned judge pronounced, 'The testimony... is voluminous, and on some points conflicting and irreconcilable. The case, in many of its circumstances, is novel and interesting... the amount of property involved is large, and the decision we make may have an important bearing upon the reputation and character of some of the parties.'

What evidence was there to support the plaintiffs' claim of Alice's insanity? The main witness for the defence was Nathaniel L. Mitchell, Alice's nephew. Mitchell had known Alice for several years, and had been aged five when her first husband died. Crucially, Alice had assumed guardianship of Mitchell, raising him in her plantation house, and according to Mitchell, he 'regarded her as a parent'. Aged seventeen at the time of Alice's marriage to Dulaney, Mitchell suggested that as he had resided in Alice's home, and had been present at the marriage, he could speak with authority as to his aunt's mental state before, during and after the marriage. It should be noted that Mitchell stood to gain a substantial share of Alice's property should the plaintiffs win their case, and so his evidence must be approached with some caution. To do him justice, Mitchell spoke highly of Alice, whom he described as fashionable and 'remarkable for her good judgement in all business matters, having speedily settled up the affairs of her deceased husband... whose estate she had administered'. Alice's wealth, social status, her industriousness, warmth of personality and intelligence made her potentially a 'good catch', and throughout her widowhood she was not without suitors, but had declined a good number of 'brilliant offers of marriage'. Indeed, Dulaney had been among those suitors, though Alice had twice previously rejected his hand.

The court heard further evidence about Alice's life. After eight or nine years of widowhood, Alice formed a passionate but unrequited attachment to Harris Loomis, nephew of her deceased husband. Loomis was an entirely unsuitable candidate for Alice's attachment. Several years her junior, like Mitchell he had been raised by Alice, and probably also similarly regarded her as a parent. Loomis's engagement greatly unsettled his aunt. According to Mitchell, the change in Alice's conduct and behaviour exhibited itself before her nephew's marriage. 'She grew callous and indifferent about the success of her business, negligent of her husband's affairs, and alive only to every interest and whim of Harris. He did not reciprocate her love. She became restless, would frequently cry all night, throwing herself first in bed, and then out of it, before the fire, indulging her grief in the wildest manner.' Loomis's eventual marriage pushed Alice further beyond reason, and her misery could not be abated. Such behaviour was entirely unlike Alice, who had previously been actively involved in business and household matters but now, 'for a length of time she seemed unconscious, that she was the head of a family or household or large estate'.

Harris Loomis was widowed about a year after his marriage. Alice's passion for him was rekindled and, according to Mitchell, her 'insanity' returned. Alice now redirected her energies into frenzied efforts to impress and attract Loomis. In the depths of misery, she had been slothful and neglectful of her affairs. Now, Alice

> aroused herself to the most intense action and as if spurred on in the daring enterprise to accumulate still more wealth to lay at the feet of Harris, she would labor almost night and day. Her economy was niggardly thrift. She spun and wove with her own hands, and wore her own home-made frocks, such as before she had never been used to. She would go and remain whole days on her plantation, and return covered with dirt and dust, and blistered by the sun and the hardest labor, and so for a season she would continue, and then relapse of despair into entire indifference.

To no avail, it would seem, for Loomis soon remarried, taking as his second bride the sister of his deceased wife. Harris's second marriage was a painful blow to Alice, who took this second rejection badly, and her alleged insanity returned. Mitchell conceded, however, that for short intervals, Alice appeared lucid and more like her former rational self, so much so that 'A stranger, or long absent acquaintance, would think her herself again, for a half hour or such a time'. Mitchell's claim that Alice experienced periods of lucidity is important here, for it would later serve to substantiate the claims of defence witnesses who denied ever witnessing Alice behaving in a manner that might be construed as insane.

According to the plaintiffs, however, Alice's grief knew no bounds. She became melancholic, took little interest in life, and ignored the plantation's business affairs. Indeed, she moved out of her spacious and elegant home, choosing instead to reside in a smaller plainer dwelling. Overseers now managed her plantation affairs, and apparently under the watchful eyes of expectant heirs they did so credibly well, for Alice's plantations continued to prosper, a fact that made her relatives hesitant to 'make a move to take her business out of her hands'. Alice's relatives discussed ways of relieving her misery and distress. Some counselled that she relieve herself of the worries of her plantation by hiring out her slaves and lands, and embark on a period of restorative travel. Throughout her alleged illness, Daniel Dulaney, the twice-rejected suitor, had maintained his attachment to Alice. He had taken an active interest in her affairs, proffering advice, and negotiating with creditors and merchants. As Alice's emotional health continued to decline, some relatives proposed a second marriage, and Dulaney was 'by some motive unknown to [Mitchell] . . . induced to renew his suit'. Certainly, Daniel Dulaney made an attractive potential husband. He was a Colonel, popular and respected, and known for his integrity throughout the county. He was about the same age as Alice, and was himself possessed of substantial wealth and property. Mitchell certainly held no qualms about a marriage between his aunt and Dulaney, and encouraged the romantic relationship between the two. He acted as their go-between, chaperoned their meetings, spoke to Alice on Dulaney's behalf, and helped Dulaney prepare romantic speeches to Alice. Still locked in misery, however, Alice at first refused to contemplate remarriage, and often scornfully laughed off such advice. Eventually though, Dulaney's persistence proved fruitful, Alice accepted his proposal, and the marriage was arranged. Mitchell, however, averred that up to the day of the marriage, his aunt continued to display reluctance to the match. In Dulaney's absence, she would claim no knowledge of their engagement, and made no preparation for the marriage day. Indeed, Mitchell claimed that he himself had allowed his aunt to 'forget' the forthcoming wedding, but had himself taken the precaution of arranging for suitable clothing and other necessaries to be brought down from her abandoned plantation home. On the morning of the wedding, Alice remained 'ignorant of it; chanced to be seized with one of her industrious fits; drew on one of the two old home-spun coats she had fabricated at home, and went into the field, a mile from the house, there remained till [Mitchell] went and brought her home, to prepare for the marriage, by some plausible pretext'. Apparently reminded by Mitchell of the reasons for the elaborate preparations, Alice appeared greatly astonished, and strongly denied her agreement to the marriage. She resolved, said Mitchell, to tell Dulaney, on his arrival that he should 'harbor no longer so mistaken an expectation. Such was her condition when Dulaney drove up in his gig.' Two maids were summoned, and by means of persuasion and deception, Mitchell finally succeeded in getting his aunt clothed, 'though, in simple, plain ever-day style, except her shoes and stocking, which it is his impression he could not get her to change', rather than the traditional wedding finery. Mitchell then escorted Dulaney into the room where his future bride sat, and after some talk, laughter, and some cajoling, once more reminded Alice of the purpose of Dulaney's presence. The magistrate and witnesses having by this time arrived, Alice continued to protest, and 'She laughed as if at a farce, and oft repeated, "oh! no! no!" &c. but, at the same time, not struggling hard to get away, caused Dulaney to rise and pull her with reluctant steps along, with her feet in her old slipshod shoes.' Mitchell went on to describe the wedding scene:

> They were standing before the squire and Benjamin F. Dulaney and myself, during the whole of which time she never ceased to struggle gently to be released, and to exclaim, 'No! no! never! It is preposterous. What consummate folly! what are you doing?' laughing the while. The question as usual being put to Dulaney, he gave the customary assent. The question, when put to her, she heard not, or heeded not if she heard, keeping up her everlasting 'No! no!' &c. but laughed and appeared pleased to have done with it, as if really it was not a wedding, but a sham representation of one. That evening she presided at the head of the table, appeared quite cheerful, as much at least as her shattered faculties could indicate, and then it was, at the table, she for the first time seemed to reflect about it, and think she 'had committed a great folly,' to use her own words.

Alice, Mitchell testified, had finally realised the enormity of her actions, yet, puzzlingly, appeared to accept the marriage. She actually seemed happy, more like her former reasonable self, and certainly offered no protestations when on the next day Dulaney took his bride to her new home. Indeed, Mitchell conceded that on the twelve-mile journey, Alice appeared 'composed, serious, but reconciled'.

Thus ended Mitchell's evidence against his aunt. When subjected to close scrutiny his statements reveal an individual struggling to construct a self-representation as a loving and concerned nephew, forced to make public his aunt's private hell as she descended into insanity. Yet, his evidence describing Alice's supposed insanity was extremely damning. Alice emerges from Mitchell's statement as an insane woman of questionable morality, driven to madness by an incestuous and immoral passion for her nephew. He acknowledged that before her grand passion for Harris had bloomed, Alice had been widely respected and admired for her efficient and successful management of her plantations, and her sensible administration of her deceased husband's estate, which she had single-handedly expanded. Only when her mental health degenerated did Alice's own relatives have cause to question her ability to manage her affairs. Alarmed that her neglect of the plantation business might result in the eventual dissolution of her substantial estate, they attempted to exert influence over her affairs. The implication of Mitchell's evidence was plain. Alice had become deranged, and could no longer expect to enjoy unrestrained rights over her property, and it was the family's *duty* to ensure that the property remained intact. He was careful to allude to his own role in encouraging the marriage between Alice and Dulaney, though he was at pains to suggest that his own actions sprung from altruism and concern about Alice's mental state.

Other witnesses for the plaintiff provided evidence that would seem to support Mitchell's testimony. Many had known Alice for years, were familiar with her family, and some had even lived in her home. Some said that she was reputed to suffer periodic fits of hysteria, but they did not consider her insane until 1822, when her disastrous passion for Harris Loomis was aroused. Relatives, neighbours and friends reported witnessing her subsequent acts of insanity, 'tearing her clothes, attempting to set the house on fire, exposing her person, &c., and other acts of extravagance as evidence of derangement', and it was claimed that neighbours commonly referred to Alice being 'As crazy as the devil, as crazy as a loon, and the crazy widow'. Nearly all confirmed Alice's previous 'industry, economy, and notableness', and remarked that she had undergone a noticeable change. Some even hinted that Dulaney, who had known Alice since childhood, had been fully aware of her mental illness, and had schemed to take advantage of her. One and all offered the opinion that for a considerable time before and after her marriage, Alice was incapable of entering into any form of contract.

As would be expected, Dulaney's witnesses told a very different story. Many had also known Alice before and after her marriage to Dulaney, and again all spoke warmly of her, painting her as an intelligent and industrious woman. They reminded the court that Alice had independently 'administered [her deceased first husband's] estate, and settled the same with energy and skill'. None of Dulaney's witnesses could ever recall observing Alice's alleged displays of insanity and not a single resident of Onslow County had ever suggested anything other to the contrary. One witness went on to dismiss the plaintiffs' suggestions that Dulaney had married Alice for her wealth, pointing out that Dulaney was worth about twice as much as his wife when they married. He had never heard a bad word spoken about Dulaney, either before or after his move to Mississippi. The separation between Dulaney and Alice, Dudley went on, 'was a source of great surprise and regret to the community Generally'. Dulaney's generosity towards Alice in the wake of their separation was also highlighted, and it was generally known that even after Dulaney's move to Mississippi after Alice's death, he still 'possessed the friendship, entire confidence and good-will of the family and relations of his wife'.

Witness after witness repeated previous claims of Alice's sound financial judgement and abilities. Leonard B. Lipsey, a distant relative of Alice, also knew Dulaney well, for they were close neighbours in Onslow County. Lipsey had boarded with Alice for six or eight months in 1831, and always considered her sane, and 'a woman of better sense than the generality of women in [the state]'. Crucially, Lipsey also testified that he had often seen Alice visiting at the house of Dulaney's father prior to the marriage. This was vital evidence, for it implied that Alice had possibly spent a great deal of time with Dulaney Snr and Jnr, engaged in discussions about the forthcoming marriage. Another witness agreed, citing Alice's 'proverbial [reputation] for industry and tact in the management of her domestic matters to great advantage, and never exhibited the least symptom of insanity'. Daniel Ambrose conceded that Alice had had sporadic fits of hysteria, but strenuously denied that her mental capacity had been impaired. Ambrose could assert this with some confidence, for he had helped her untangle and sort out her deceased husband's estate, and in the process had come to admire her sound judgement. Ambrose also offered some previously undisclosed evidence to the court that was perhaps to play a large role in the judge's decision. Eli W. Ward, Alice's nephew and father of the plaintiffs, had along with Alice's brother Seth, borrowed substantial sums of money from Alice over the years. The import of this would become clear as the trial progressed. David Ward, a relative of Alice's, gave evidence that Alice often complained about Eli W. Ward because he refused to repay the loans and thus threatened Alice's financial security.

A crucial piece of evidence to the state of Alice's mind *after* her marriage was given by Elizabeth Mitchell, who had enjoyed a long friendship with Alice and had known her before her marriage to Dulaney. The two women visited each other often, and Alice had stayed temporarily in Elizabeth's home after her separation, while she waited for her new house – built by Dulaney – to be made ready. Elizabeth was therefore in a position to speak knowledgeably and authoritatively on Alice's mental condition. Elizabeth firmly rebutted allegations of her friend's insanity. Neither before, during, nor after the six months that Alice had lived with her, did Alice ever give her reason to question her intellectual capacities. Another witness told how Alice had superintended the wedding supper of Dulaney's daughter from his former marriage with aplomb, displaying as much efficiency and good sense as she brought to every other aspect of her household and business affairs. Another witnessed remembered attending a large wedding party at the Dulaneys' house, and on another occasion prior to the marriage, a grand party hosted by Alice at her house. On both occasions

Alice played her role as hostess to perfection, displaying 'as much intelligence in receiving and entertaining the company, as any lady of [his] acquaintance'.

Without exception, witnesses for the defendant all testified to Alice's sanity, intelligence, industriousness and decent conduct, both before and after her marriage. All provided character references for Dulaney, and the consensus was that the defendant was a man of honour and well-regarded by all who knew him in North Carolina and Mississippi.

When Daniel Dulaney eventually took the stand in his own defence, he produced in evidence a bond executed in November 1822 by Alice Loomis, and sureties for the guardianship of Nathaniel L. Mitchell, the chief witness for the plaintiffs. He also produced the record of a suit brought in 1829 by himself and Alice against Eli W. Ward, the father of the complainants, on two bonds made by him, payable to Alice before her marriage to Dulaney. One bond, in the amount of $793, was dated 14 November 1822, the other dated 1 June 1824, for $1,100. The last plea was rendered against him for approximately $3,000. Eli W. Ward had refused to settle his debts and Alice had been forced to institute court action to recover them. Subsequently, on 6 March 1832, Eli W. Ward paid Dulaney $500 on account of this judgement, and Dulaney released the balance. Daniel Ambrose, a witness for the defendant, confirmed that this money was advanced by the father of Eli W. Ward (Eli being insolvent), in consideration that Dulaney would release the remainder. Dulaney's purpose in producing this evidence was to reveal Alice's state of mind both before and after their marriage. If anything, it was plain that Eli W. Ward had taken advantage of Alice's distressed state, for he had borrowed substantial amounts of money from her in 1822, when Alice was distracted by her passion for Harris, and he continued to do so even after her second marriage. Dulaney also clearly hoped to show that he had no financial motives for marrying Alice. He himself had set aside debts owed to him by Eli W. Ward. Dulaney's production of these bonds ended the defence's case, and the learned judges retired to deliberate over the volumes of witness statements, briefs and other evidence entered before the court.

Was Alice Ward Loomis Dulaney insane at the time of her marriage, and if so, was the marriage therefore void? This was the first and most crucial question to be decided upon. In reaching their judgement, the court had to weigh up two opposing claims. The first, put forward by the plaintiffs, that Alice had been insane when her marriage took place and so the marriage should be declared void (making Dulaney's inheritance of her estate illegal), and secondly, Dulaney's assertions of his wife's sanity. No doubt both plaintiffs and defendant awaited the court's judgement with bated breath, for much was at stake. The decision, when it eventually came, found in favour of the defendant Daniel Dulaney. The reasons for the judgement were these: on weighing up the evidence before them, the court first addressed the likelihood of a match between Alice and Dulaney. Both had grown up in the same county, knew each other's families, were almost equal in wealth and property, were of similar age, both commanded respect within their community, both were said to be intelligent and possessed of honesty and integrity. Alice, in particular, impressed those she met with her intelligence, her flair for business, her single-handed management of her plantations and her conversational skills. Dulaney was also widely respected, and the judges agreed that neither party had anything unsuitable in their background or circumstances that would cause the other's family to raise objections to their match: 'The marriage under such circumstances was not unnatural or unreasonable, and it must, therefore, require no slight degree of proof to annul or set aside a contract so equal in all respects, and which in itself has nothing that is calculated to awaken a suspicion of imposition or unfairness.' Nevertheless, the fact of their suitability was in itself insufficient to prove the defendant's case. Turning to the evidence before them, the judges agreed with the plaintiffs' briefs that the witnesses for the defence had merely presented their *impressions and opinions* of Alice. More substantially impressive were the statements of the plaintiffs' witnesses, describing the numerous acts that had caused them to doubt Alice's sanity. Yet, what 'truth' could be discerned within the individual statements of the plaintiffs' witnesses? The evidence of Nathaniel Mitchell, in particular, was subjected to critical scrutiny. Even if, as Mitchell alleged, Alice had formed an 'unnatural and incestuous' attachment to her nephew, this did not in itself constitute an act of insanity. 'Improper, immoral and very reprehensible' perhaps, but it was not against Mississippi law, and the judges had no reason to believe that North Carolina statutes were any different. Moreover, 'on the scale of morality', were Harris Loomis's subsequent marriages to two sisters not equally reprehensible, even though legal? Alice's attachment might be considered immoral, but immorality was not symptomatic of insanity. Nathaniel Mitchell's evidence did not satisfactorily prove insanity on his aunt's part; rather, in the view of the judges, it tended to show the very opposite. It was true that when Harris Loomis spurned her in favour of another, Alice had sunk into misery, but this was only to be expected in one disappointed in love. To be expected, also, was Alice's more visible cheerful countenance and renewed industry after hearing of the death of her love rival. Surely this could not be construed as anything other than the rational behaviour of a woman hoping to attract Loomis's attentions? Even the alleged abandonment of her fine house, her adoption of plain homespun clothing, and her working in the field alongside her hands could be perfectly reasonably understood, once the circumstances of her life at that period came to be known. Recall that Eli W. Ward, Alice's nephew, had borrowed vast sums of money from her, and had compounded his offences by stealing her slaves and fleeing, leaving Alice indebted. Harris's betrayal, combined with the duplicitous actions of Eli W. Ward, almost certainly conspired to oppress Alice. In the judges' view, Alice's behaviour was perfectly understandable.

> What is there more natural, than that she should have been much harassed by this condition of her affairs, and should have been seen frequently in tears, and exhibiting other evidences of grief: What more probable and reasonable, than her withdrawal from her finely furnished home, the resort of the gay and fashionable, to another more distant and retired, where she could practise the economy and thrift necessary to reinstate her affairs, and relieve herself from pecuniary embarrassment? And what more natural, under such circumstances, than that she would dress more plainly, and exercise more than her usual economy and industry?

And, turning to the marriage itself, if it had indeed been the case that Alice had objected to a union with Dulaney, why did she permit the wedding to proceed? If it were also true that Alice had exclaimed at the wedding supper that she had committed a folly, surely this indicated that she had reflected on her actions; and if she was able to arrive at such a conclusion, did this not provide evidence of 'mind enough to know what she did, memory enough to remember it afterwards, and judgement enough to reflect and comment upon the matter and character of the act she had committed?' Clearly, Alice at her wedding supper was sufficiently *compos mentis* to suggest the validity of the marriage contract, a matter that Alice herself did not query. Crucially, apart from Mitchell, not a single witness for the plaintiffs – some of whom we must assume also attended the wedding – commented on Alice's objections to the wedding, and none claimed to have heard her subsequent expressions of dismay at having committed such an act of folly. Moreover, why did none of those involved in the wedding ceremony – the magistrate, the witnesses – testify to Alice's behaviour on the day of the wedding? And if Alice had indeed voiced objections to the marriage, or even appeared reluctant to participate in the ceremony, why did the presiding magistrate proceed with the marriage? In the view of the judges, Nathaniel's evidence could not be accorded any degree of credibility. That Mitchell might have embellished his accounts of Alice's insane behaviour in order to give added colour to his evidence was a distinct possibility that could not be ignored. He certainly had much to lose should the court find in favour of his uncle-by-marriage, the defendant Daniel Dulaney. Besides, the incidents of which he spoke had occurred during his adolescence, years in which he could not possibly have been sufficiently knowledgeable about mental illness to arrive at a competent and qualified assessment of Alice's sanity. To be sure, Alice had been subject to fits of irritability and bad-temper, as even the witnesses for the defence concurred. However, such 'eccentricities of conduct' did not imply insanity. As to claims that Alice was commonly referred to as 'crazy', or 'mad', such terms were commonly used to describe individuals who exhibited extravagant or eccentric behaviour. That Harris Loomis's betrayal had caused Alice to behave in ways described by some neighbours as crazy was possible, but few had actually witnessed Alice's insane behaviour, and much of their evidence was based on mere hearsay. In the judges' view, some 'very ignorant and illiterate' witnesses had clearly colluded together. Moreover, '[S]everal of the women [witnesses for the plaintiffs] are proved to have been of unchaste conduct; and while this kind of evidence is not in itself sufficient to impeach their veracity, yet as it would tend to show that they could not in all probability have been on terms of intimacy with Mrs Loomis, and would not, therefore, have had an equal opportunity with others differently situated, of forming a correct opinion in regard to her capacity and intellect.'

As for the attacks that regularly beset Alice, these could be easily explained by reference to a good medical dictionary, which would confirm that Alice's often agitated behaviour was symptomatic of hysteria.

Turning to the defendant's evidence, the judges reviewed Dulaney's assertions that his wife had indeed been of sound mind before, during and after their marriage. Despite their statements otherwise, witnesses for the plaintiff had been unable to offer satisfactory evidence to contradict Dulaney's claims. It was also significant that Eli W. Ward had 'permitted himself to be sued by Dulaney in right of his wife as late as 1830; and after having pleaded the statute of limitations, withdrew it, and suffered the defendant to recover a judgement against him for nearly $3,000 without opposing his right to sue or attempting to resist a recovery, because of the invalidity of the marriage or the insanity of his aunt'. By all accounts Eli Ward was an unscrupulous individual, and it somewhat stretches the imagination to believe that he would not have exercised his right to sue or attempt to contest the judgement made against him on the grounds of Alice's insanity. Finally, there was the matter of William Mitchell, uncle of Nathaniel Mitchell, and the officiating Justice of the Peace who conducted the marriage ceremony between Alice and Daniel Dulaney. Would Justice Mitchell have knowingly involved himself in a 'sham' marriage ceremony that would ultimately have profound implications for his nephew's future financial security? In joining together Alice and Dulaney, Justice Mitchell must have been aware that his nephew's chances of inheriting Alice's substantial estate might be considerably diminished. Alice had no children of her own and so long as she remained unmarried it was highly possible that she might bequeath her estate to Nathaniel. Marriage changed that of course, for when she married Dulaney all her property passed into his hands.

Still remaining, however, was the question of why Dulaney had married Alice. Had he, as witnesses for the plaintiff implied, married her solely to acquire her property assets? Had he indeed, known her to be insane before the marriage? It was after all entirely possible that this might have been the case. Yet the judges concluded otherwise. And even supposing Alice had been insane when she married, why had she herself not taken steps to have the marriage annulled in the following years? Witnesses for the defence all claimed that she had been sane up to and after the wedding, and after the subsequent separation. Why, if Alice herself believed her marriage to have been illegally contracted, did she not take action after the marriage had been dissolved to recover her property from Dulaney? Legally, her separation from Dulaney would have restored to her *femme sole* status, thereby enabling her to sue him for the return of her property in a court of law. According to the statute of limitations, Alice had had a period of six years after she had contracted herself in marriage to Dulaney in which she could have had her marriage declared null. Yet she made no attempt to do so, and her inaction proved the decisive factor shaping the judges' decision in favour of Daniel Dulaney. The decision effectively denied Alice's relatives' claims to be her rightful heirs, and meant that Daniel could legally retain the property he had gained through his marriage to Alice. Since there is no evidence to suggest that Alice's relatives appealed against the decision, we can only assume that Daniel Dulaney was left alone to live out his remaining years in peace. Following the court case, Alice and Daniel Dulaney seem to have disappeared from historical records.

Alice Ward Loomis Dulaney would probably never have secured her place within historical memory were it not for the fact that she was a white woman of substantial wealth and property. She was, it is said, a remarkably shrewd woman financially, possessed of good sense and intelligence, who skilfully and profitably managed two plantations and several negro slaves, property probably inherited from both her father and Dr Nathaniel Loomis, her first husband. Male and female witnesses alike testified to her sound business strength and expressed admiration at her efficient management of her property. Strikingly, though the business of plantation and property management was assumed by nineteenth-century Southerners to be a masculine endeavour, not a single witness on either side questioned Alice's rights of ownership and management of her property.

Southern white women's rights over property were always subject to legal restraint once married, but as a widow Alice's full rights in property were restored. In the absence of children, Alice could do as she wished with her property; she could freely make gifts of it, she could sell it, or bequeath it to whosoever she desired. That she derived pride and satisfaction from her ownership of land and slaves is evident. Alice accepted the challenges of plantation management, immersing herself in the day-to-day operations of her plantation. Small wonder that she seemed reluctant to embark on remarriage, a step that would certainly have meant relinquishing her property to a new husband, and considerably reducing her involvement in its operations.

Alice's story brings to the fore two significant aspects of Southern gender relations that have not received systematic attention. Alice's sanity is not of concern here. Rather, I want to signal the linking of property rights to gender relations, and secondly, to point to women's agency as plantation owners, and as owners of slaves. As Ann Whitehead has pointed out, an examination of 'women' and 'property' indicates the social character of property. Legal and ideological practices construct women and men's ability to act as fully independent subjects in relation to property in quite different ways.[2] Access to property – who has legitimate rights to property – and the limits of property ownership are a crucial indicator of the balance of power between women and men. The significance of property ownership as a key dimension in shaping gendered social relations has received insufficient attention.[3] Therefore, it is the intention here to explore the ways in which Southern social relations structured white women's access to property, and white women's relationship to that property and, in particular, their ownership of slaves.

In North Carolina, as elsewhere throughout the South, white women's access to property was determined primarily by their marital status. Unmarried and widowed women were not constrained from owning property, but marriage imposed severe limitations on women's access to property. On marriage, women's identity and person were subsumed into a single individual, and that individual was represented in the body of the husband. According to William Blackstone, marriage required the suspension of women's individual existence, 'or at least incorporated or consolidated it into that of her husband'.⁴ Marriage then removed a woman's right to own or control property independently. Whatever rights in property a woman brought to her marriage – down to ownership of her petticoat – passed to her husband.⁵ Alice Ward had spent the years of her widowhood improving on her property and in the process had amassed a sizable fortune, but when she married Daniel Dulaney she effectively surrendered all ownership and control of property that she had worked so hard to maintain and expand. Married women such as Alice generally regained sole control of property only on the death of their husband. When her first husband Nathaniel died, Alice regained ownership of property that she had brought to her marriage. As in Barbados, by law widows were entitled to a dower which gave them one-third of their husband's property, but because her first marriage had produced no children, Alice inherited the bulk of her deceased husband's estate.⁶ Most commonly, husbands ensured that wives at least received their dower, while sons inherited the greater part of their father's estate, with the expectation that male heirs would provide for their mothers. If the heir had not yet reached the age of majority, trustees and executors commonly advised widows to sell the plantation business (while retaining some of the slaves), or persuaded them to place control in the hands of other male heirs or executors. Some women of the elite classes sought to protect their property interests through the use of premarital contracts. Mary Young, who married Alice's brother Seth in 1807, took such a precaution. Seth, a planter, agreed to establish for his wife a separate trust to protect Mary's several interests in land, slaves and monies inherited from her deceased father.⁷ Without the existence of a prenuptial agreement, white women lost rights over any property they had brought to the marriage. The denial of married women's property rights effectively rendered wives socially, economically and politically powerless, forcing them to be dependent on their husbands. Recall that following her divorce, Alice Ward, who as a widow had built a thriving, profitable plantation business, was forced to rely for her maintenance on her former husband, into whose hands her property had passed on their marriage.

Legal restrictions notwithstanding, many married women found ways to circumvent the limitations placed on their rights to own and control property. Mary Young represents only one of the numerous white Southern women who determined to retain ownership rights of property they considered rightfully theirs. Sarah Nutall, a divorcee, devised a premarital agreement with her second husband that established her sole and separate ownership of all her property, real and personal, declaring it exempt from the 'control, management, or authority of any person whatsoever'.[8] That Sarah Nuttall was able to assert her right to retain sole interests in and control of her property was due to innovations in equity law that made provision for couples to retain rights over their separate estates. However, as Bynum argues, this legal mechanism was strictly limited, and when it was used it placed women in a defensive situation. Wives could rarely, if ever, convey the property they possessed in their own names.[9]

Property ownership provided the basis of wealth in North Carolinian society, where, as the transplanted Northerner Sarah Hicks Williams observed, the ownership of property – whether land, slaves and/or plantations – represented the most visible signifier of status. With the exception of a numerically insignificant population of free blacks and coloured people, only white individuals could legitimately gain access to property. The doctrine of separate estates through which some married women maintained independent property rights provided those women with security against a future divorce or separation, or against the wasteful predations of a profligate husband. Even the creation of a separate trust for her own use and benefit did not always guarantee a married woman's hold over her property, as evidenced in the court case brought by Ann 'Nancy' Tull against her husband William Tull in 1857. Before her marriage to Tull, Ann Lovick persuaded her intended husband to agree that she could hold in separate estate some property she had owned for some years, 'one negro man named James or Jain, one negro woman named Beck and one negro girl named Betsey, which said negroes were of great value'. Ann's family were by no means among the wealthiest of Lenoir County's planters, and the three slaves she owned represented the extent of her property. Tull apparently entered freely into the marriage settlement and the nuptials went ahead. Some time after, Ann made arrangements for the three slaves to be held in trust by her father William Lovick and conveyed them in a deed of gift to him. A family friend and probable lawyer, Thomas Woodley, took possession of the slaves on her behalf. Ann understood that unless she herself had cause to sell or dispose of the three slaves during her marriage, they would remain her property until her death. Moreover, an additional clause stipulated that Ann was to retain the right to dispose of the slaves in her will in any way that she saw fit. According to Ann, her father had made clear to her his intention that he should act as trustee of the slaves only. Both the deed of gift and the marriage settlement were intended solely 'to prevent Tull from taking them or his creditors to take them for debt', and Ann's father promised to convey the slaves back to her. By settling the slaves in trust to Woodley and her father, Ann's intention was clearly to remove the slaves beyond the reach of her husband. Ann must have had good cause to harbour doubts about her husband for within a few years the marriage ended. According to Ann, Tull had attempted to force her to cede ownership of the slaves to him but she refused, telling her father and Woodley that 'she didn't want her husband to ever have the slaves or even the use of them' because, she stated 'he had whipped her and then deserted her because she would not give a right to the slaves'. Ann further stated that Tull had agreed to live with her again if she would convey the slaves to him. Perhaps wishing for a peaceable reconciliation, Ann agreed, and asked her father to do so, but probably to protect his daughter's interests Lovick refused. In his deposition to the court, Woodley suggested that Lovick had refused because he feared that once his son-in-law gained ownership of the slaves, he was likely to sell them, leaving Ann without means of support. When Lovick died in 1856 Ann approached Woodley, requesting that the three slaves be released back into her custody, a request that for some unknown reason he refused to comply with. This left Ann with no recourse but to seek judicial action to regain her property. Witnesses involved gave conflicting opinions as to Lovick's intentions regarding the three slaves. Despite attempts by some of the main witnesses to portray Ann as a violent and disagreeable woman, the court found in her favour and she was able to regain her rights in negro property.[10]

While some women appreciated the security of a separate trust, the Southern ruling-class patriarchy no doubt viewed the practice with a good measure of unease, for a married woman's insistence on maintaining a separate estate could potentially undermine the wealth of the great property-owning families. Courts of equity were therefore more likely to use the mechanisms afforded to them in order to prevent the dissolution of great estates, and the protection of an individual woman's property interests might be of secondary importance. For the most part, however, elite wives did not maintain property independently of their husbands.

While there has been little research into the specificity of women as property owners in North Carolina, it is clear from research undertaken in other slave societies of the same period that many elite women struggled to assert their rights to property. Even poorer women exercised their rights to own property, buying slaves and land when their economic circumstances permitted. Hilary Beckles and Mary Butler both offer conclusive evidence of the importance of women's participation in the property and economic markets of Jamaica and Barbados.[11] White women in those plantation societies clearly asserted their rights to own property not simply as a matter of principle, but as a means of securing a livelihood and hence wealth and status.

The fact that married women had limited property rights does not imply that married women were not interested in property ownership. Neither should it suggest that limited property rights precluded women's economic involvement. Elite married women were at all times conscious that their social status derived from the ownership of family-held property, and were as interested in increasing and preserving family property as were their husbands. The death of a husband, even a wealthy one, could have devastating financial consequences for his widow and children, and married women therefore understood the importance of property ownership in sustaining them in their future widowhood.

Although white Southern husbands assumed control of jointly held property, white plantation women did not view marital property as belonging solely to their husbands. Despite her professed ambivalence towards slavery, Sarah Hicks Williams casually referred to the slaves she acquired on her marriage as 'our slaves', throughout her letters home to New York – thereby asserting her joint ownership of human property. Neither could Southern mistresses abdicate responsibility for the plantation's business, for they lived daily with the knowledge that their privileged livelihoods rested on the productivity and financial success of the plantation. Most women viewed their roles as plantation mistresses as a partnership, in which the master assumed responsibility for agricultural production and labour outside of the Big House, while mistresses claimed the domestic sphere as their responsibility. Many of North Carolina's planters combined agricultural production with political and professional roles that frequently took them away from their plantation homes for extended periods. In their husbands' absences, white plantation women assumed responsibility for management of the plantation, sometimes in conjunction with an overseer or a male relative, though many carried out their responsibilities without assistance. The many letters that flowed between absent husbands and their wives left behind to manage the family plantation business reveal the mistresses' everyday participation in plantation matters.

In an 1859 letter to her absent husband, Julia Joyner could not refrain from gently boasting of her success in collecting a long overdue debt owed her husband. 'I have got the money you had been fifteen years trying to get. Mr. Cook came round last Saturday and paid it and said he had just got it but I reckon if I had not been so close on him I should not have got it as soon as I did.'[12] Other correspondence between absent masters and plantation-bound mistresses are replete with detailed discussions of the plantation's business affairs, as mistresses reported on plantation and family matters, sought advice on crop cultivation, slave purchases or sales, the organisation of the slave labour force, slave discipline, crop planting, and various financial matters. For over twenty-five years Isaac Jarrett, a slave trader, spent long months travelling throughout the Southern slaveholding states buying and selling slaves, a business that demanded lengthy separations from his wife Harriet and their children. Though her children and domestic concerns took up a great deal of her time, Harriet was often lonely and in her letters to her husband frequently bemoaned the long periods of separation, and entreated him to engage in other forms of business that would enable him to remain at home.

> I spend my time very lonely but it is not worth while to complain for it is what I expect to do the balance of my life ... I hope you will not stay in Alabama longer than you can help for if you were here as lonesome as I am I would certainly try and be with you. I am afraid my dear husband that you and your friend Mr. Carson will keep up negro trading as long as you can buy any negro to trade on and when you can't buy any through the country you will carry off all you can parade at home but one good thing Mr Carson has no wife to leave behind when he is gone.[13]

Isaac wrote regularly home to his 'beloved wife', conveying his own sorrow and distress at being apart from her and his children, and sharing Harriet's desire for a stable family life. Although slave trading provided the wealth on which his plantation was grounded, the nomadic life of a slave trader was not to Isaac's satisfaction, and he often expressed his wish that he might one day be able to engage in some profitable business that would not take him away from his family. Isaac's business was frequently in difficulty as his creditors failed to settle their accounts on time, and he relied heavily on the profits from his plantation business to maintain his family. 'The only chance I see is to try and make as much on my farm for this year and live as Economical as I can and try to make my farm support my family expenses and perhaps in one or two years I may be able to wind up my business here.' Isaac's letters made it clear that the responsibility for wrestling the hoped-for profits out of the plantation would fall on Harriet's shoulders alone. Each letter home contained detailed advice and directions for the management of their plantation enterprise. Directing Harriet in February 1839 Isaac wrote,

> I want [my negroes] to push on with their work as hard as they can. Try if possible to let them have their breakfast by sun-up or as soon after as you can. My negroes have never worked but they must begin and do it this summer both in the house and them in the field. Try and get as much spinning done as possible but I fear you can't get much done. I

want them to prepare their own grounds well for a full crop and sew the oats as soon as they can and take good care of my sheep for I make strong calculation of them ... I want good care taken of the cattle and the hogs I want kept gentle.[14]

Isaac went on to issue further instructions: the specific crops to be planted (Irish potatoes and sweet potatoes), those fields to be cleared, ploughed and planted, and those to be left fallow, the meats to be smoked and preserved, the woods to be used, which slaves should be put to which tasks. Isaac and Harriet had been married for less than five years, but already Isaac had come to depend heavily on his wife's good managerial skills, and he preferred to leave his plantation in her capable hands rather than entrust its management to an overseer.

Isaac Jarrett certainly did not expect Harriet to assist in the arduous labour of clearing and planting fields, chopping trees or building ditches, but he did expect that she be able to direct and manage the work of the slaves who actually performed such labour. Harriet's responsibilities on the plantation were many and wide-ranging. In addition to overseeing the labour of the field and domestic slaves, Harriet kept the plantation accounts, engaged in trade with local seed, oats and other merchants who supplied the plantation, arranged for crops to be sold, ensured that livestock was well cared for, bought, sold and hired slaves, oversaw the spinning of wool, the sewing of clothing for the slaves and her own family, and wrote regular progress reports to Isaac. And always the needs of her young children had to be met. Scarce wonder that Harriet could neither keep up the regular correspondence that Isaac expected of her, nor accept invitations to visit family and friends. Every letter from Isaac came with new directives, and each directive had to be put into effect.

> Try and get as much work out of my home gang as possible and you will have to make the house folks do as much in your garden as possible, and Jim had better break up the ground round the barn ... and feed all the stock in the potato lot, give them a plenty of straw and shucks ... you don't know anything about ploughing but if you will tell him, he knows, and Eliza must plough whenever Jim does, or whether he does or not, she can plough.[15]

Harriet's knowledge of ploughing might be limited, but Isaac patently trusted his wife's judgement in all matters concerning the plantation.

Planters' wives such as Harriet, entrusted with the responsibility of buying slaves in their husband's absence, needed sound knowledge of the slave market when purchasing slaves. They needed to know which slave traders could be trusted and which were unscrupulous. They had to be able to distinguish between a healthy slave and one in poor health, which slaves might be troublesome, and which were likely to be good workers, the current capital worth of a slave, and of course, they needed the acumen and tenacity to negotiate and secure a good bargain at the slave market. Transactions involving slaves – buying, selling or hiring – regularly featured in plantation mistresses' letters. Harriet Jarrett wrote to tell Isaac of her current negotiations with a local trader to procure a slave boy: 'to help on the farm [if I can get one] I shall be satisfied and try to do without a nurse for I find I can do better without, than I thought I could for necessity as you know is the mother of invention'.[16] Harriet went on to reassure her husband that despite his absence, all was well at the plantation under her management. 'Your home affairs are going on as well as can be expected without your presence,' she told him,

> Mr Joiner has had the ploughs going continually for the past month. He says he is preparing sixty acres of corn ground. He thinks he will get the oats all in this month. Your sheep are doing very well, there is six very pretty lambs among them, the cows look pretty well also . . . your stock of hogs are all in right good order.

Harriet rarely complained about the responsibilities of plantation management, and her letters suggest that she derived satisfaction and pride from her ability to manage the plantation. To be sure, she did not manage the plantation independently, for she relied heavily on Isaac's advice, and she often sought the advice of neighbouring planters, but then, in this she was not alone, for all planters frequently exchanged advice on a diverse range of matters – the best crops to plant, when to plant, how many slaves should be allocated to clearing a field. When her husband's slave trading business ran into difficulties as a result of his creditors' inability to settle their bills, Harriet's responsibilities increased further, though she appeared to take the new challenges in her stride. Eliza, the slave nurse of Harriet's young children, had recently run away, and though Eliza's absence must surely have added to her mistress's many burdens, Harriet's determination to maintain her economy drive led her to make do with the help of Mary, a slave woman untrained in childcare, rather than incur the expense of purchasing or hiring a new nurse.

Management of domestic slaves commonly fell into the area of 'women's work' within the plantation, and it was here perhaps that the reality of Southern imaginings of ideal white womanhood met and collided. Southern men such as Thomas Dew and George Fitzhugh might deify the ideal Southern mistress as a frail and gentle creature, physically incapable of hard labour, but the responsibility of managing the plantation's business, directing the work of the slave labour force and still attending to their 'natural' duties as mothers and housewives, surely demanded strength, stamina and courage. Few, if any, planters would expect their wives to perform the heavy physical labour that fieldwork demanded. Field labour was reserved for black and white males and black women, and though it was an open secret that many poorer white women laboured alongside husbands and slaves in cotton, tobacco and cornfields, wealthier planters insisted on their wife's exemption from fieldwork. By the gender conventions of the day, genteel women confined their labour to the household and its immediate surroundings. Recall that when Alice Ward's nephew, Nathaniel Mitchell, gave evidence attesting to her insanity, he had cited as evidence of her disturbed mind the fact that she had gone out for several days to work in her plantation fields, returning 'covered with dirt and dust, and blistered by the sun and the hardest labor'. To Nathaniel's mind, a wealthy white woman such as his aunt had no business involving herself in such physical labour, for fieldwork was unbecoming for a white woman of quality; only black women, or a poor or deranged white woman would stoop to such labour.

Though they were shielded from the most strenuous forms of labour, the business of plantation management had its own particular hardships and imposed wearisome burdens on the mistresses' shoulders. Recall Sarah Hicks Williams's repeated complaints to her parents in New York. Newly married Sarah resented what she regarded as her mother-in-law's interference, and desperately longed to set up housekeeping alone with her husband Benjamin. Once in their own home, far from Mother Williams, full responsibility for the household and their slaves devolved on to Sarah's shoulders, and the realities of being a plantation mistress soon brought disillusionment. Harriet Jarrett probably derived satisfaction from her responsibilities but countless other women clearly did not. Left alone for many months to manage the plantation while her husband was away, Julia Joyner found the responsibilities overwhelming. She wrote to her husband imploring him to return home soon,

> for I am almost worn out with you staying away from home and there is so many here doing nothing and they all have to eat and wear. Pen offered me two dollars a month for Fed from now until Christmas. I told him your price, he said Fed knew so little about work, he thinks that is about as much as he is worth and I think we had better take that than to keep him here unless we had more land to work.[17]

Most mistresses viewed the management of household slaves as a tiresome burden. From the perspective of the mistress, slavery made slaves of slave-owning women, and mistresses commonly complained without irony that there was no greater slave on a plantation than the mistress. In their journals and private letters, mistress after mistress complained of malingering slaves, of sullen slaves who ignored orders, deliberately burned food, ruined a good dress by poor starching, broke valuable household items, stole clothing and jewellery, brought meals to the table cold, and were guilty of a thousand other misdemeanours. As much as the physical hardships, the psychological toll of managing recalcitrant slaves was severe, and relations between slaves and mistresses could sometimes flare into violence.

The ex-slave Harriet Jacobs remembered in her narrative that Mrs Wade, a neighbouring plantation mistress, did not shirk from administering physical punishment. At Mrs Wade's house, 'at no hour of the day was there cessation of the lash. Her labours began with the dawn, and did not cease till long after nightfall. The barn was her particular place of torture. There she lashed the slaves with the might of a man.'[18] The ex-slave abolitionist and advocate of women's rights, Frederick Douglass, also recalled a mistress, Mrs Giles Hicks, who had murdered his wife's cousin, 'a young girl between fifteen and sixteen years'.[19] This poor girl, who had served as nursemaid, had fallen asleep one night, and fatigued from the loss of sleep caused by her charge's crying over a period of nights, had failed to wake when the baby starting crying yet again. Mrs Hicks, asleep in the same room as her baby and its nurse, was woken by the plaintive cries and enraged by the slave girl's failure to respond to the crying infant in quick time, leapt from her bed and with an oak stick proceeded to beat the slave girl about her body, with fatal results, 'mangling her person in the most horrible manner, breaking her nose and breastbone with a stick, so that the poor girl expired in a few hours afterwards'. Douglass recalled that the murder of a slave girl by a white woman created a short-lived sensation in the local community. A warrant was subsequently issued for Mrs Hicks's arrest. Ultimately though, 'this murderess' escaped the indignity and humiliation of appearing before the court, as the scandal over the killing of a black enslaved woman by her white mistress soon abated, and Mrs Hicks escaped punishment.[20] For mistresses (or masters) too timid or unable to wield the whip themselves, the Work House – premises where slave-owners sent their slaves to be whipped or punished for a fee – offered an alternative.

Kirsten E. Wood has suggested that mistresses used less violent force against their slaves than did male planters. Wood argues that notions of genteel lady-hood constrained women's ability to resort to violence when confronted with recalcitrant or unruly slaves. The deployment of physical violence was a force strongly associated with the prerogatives of masculinity and mastery, not genteel femininity. The desire of the white patriarchal ruling class to maintain white hegemony entailed absolute control over the enslaved, and that control was secured only through resort to violence. Whether threatened or actual, violence was the perpetual backdrop of slave society, as owners struggled to assert their dominance, and the enslaved to assert their human rights. Mistresses as well as masters were drawn into the structures of slave control, and even though violence went against the grain of genteel womanhood, few mistresses could maintain control of their slaves without resorting to violence. Enslaved peoples certainly experienced violence at the hands of their mistresses. Formerly enslaved Bob Jones of Raleigh remembered that his masters were 'as nice as could be' but 'Miss Betsy was crabbed and hard to get along with. She whupped the servants what done the housework, and she fussed so bad that she might run us crazy. It was her what sold my aunt Sissy Ann, and it was her that whupped my sister so bad. There warn't but six of us slaves, but them six run a race to see who can stay out of her sight.'[21] Ex-slave Ria Sorrell, also of Raleigh, perhaps inadvertently drew attention to what might be read as the enslaved's more general acceptance of the master as the source of authority. Mistresses and slaves understood that the household represented the limits of white female power, but that power was only a delegated power; ultimate authority resided in the hands of the master, and the mistress was only ever a representative of that authority. Her master, Ria recalled, rarely whipped his slaves, though his shrewish wife was quite another matter. Ria's mistress 'was a pure devil, she just joyed whipping Negroes ... When Marster [went] to town, she raised old scratch with the slaves. She whupped all she could while Marster was gone.' Perhaps it was indeed the case that, as Ria claimed, Master Sorrell was 'a good man' who rarely whipped his slaves, and ensured that they were well housed, clothed and fed. According to Ria, Master Sorrell ignored his wife's insistence that 'underleaves of collard was good enough for slaves'. Knowing the advantages of a well-fed, healthy slave labour force, Sorrell brushed aside his wife's suggestion of feeding the slaves collard leaves, reminding her that 'people couldn't work without eating'. Sorrell refused to employ an overseer, maintaining that he 'didn't believe in them and he didn't want any', a decision possibly taken because he had little confidence that an overseer could manage his slaves or his plantation affairs well. Equally possible, Sorrell's insistence on managing without an overseer possibly derived from confidence in his own ability to successfully impose and maintain order and control among his slaves without resorting to the whip. That Mistress Elizabeth resorted to more frequent violence might simply be a reflection of her frustration and resentment of the slaves' rejection of her feminine authority. Sorrell emerges from Ria's narrative as a paternalistic master, mindful of his slaves' welfare. Yet though masters might display paternalism in their relationships with their slaves, this did not mean that they hesitated to use brute force when they believed that a slave threatened their authority. Ria herself knew that the one form of disobedience calculated to bring down her master's wrath and provoke a whipping was defiance of his order that slaves were not to be allowed to read and write. Recalled Ria, 'There was one thing that wasn't allowed, that was books and papers. I can't read and write.'

Mistresses might shirk from administering physical punishment, but slaves well knew that such reluctance did not mean that wrongdoings would go unpunished. That prerogative could always be delegated to others – an overseer, a brother, uncle, father, some other male friend, or the local sheriff. Slave-owning women's struggles to conform to gendered notions of genteel womanhood involved a conscious distancing of themselves from violence, in choosing to delegate whippings and other punishments to male proxies. Wood has argued perceptively that devolving responsibility on to white males 'protected [the mistresses'] self-image as gentlewomen, without critically sacrificing violence as a tool of racial control'.[22] Physical violence, of course, was not the only form of violence mistresses used on their slaves. Emotional violence could be just as devastating in its effects. Threats to sell and separate an enslaved family could be as psychologically traumatic for the enslaved as a physical whipping, perhaps even more so, and represented an effective controlling tool in the hands of the mistress. So powerful was the threat to separate a mother from her children or a husband from his wife that it left a lasting impression. Sarah Debro recalled the controlling power of a threat made by her owner Miss Polly White to sell her grandfather. Sarah's grandfather one day 'sassed Miss Polly White and she told him that if he didn't behave hisself that she would put him in her pocket. Grandpappy was a big man, and I ask him how Miss Polly could do that. He said that she meant that she would sell him, then put the money in her pocket. He never did sass Miss Polly no more.'[23] When Sarah Devereux found her slave Sally too unruly to manage, she turned to her brother Thomas, manager of her Halifax County plantation, for advice: 'I have pondered much upon Sally's conduct . . . I told Sally if such should be the case I would sell her but in the very face of my threat . . . now it is very hard to sell her, and three children, for without them, I am much perplexed and do not know what is my duty'.[24] Rather than take decisive action herself, and perhaps wanting to avoid the personal guilt of having separated Sally from her children, Sarah Devereux delegated the onerous task to Thomas, leaving it to him to decide the future of Sally and her family: 'if you think it best to make her an example sell her, you spoke of selling some of yours and may include her if you think best'.[25]

Threatening to separate enslaved families by sale represented one of the strongest psychological weapons in the mistress's armoury. However, putting such a threat into effect might provoke further trouble among her slaves, and for many owners the sale and subsequent separation of enslaved families was a last, desperate resort. One mistress devised a particularly humiliating punishment for a female slave. Ex-slave Lizzie Baker recalled that her mother, Teeny McLintire, had been accused of stealing some food from her mistress, who punished Teeny by forcing her to wear trousers for an entire year. Teeny's punishment was especially cruel and wounding, for it struck at her identity as a woman. In forcing Teeny to adopt male garb, Teeny's mistress wilfully deployed shaming tactics to undercut the enslaved woman's sense of femininity.[26] Of courting age, the young Teeny would almost certainly have relied on her feminine charms and dress to secure a male partner, and the enforced trousers probably made her a target of ridicule among the plantation's enslaved community. Enslaved women such as Teeny had good reason, then, to fear their mistress's wrath, even though they might not accept her authority. Indeed, it was a common complaint among mistresses that female slaves were more troublesome than males. Relations between mistresses and their female slaves were often fraught with tension, and many enslaved women did not hesitate to retaliate when a mistress attempted to enforce punishment. As one female slave in North Carolina commented, 'No Sir, Missus, ain't 'llowing nobody what w'ar de same kind of shirt I does ter whip me'.[27] Hence, we see that both enslaved women, and their mistresses struggled to establish the boundaries of the mistress/maid relationship.

At times, the relationship between slave and mistress was tinged by genuine affection, as illustrated in the exchange of correspondence between Patsy Padison and her ex-slave Violet Lester. Violet and her children had earlier been sold to settle a family debt. Violet's family had been separated, and she had lost contact with her children. Now settled with a kind master who had promised 'that he will keep me til death separates us unless some of my old North Carolina friends wants to buy me again', Violet wrote to her 'loving mistress Miss Patsy' to enlist her help in finding her daughter, whom her new master had agreed to purchase if she could be located.[28] Former slave Sarah Debro also recalled her Mistress, Polly White, with fondness:

> I was kept at the Big House to wait on Miss Polly to tote her basket of keys... whenever she seed a child down in the quarters that she wanted to raise by hand, she took them up to the big house and trained them. I was to be a housemaid. The day she took me, my mammy cried, 'cause she knew I would never be allowed to live at the cabin with her no more. Miss Polly was big and fat and she made us niggers mind, and we had to keep clean. My dresses and aprons was starched stiff. I had a clean apron every day... I toted Miss Polly's bags and bundles, and if she dropped her handkerchief I picked it up. I loved Miss Polly and loved staying at the big house.[29]

Mistresses as well as masters were aware of the economic value of slaves, who represented a considerable investment. Slave-owners recognised that habitual brutality against the enslaved might help to ensure a compliant and disciplined workforce, but should the slave die or suffer permanent injury as a consequence of harsh punishment, the slave-owner not only suffered the loss of a valuable unit of property, but ran the risk also of provoking unrest among the enslaved. Slaves were workers first and foremost, the producers of profit, and the loss of a single slave on a small plantation could have significant repercussions for the owner's economic wellbeing. For this reason, most owners tried to afford their slaves a modicum of care. That many plantation mistresses also bore responsibility for nursing and caring for sick slaves, demonstrates not merely their acceptance of these roles as an extension of their 'natural' qualities, but also their awareness of the slaves' economic value. Indeed, few plantation mistresses could remain ignorant of current prices on the slave market. Sarah Keenan kept her absent brother up to date with the family's plantation business, and her letters reveal an acute knowledge of slave prices. 'The negroes were hired out on the 13th February. They did not hire for as much as the last year.' Their aunt, however, fared better. 'She hired out Albert and her two negro girls, Albert went for nine dollars. I think that was right smart, he is only nine years old; negroes generally at all the hirings in the county went for less than they did last year.'[30]

Investment in slave property enabled all but the poorest whites to earn an independent income. Enslaved peoples themselves well understood that the wealth and social status of their owners was derived from unfree black labour. Sarah Debro's aunt Charity was acutely aware of the social and economic implications that emancipation would have for those white women dependent on slaves for their survival. As she told Sarah at the height of the Civil War, when her apparently hard-hearted mistress broke down in tears, Charity could only look on with cynicism. 'She ain't crying 'cause the Yankees killing the mens; she's doing all that crying cause she's scared we's going to be set free.'[31] Miss Polly wept not for the thousands of white Southern men who lost their lives, but for the possible loss of her slaves, and the privileges that slave ownership conferred. Perhaps more than any other form of property, the ownership of slaves was crucial to the economic survival of widowed or unmarried white women. Investment in slaves represented more certain returns than land, which could lose its value. Even when land values held, planters might have to contend with droughts and the inevitable poor harvests that followed, heralding financial disaster. When the price of cash crops fell, women slaveowners invariably responded to slumps by working their slaves more intensively.[32] Planters sought to stave off economic vulnerability by making their slaves increase the production of cash crops such as cotton, tobacco or rice. As the south began to industrialise, slaveowners recognised new sources of income to be derived from slave labour. Male slaves were contracted out to work on railroads, bridge building, or various construction projects, and women slaves sent to labour in textile mills. Slave prices fluctuated throughout the antebellum period, but still human property represented a safe form of investment. In times of economic crisis, land and houses might be sold, but sensible planters held on to their slaves at all costs. As long as they could afford to maintain even a single slave, women slaveowners could be guaranteed a source of income. When Alice Ward's behaviour became sufficiently eccentric to alarm her family, their advice that she sell off her lands and plantation and to put her slaves out to hire, was economically sound, for they rightly rationalised that the income from the hiring-out of her slaves would be sufficient to maintain Alice's livelihood. Less understandable to her relatives was Alice's insistence on undertaking physical labour when she had at her disposal a retinue of field and domestic slaves. Yet, as the judges in *Ward* v. *Dulaney* correctly perceived, Alice's 'unwomanly' behaviour, evidenced in her performance of fieldwork, represented a rational economic strategy by which she could hope to recoup some of her losses. Alice may well have reasoned further that her physical presence in the fields would have the effect of spurring her slaves on to work harder.

Mistresses might bemoan the irritations and inconveniences that ownership of human property imposed upon them, but few would relinquish ownership of such valuable sources of income. The economic value of slaves to white women is borne out in an analysis of divorce petitions presented by white women abandoned by their husbands. Many wives specifically charged in their divorce petitions that the errant husband had either 'wasted' their property by selling their slaves, or had run off taking slaves that their wives had brought to the marriage. Arnold and Euphan Rhodes of Beaufort County jointly petitioned for divorce in 1803, after having lived apart for two years. On her marriage to Arnold in 1795 at the age of seventeen, Euphan had brought considerable property consisting of 'a valuable estate in land and slaves' to the marriage. Euphan's petition accused her husband of 'abandoning himself to Idleness, intoxication, gambling &c' shortly after their marriage. His dissolute behaviour culminated in the wasting away of the property, the loss of all the slaves and a large portion of the real estate.[33] Another abandoned wife, Sarah Johnson, also requested divorce on the grounds of her husband's desertion and his 'squandering' of property, including nine slaves she had brought to their marriage. Sarah was left considerably indebted and had to sell two of her three slaves.[34] The 1808 petition of Lucy Crockett of Person County alleged that her husband William had abandoned her shortly after their marriage, but not before he had 'squandered her property, including several valuable slaves'. Lucy had been left pregnant and without funds, and the loss of her slaves placed her in a precarious economic position, for without them, she had few means of securing an income.[35] A year later, Frances Murdin [or Mundin], also filed for divorce, stating that her 'unfeeling monster' of a husband had run off to Georgia after nine years of marriage, taking with him their eight slaves, leaving her and their three children without care or protection.[36] Barbara Wilkinson's divorce petition charged that she had been left in opulent circumstances when her former husband died, leaving Barbara with 'a manor house, outbuildings, plantation lands, orchards, livestock, household and kitchen furniture, and slaves'. Her second husband, a young physician, stripped Barbara of her property before finally abandoning his now-destitute wife.[37] Elena Cobb's petition also revealed the deceptions of some unscrupulous white males seeking to garner property. Her husband John Cobb had represented himself to Elena and her father as a wealthy slave-owner and practising physician. Convinced of his status, Elena married John Cobb, only to discover two days after the nuptials that her husband was an abusive drunkard who owned neither slaves nor land, and 'had not the slightest idea how to practise medicine'.[38]

Slaveholder Cassandra Houston of Mecklenberg County also charged her husband with abandonment, and requested that she be granted a divorce. Cassandra's claim made public aspects of male and female sexuality that remain unexplored in the context of Southern slave society and are worth recounting in some detail. Cassandra and James Houston were married on 4 January 1803, and lived together until November that year when she left him because, she alleged, of his impotence. The marriage had not been consummated, for according to Cassandra, James had been unable to perform his duties as a husband and, 'as a man in procreating his species'. Depositions were taken from Cassandra's relatives and others who gave evidence that their observations of him attempting to urinate had led them to suspect that Houston was 'not a man like other men'. Houston himself had apparently admitted that 'he was not as complete as to genitals as other men', and that he had on several occasions attempted to engage in homosexual sex with other men. Cassandra's brother Marshal testified that he had himself been the object of James's sexual attentions, and had noticed that James lacked testicles. Cassandra's family told the court that it was their belief that James had married Cassandra solely to obtain her slaves and other property. Cassandra's petition requested that the court allow her to retain all the property that she had brought to the marriage. In publicly stating the grounds on which she sought a divorce (the unconsummated marriage), Cassandra not only broke early nineteenth-century silences surrounding women's sexuality and sexual agency, but in alleging James's homosexuality, also revealed a rarely acknowledged aspect of Southern white male masculinity. Although a few isolated instances of homosexuality between men in the antebellum south have been uncovered, Southern mastery was firmly grounded in heterosexuality and homosexuality was perceived as threatening to the reproduction of patriarchal power. Southern historians have barely begun to explore the relationship between white male mastery, heterosexuality and slavery, and there is a rich field of scholarship waiting to be developed. However, the 'truth' of James's sexuality is not the central issue here.[39] In an era in which silence cloaked white female sexuality, and sexual passivity and propriety was demanded of respectable white women, Cassandra's willingness to publicly proclaim her desire for a sexual life is striking. Cassandra's divorce petition not only exposed her sexual desires, but also revealed her strong interests in and attachments to property she considered rightfully hers, and the lengths to which she was prepared to go to assert her rights to that property. We can only surmise that James's venture into matrimony was, as Cassandra alleged, committed solely to obtain her property.

Individual white women waged struggles against the patriarchal order to assert their rights of ownership over property, but one fact remains clear. Legally defined as property themselves, enslaved black women were denied the right to own property, and it was this – the distinction between women who could legally own property, and women who could not – that signalled the crucial indicator of the power imbalance between white and black. An examination of the experiences of white Southern women such as Alice Ward Loomis Dulaney, Harriet Jarrett and their contemporaries, reveal the tangled complexities of race, class and gender in North Carolinian slave plantation society. It also points to the significance of conceptualising slavery, not simply as a system of social relations between the free and the enslaved, but as spawning a particular set of relations between white women and men. The stories revealed in this book have indicated how structural factors interwove to shape the contours of women's lives and their material experiences. In analysing these experiences I have challenged prevailing conceptions of white plantation women as mere passive victims of slavery, indicating the possibilities for female resistance and agency. When circumstances demanded or permitted, white women of all social classes pursued a range of economic strategies that ranged from waged labour to the buying of slaves. McLintock reminds us that 'the rationed privileges of race, all too often put white women into positions of decided – if borrowed – power, not only over colonised women, but over colonised men. As such, white women were not the helpless onlookers of empire, but were ambiguously complicit both as colonisers and colonised, privileged and restricted, acted and acted upon.'[40] McLintock speaks here specifically of white women in the British colonial complex, but her words attest equally well to the experiences of antebellum North Carolina's slave-owning white women, as well as to the white women of Barbados.

Notes

1. *Edward Ward et al v. Daniel M. Dulaney*, Onslow County Court, North Carolina (January Term, 1852) (http://www.rootsweb.com/pub/usgenweb/nc/onslow/court/ward12.txt).
2. Ann Whitehead, 'Women and Men; Kinship and Property: Some general issues', in Renee Hirschon (ed.), *Women and Property, Women as Property* (Kent: Croom Helm, 1984), pp. 176–192.
3. Hirschon, *Women and Property*, pp. 1–2.
4. William Blackstone, cited in Victoria Bynum, *Unruly Women: The politics of social and sexual control in the Old South* (Chapel Hill: University of North Carolina Press, 1992), p. 60.
5. Linda G. De Pauw, 'Women and the Law: The colonial period', *Human Rights* 6:2 (Winter 1977), pp. 107–113.
6. Bynum, *Unruly Women*, p. 62.
7. Marriage Contract: Seth Ward & Mary Young, 10 Oct, 1807: Onslow County, North Carolina, Deed Book 1, page 133 (http://ftp.rootsweb.com/pub/usgenweb/nc/onslow/court/ward15.txt).
8. Bynum, *Unruly Women*, p. 59.
9. Ibid., p. 65.
10. *Ann H. Tull v. William Tull and others*, Court of Equity, Lenoir County, State of North Carolina, Spring Term 1857 (http://www.rootsweb.com/~usgenweb/copyright.htm).
11. See Hilary Beckles, 'White Women and Slavery in the Caribbean', *History Workshop Journal* 36 (1993), pp. 65–82; Kathleen Mary Butler, *The Economics of Emancipation: Jamaica and Barbados, 1823–1843* (Chapel Hill: University of North Carolina Press, 1995).

SHE WOULD LABOR ALMOST NIGHT AND DAY

12 Julia Joyner to her husband, May 10 1859, Joyner Family Papers, SHC, UNC-CH.
13 Ibid.
14 Isaac Jarrett to Harriet Jarrett, Jarrett Family Papers, Perkins Library, Duke University.
15 Ibid.
16 Ibid.
17 Julia Joyner, Joyner Family Papers, SHC, UNC-CH.
18 Harriet Jacobs, *Incidents in the Life of a Slave Girl* (Oxford: Oxford University Press, 1988).
19 Frederick Douglass, *The Life of Frederick Douglass, An American Slave* (London: Penguin 1986 reprint), p. 68.
20 Ibid., p. 69.
21 Bob Jones, in Belinda Hurmence (ed.), *My Folks Don't Want Me to Talk About Slavery: Twenty-one oral histories of former North Carolina slaves* (Winston-Salem: John F. Blair, 1984), p. 57.
22 Kirsten E. Wood, *Masterful Women: Slave-holding widows from the American Revolution through the Civil War* (Chapel Hill: University of North Carolina Press, 2004), p. 53.
23 Sarah Debro, in Hurmence, *My Folks Don't Want Me to Talk About Slavery*, p. 55.
24 Sarah E. Devereux in New Haven to Thomas Devereux in Halifax County, North Carolina, Devereux Family Papers, 1791–1936, Folder III, Correspondence 1791–1841. Rare Book, Manuscript and Special Collections Library, Duke University.
25 Ibid.
26 Lizzie Baker, in George Rawick (ed.), *The American Slave: A composite autobiography. Vol. 14, part 1* (Connecticut: Greenwood Publishing Company, 1972), pp. 67–68.
27 Elizabeth Fox-Genovese, *Within the Plantation Household: Black and white women of the Old South* (Chapel Hill: University of North Carolina Press, 1998) p. 313.
28 Violet Lester to Patsy Adison, Joseph Allred Family Papers, Perkins Library, Duke University.
29 Sarah Debro in Hurmence, *My Folks Don't Want Me to Talk About Slavery*, pp. 55–56.
30 Sarah Kenan, Kenan Family Papers, SHC, UNC-CH.
31 Ex-slave Aunt Polly to ex-Slave Sarah Debro, in Hurmence, *My Folks Don't Want Me to Talk About Slavery*, p. 57.
32 Wood, *Masterful Women*, p. 46.
33 Race and Slavery Petitions Project, Petition of Arnold Johnson and Euphan Rhodes to General Assembly, Session Records, PAR No. 11280301, NCDAH.
34 Ibid., Petition of Sarah Johnson to General Assembly, Session Records, PAR No. 11280504, NCDAH.
35 Ibid., Petition of Lucy Crockett to General Assembly, Session Records, PAR No. 11280809, NCDAH.
36 Ibid., Petition of Frances Murdin to General Assembly, Session Records, PAR No. 11280903 NCDAH.
37 Ibid., Petition of Barbara Wilkinson to General Assembly, Session Records, PAR No. 11281006, NCDAH.
38 Ibid., Petition of Ellena Cobb to General Assembly, Session Records, PAR No. 11283401, NCDAH.
39 Ibid., Petition of Cassandra Houston to General Assembly, Session Records, PAR No. 11280405, NCDAH. From the descriptions of James's genitalia provided by male witnesses, it is possible that he suffered from a medical condition known as Reifenstein syndrome, an inherited disorder that causes underdevelopment of the male reproductive tract and sexual dysfunction in males. In severe cases, the genitals may appear to resemble female genitalia, giving rise to its alternative name of *pseudohermaphroditism*, a condition in which the male has testes but possesses

both male and female sexual characteristics. Were this the case, James would have been rendered infertile, a possibility of which he may well have been aware of prior to his marriage to Cassandra. Conversely, he may have been unaware of his infertility, and sought to strengthen his claims to her property in the event of a child being born. His pitiful and rebuffed attempts to engage in sex with other males raises the distinct possibility of James's own awareness of his medical abnormality.

40 Ann McLintock, *Imperial Leather: Race, gender and sexuality in the colonial contest* (London: Routledge, 1995), p. 6.

Conclusion

This study represents a socio-historical analysis of the intersections of gender, race and class in the slave-based plantation societies of Barbados and North Carolina. Specifically, it brings to the fore the material experiences of white women who inhabited these worlds, and attempts to generate greater understanding of their complex integration within the colonial slave economies. The white women who inhabited the slave societies of North Carolina and Barbados were willing and unwilling participants in the extraordinary and peculiar institution that was slavery. They were integrated at various levels and in diverse ways into social system grounded on the enslavement and brutalisation of millions of African men, women and children. Though they shared much in common with other white women in non-slaveholding societies of their time, the specific social structures of slave societies shaped their worlds in fundamentally distinct ways. Slavery permeated and indelibly shaped the contours of every individual's reality: white and black, male and female, rich or poor, slave or free, and slave-owner and non slave-owners alike. No individual remained untouched by this most barbaric institution, for slavery was critical to the shaping of the gender, class and racial identities and relations that structured these societies. As these different slaveholding societies developed, matured and diversified over time and space, the intersections of whiteness, class and gender produced both similarities and difference in white women's material realities.

I stated in the introduction to this study my conviction that existing conceptualisations of white women in slave-based plantation societies are inadequate for understanding the material realities, social positioning and agency of white women in North Carolina and Barbados. Certainly, some white women enjoyed the leisured lives of the plantation mistress popularised in films and novels of the plantation genre. But the plantation experiences of women such as Sarah

Hicks Williams and Alice Ward Loomis Dulaney reveals a far different and more complex reality. Women's labour was an essential component of the development and reproduction of North Carolinian and Barbadian plantation economies. The daily lives of most white women bore little resemblance to the pampered and leisured lifestyle enjoyed by Scarlett O'Hara before the Civil War spun the South into turmoil. Ruling-class patriarchs in both societies constructed white women as dependent subjects, an ideology that could be maintained only so long as white women's labour – whether waged or unwaged – remained undervalued and unacknowledged. Yet, contrarily, white males expected that 'their' women be industrious, and appropriated white women's labour power on plantations and farms, in textile mills, and in diverse work settings. Though most of North Carolina's white women enjoyed access to slave labour, the majority were neither slave-owners nor wealthy, and their daily labour was, in many instances, critical to the survival of their families.

Elite plantation mistresses inhabited a world far removed from that of poor white women, but even among the former group, distinct differences could be discerned. Whether mistress of 100 slaves or mistress of five, plantation mistresses nearly all carried on their shoulders the accompanying responsibilities of wives and mothers and the onerous domestic duties that flowed from these roles. But it was one thing to be a wealthy plantation wife with a retinue of domestic slaves to do one's every bidding, and quite another entirely to be the widowed mistress of four or five slaves struggling to secure and maintain economic security in a world unfriendly to lone women.

Not all white women belonged to the planter class, not all owned slaves, and not all white women were considered ladies. Poor white women represented a numerically significant but socially liminal group, existing on the fringes of respectable white society. Denied the social and racial privileges that accrued to whiteness, it was inevitable that many would slip entirely from the white cultural milieu. With little social status to lose, many rejected the gender and racial norms of their society, engaging in unmarried sex and bearing illegitimate children. In their social and sexual behaviour, unruly white women challenged and pushed against dominant social values that sought to maintain their subordination to the white male patriarchy. Ruling-class white males were not hesitant to exercise a degree of savagery in their dealings with these female 'race traitors', to deploy a contemporary term. Such women could be stripped not only of their rights to motherhood, but effectively also of their claims to whiteness and its accompanying social and racial privileges. Time and space separated the poor white women encountered in this study, but they shared

CONCLUSION

beyond their gender a dubious quality of whiteness. And when their transgressive social behaviour brought them to the attention of the authorities, they suffered identical fates – forced separation from their daughters.

Within these two societies, emerging white racial identities in the seventeenth to eighteenth centuries were secured in part through patriarchal control of white women. That the plantocracy recognised the greater propensity and possibility of poor white women's resistance, is evident from the legal measures they took to control the social and sexual behaviour of lower-class white women in both sites. In both North Carolina and Barbados, the reproductive capacities of white women in general, and poor white women in particular, identified them as potential threats to the reproduction of white racial purity and the stability of the racially stratified social order. A critical site of antagonism between white women and the authorities in both societies was that of sexual relationships between white females and black males. White female sexuality therefore, had to be brought under the control of dominant white male authority, whether exercised by individual men or by the state. Parish records in Barbados reveal the implication of the vestry in the regulation of poor white women's behaviour, through the dispensation or withholding of poor relief. Across the Atlantic, North Carolina's authorities similarly deployed the legal apparatus to punish unruly women. Few court records of the plantation era in Barbados have survived, so it is difficult to know just how far the Barbadian legal system was also brought to bear on transgressive white women, and how poorer white women who were not claimants of poor relief were socially regulated. The threat of potential removal of white privileges undoubtedly served to control some women, but ultimately, for the very poorest, such privileges could only have been negligible. Were such women simply allowed to 'slip' from within the white cultural milieu, and with what consequences?

The relative economic insecurity of poor women, whether married or single, undermined white ideals of dependent womanhood, and the necessity to secure or contribute to the family income compelled poorer white women to labour outside the domestic sphere. Women of the poorer classes could test the limits of the dominant class power to reproduce whiteness as a privileged identity and in doing so, contest the limits of normative, feminine, white identities. Patriarchal rule was never so absolute as to deny possible resistance. This is demonstrated in the example of the attempts by St John's Vestry to force young poor white women into apprenticeships, which provoked their mothers to resistance.

Albeit constrained by various ideological, legal and social practices, white women were significant social and economic actors in both North Carolina and Barbados. Clearly the form and content of these ideologies, laws and social practices varied across time within each society, producing different qualitative experiences for women. The critical questions are: How did geographical location differentially affect the lives of white women within each society? What commonalities and differences may be discerned? The most important commonality in white women's lives in North Carolina and Barbados was their subjugation to a patriarchal, racialised social system that demanded the subjection of all women, white and black, to white male authority. White women were – at least in theory if not in practice – excluded from participation in the public realms of their respective societies and barred from holding political office in both North Carolina and Barbados. But despite their supposed confinement to the domestic sphere, the imperatives of maintaining slavery as an institution and as an economic mode of production required the co-option and co-operation of white women in the reproduction of whiteness, and it was within the domestic household that much of the cultural work of reproducing whiteness took place. On both sides of the Atlantic, women's domestic labour was critical to the maintenance of white economic power, white cultural values, and by extension, to the reproduction of whiteness.

The advent of slavery, and its maturation in both North Carolina and Barbados forced the dominant whites to produce, maintain and justify a common white identity. The imperative to maintain and reproduce white racial purity and social superiority drew white women into the patriarchal social system in a manner not apparent within European societies of the period, since slavery did not allow clear boundaries between public and private spheres. Thus, the specificities of these slave societies produced and idealised very specific white female identities and a particular range of material experiences, as surely as slavery defined the lives and destinies of enslaved Africans. Harriett Jarrett, Ann Tull, and the 'treacherous' Millisaint Jenkins, represent only a few white women in both societies who struggled to exercise a degree of personal autonomy while at the same time denying the same to their slaves. As free citizens, white women could at least exercise some degree of control over their own lives, and the white women who have appeared within these pages demonstrate the possibilities of agency and resistance for white women.

An aim of this study has been to problematise whiteness, as an unstable identity, and to show the implications that attention to whiteness as an identity might have for understanding white women's

CONCLUSION

positions in North Carolina and Barbados. In doing so, I have analysed some of the ways in which white women were socially and sexually regulated in order to secure and reproduce a unitary white identity for the plantation society. It became clear that attempts to secure a fixed and cohesive white identity in North Carolina and Barbados were always problematic. Authorities were confronted with continuing pressures to specify and regulate social and racial identities and positions.

Whiteness shaped white women's social identities, but the reproduction of white racial identity had always to be regulated and organised. Whiteness in Barbados and North Carolina emerged as a product of specific processes of racialisation and of exclusionary practices, for instance, in terms of property relations. The case study of Barbadian vestries demonstrate further struggles around the boundaries of whiteness, indicating the instability of whiteness as a socially constructed racial identity. Since it is constituted in specific social and historical relationships, discursive practices and their effects, whiteness cannot be analysed in general. It is therefore not a fixed category, but is subject to instability, and is reliant on the active participation of white people in efforts to stabilise, naturalise and regulate it. In North Carolina and Barbados, whiteness developed as a socially privileged status with social boundaries that required varying degrees of efforts to reproduce and maintain. In both societies white identity and whiteness were developed in relation to enslavement, and small but problematic intermediate categories of coloured and free people.

Patriarchal authority varied in intensity and form between and within the two societies. While Southern states promoted an idealised image of white womanhood that locked wealthier women into narrowly defined identities and roles, the cult of true womanhood does not appear to have established the same ideological power among poor whites in either society. The data presented in this study suggest that white Barbadian women were perhaps able to attain a degree of social and economic autonomy not possible for women in North Carolina. This is a critical area in which comparative study needs further development.

Of course, the degree of autonomy which white women were able to secure in either society was always mediated by their class positions and marital status. In both societies, marriage tied elite white women firmly to white male patriarchs, but there is less evidence to suggest that Barbadian white women experienced the same degree of confinement to the domestic sphere that defined the boundaries of elite women's existence in North Carolina. However, there is a great need to clarify the content of the specific gender ideologies that shaped the lives of white Barbadian women during the era of plantation slavery.

In both societies, possibilities for female agency were significantly mediated by women's class position. While wealthy Barbadian women could invest in sugar plantations, property and slaves, the possibilities for poorer women's economic participation were limited by narrow economic opportunities for women in the public sphere. Further comparative work might establish whether Barbadian women participated to a greater extent in the economic sphere than did women of North Carolina, who were geographically more isolated and dispersed. An important variable affecting white women's ability to participate in the economy may have been the relatively small number of free coloured women in Barbados and North Carolina, compared with Jamaica in the Caribbean or Louisiana in the American South, for example. In Jamaica and Louisiana, large, free, coloured populations dominated the economy, thereby competing for opportunities with poor white women. Further research might explore these questions, and show more clearly some of the factors that promoted and inhibited white women's economic participation.

Whilst it is not possible to claim for elite white women in North Carolina the same degree of economic agency identified among Barbadian women, this study has pointed to the economic activities of poor white women and yeoman farm women of that state. That some women there, and in Barbados, participated in their respective economies, is not to be read as evidence of women's absolute independence of male control and regulation, for women's labour probably only afforded, at best, semi-independence.[1] However, it did mean that such independence as they could secure, if only limited, enabled some women to diversify the conditions of white womanhood in patriarchal societies, even when their self-imposed definitions did not conform to dominant notions of appropriate white femininity. Many enterprising widows understood well that revenues derived from their successful businesses enabled them to choose between remaining in a state of widowhood and maintaining control of their enterprises, or remarrying – which would entail ceding ownership and control of their personal properties.[2] For poorer women, participation in the economy, either as waged labourers or as small traders, enabled them to escape to some extent the strictures placed on them in exchange for poor relief, as the documentation of the St John and St Michael vestries demonstrates.

By focusing on property relationships, and women's participation in the economic sphere, it has been possible to reveal white women as significant actors in the economies of their societies. When circumstances permitted, women in both societies bought, sold, mortgaged,

CONCLUSION

leased and hired property in all its varied forms, and were active owners and managers of the enslaved. While white males were the predominant owners of property in Barbados and North Carolina, some white women of all social classes pursued independent market activities. Evidence of white women's agency as slave-owners, plantation managers, and as waged labourers within the economic markets, exposes the limitations of previous conceptualisations, and suggests the need for further research to explore and clarify the diversity of white women's economically, productive roles.

No study on female agency can credibly ignore women's relationship to and with property, or fail to consider the complexities of property relations within racialised societies. Single and widowed white women could, and did, legitimately exercise their rights to own and control property in all its diverse forms. In neither society could enslaved people lay claims to property of their own. Neither Barbados or North Carolina prevented the free black and coloured populations from accumulating land but, as John H. Franklin's study of the free black and coloured populations of North Carolina demonstrates, their rights to own slaves was always less secure.[3] Uncertainty and white agitation eventually led to the passing of an 1833 Act which established the right of free non-whites to own slaves, but in the years leading up to the Civil War, this Act was rescinded.[4] Throughout the South, as civil war loomed the sight of prosperous free coloureds amassing property and wealth prompted pro-slavery Southerners to advocate the restriction of property rights of this group. Demands were even made that the property of individual black and coloured people be 'appropriated' and redistributed to whites, and the property-owners re-enslaved.[5] The property rights of free coloureds and blacks in Barbados were no less secure. At various times Barbadian authorities also attempted to restrict and limit the property rights of free coloureds. An act of 1721 removed the rights of free coloureds to testify in law courts, a move which was to have serious consequences for their ability to protect their property.[6] While this act did not directly remove or restrict the rights of free coloureds and blacks to own property, it did have the adverse effect of undermining those rights.[7] The point to be made here is that, where property was concerned, white women stood in a different relationship to that of the free coloured and black populations. While the patriarchal ethos of their societies served to restrict white women's public and economic activities, with the exception of married women, legislation enshrined white women's rights to property in all its varied forms.

There is a case to be made that the white women of Barbados and North Carolina *were* active agents of power over others, in their acceptance of, and adherence to, the pro-slavery ideologies of their society. Only a few white women in North Carolina found the personal courage to oppose slavery, and there is little evidence that a white feminist consciousness emerged in either society before emancipation. It is not known if the presence of white women in these societies lent to slavery a more humane quality, as social observers and commentators often claimed. The narratives of Harriet Jacobs, Mary Prince, Frederick Douglass, and other formerly enslaved women and men indicate that some of the worst atrocities of slavery were committed either at the instigation of, or at the hands of, white women. It would seem therefore that claims of white women's humanising influence are tenuous. It is clear that individual white women made strenuous efforts to ameliorate the conditions of individual slaves, but they did so without offering serious resistance to the slave economy on which they depended. Ultimately, most white women aligned themselves with the white, male-dominated ruling class; their interests lay not with the enslaved, but with the rulers. Few could do otherwise, for fear of losing their racial privileges, and it is this significant alignment in racial politics that the work of black feminist historians has made so clearly visible.

A comparative study such as this work inevitably raises many more questions than it has answered. It has not, for instance, investigated how the position of white women and their relations to others developed, changed and diversified over time and space. Investigation of these issues should shed further light on similarities and differences in women's identities, agency, exercise of power and resistance. The point of further research would be to qualify further inadequately grounded generalisations about white women, and to consider the implications of the evidence of the diversity of women's 'raced', 'gendered' and 'classed' lives.

Representations of women as passive victims of patriarchy illuminates how male power was exercised in constituting feminine identities, and how men controlled women's bodies and sexuality, but sheds no light on the critical differences that being socially identified as white made to what was controlled and why. Neither do they suggest how white women exercised power over the productive and reproductive labour of the black males and females that were enslaved, even though white women's social and economic circumstances varied over the period.

Feminist historians have rightly insisted on the deconstruction of 'woman' as a singular category. As this analysis of the diverse experiences of white woman within the slaveholding worlds of Barbados and North Carolina has revealed, it is quite simply not possible, or ana-

CONCLUSION

lytically useful, to ignore crucial differences between women, even within a single ethnic group. Whilst it is easy to make generalisations about white women in plantation societies if differences and specifities are ignored, it is less easy to explicate the specificities of women's varied experiences that require such generalisations to be qualified. This study has, nevertheless, attempted to demonstrate that some useful comparisons can be drawn between the various positions of white women, within and between, North Carolina and Barbados, in order to establish how evidence of significant differences and specificities might challenge universalistic notions of womanhood.

Notes

1 Leonore Davidoff and Catherine Hall, *Family Fortunes: Men and women of the English middle class 1780–1850* (London: Hutchinson, 1987). I have not been able to establish systematically the levels of independence different forms of economic activity made possible for women in differing economic circumstances over the period, but this could be explored in further research.
2 Philip Wright (ed.), *Lady Nugent's Journal of Her Residence in Jamaica from 1801–1805* (Kingston, Institute of Jamaica, 1966).
3 John H. Franklin, 'The Free Negro in the Economic Life of Ante-bellum North Carolina', in Paul Finkleman (ed.), *Free Blacks in a Slave Society* (New York: Garland Publishing Inc., 1980).
4 Ibid., p. 369.
5 Michael P. Johnson & James L. Roark, *Black Masters: A free family of colour in the Old South* (New York: W.W. Norton & Co., 1984).
6 I. A. Hoyos, *Barbados: A history from the Amerindians to independence* (London: Macmillan, 1978).
7 Pedro Welch has argued that a direct consequence of this Act was that it enabled unscrupulous whites to contest the legal status of individual free black and coloured property owners, and therefore their rights to own property; another tactic employed was to challenge the legitimacy of an individual's property ownership. To safeguard their ownership and control of property, therefore, many free black and coloured property owners found it expedient to seek the protection of friendly or sympathetic white male patrons. One of these was the wealthy and successful Rachel Pringle-Polgreen, free coloured woman of Barbados, who was manumitted from slavery and set up in business by a British naval officer. Among the regular visitors to Rachel's Royal Naval 'hotel' was Prince William Henry, later King William IV. See Pedro Welch, 'In Search of the Ostrehans and their Contemporaries: Free Coloured Women in eighteenth and nineteenth century Bridgetown'. Seminar Paper presented to the Department of History, University of the West Indies, Cave Hill campus (1994). See also Gad Heuman, 'The Social Structure of the Slave Societies in the Caribbean', in Franklin W. Knight (ed.), *General History of the Caribbean* Vol. III (New York: UNESCO Publishing, 1997).

BIBLIOGRAPHY

Andrews, J., Walker, E., and McLean, C. (eds), *Janet Schaw's 'Journal of a lady of quality: being the narrative of a journey from Scotland to the West Indies, North Carolina, and Portugal, in the years 1774 to 1776'* (New Haven: Yale University Press, 1921).

Bardaglio, Peter, ' "Shameful Matches": The regulation of interracial marriage and sex in the South before 1900', in M. Hodes (ed.) *Sex, Love, Race: Crossing boundaries in North American history* (New York: New York University Press, 1999).

Barnes, Albert, *An inquiry into the Scriptural Views of Slavery*. Philadelphia, 1846.

Barrow, Christine (ed.), *Caribbean Portraits: Essays on gender ideologies and identities* (Jamaica: Ian Randle Publishers, 1998)

Beatty, Bess, *Alamance: The Holt family and industrialization in a North Carolina county, 1837–1900* (Baton Rouge: Louisiana State University Press, 1999).

Beatty, Bess, ' "I can't get my bored on them old lomes": Female textile workers in the Ante-bellum South', in Susanna Delfino and Michele Gillespie (eds), *Neither Lady nor Slave: Working women of the Old South* (Chapel Hill: University of North Carolina Press, 2002).

Beckles, Hilary, 'White Women and Slavery in the Caribbean', *History Workshop Journal* 36 (1983), pp. 66–82.

Beckles, Hilary, 'Class Formation in Slave Society: The rise of a black labour elite and the development of a white lumpen-proletariat in seventeenth century Barbados', *Journal of the Barbados Museum and Historical Society* 37:1 (1983).

Beckles, Hilary, *Natural Rebels: A social history of enslaved black women in Barbados* (London: Karnak House, 1988).

Beckles, Hilary, *A History of Barbados: From Amerindian settlement to nation-state* (Cambridge: Cambridge University Press, 1990).

Beckles, Hilary, 'Centering Women: The political economy of gender in West African and Caribbean slavery', in Christine Barrow (ed.), *Caribbean Portraits: Essays on gender ideologies and identities* (Kingston: Ian Randle Publishers, 1998).

Beckles, Hilary, 'Historicizing Slavery in West Indian Feminisms', *Feminist Review* 59 (Summer 1998).

Beckles, Hilary, *Centering Woman: Gender discourses in Caribbean slave society* (London: James Currey, 1999).

Billings, Warren M., 'The Cases of Fernando and Elizabeth Key: A note on the status of blacks in seventeenth century Virginia', *William and Mary Quarterly* 3rd Ser., 30:3 (Jul. 1973), pp. 467–474.

BIBLIOGRAPHY

Bolton, Charles C., *Poor Whites of the Ante-bellum South: Tenants and labourers in central North Carolina and Northeast Mississippi* (Durham, NC: Duke University Press, 1994).

Bonner, James C., 'Plantation Experiences of a New York Woman', *North Carolina Historical Review* 33: 2 & 3 (July and October 1956), pp. 384–412 and 529–586.

Bridenbaugh, Carl and Bridenbaugh, Roberta, *No Peace Beyond the Line: The English in the Caribbean 1624–1690* (New York: Oxford University Press, 1972).

Brown, Kathleen M., *Good Wives, Nasty Wenches and Anxious Patriarchs* (Chapel Hill: University of North Carolina Press, 1996).

Bryan Mary Norcott, *A Grandmother's Recollection of Dixie* (New Bern: Owen G. Dunn, 1912).

Bryant, Keith L. Jr., 'The Role and Status of the Female Yeomanry in the Antebellum South: The literary view', *Southern Quarterly* 18:2 (Winter 1979–80), pp. 73–88.

Buhle, Mari Jo, 'Needlewomen and the Vicisssitudes of Modern Life: A study of middle-class construction in the antebellum Northeast', in Nancy A. Hewitt and Suzanne Lebsock (eds), *Visible Women: New essays on American activism* (Urbana and Chicago: University of Illinois Press, 1993), pp. 145–165.

Burnard, Trevor, 'Inheritance and Independence: Women's status in early colonial Jamaica', *William and Mary Quarterly* 3rd Ser., 48:1 (January 1991), pp. 93–114.

Burnard, Trevor, 'Family Continuity and Female Independence in Jamaica, 1655–1734', *Continuity and Change* 7:2 (1992).

Bush, Barbara, 'White "Ladies", Coloured "Favourites", and Black "Wenches": Some considerations on sex, race and class factors in social relations in white Creole society in the British Caribbean', *Slavery and Abolition* 2:3 (December 1981).

Bush, Barbara, *Slave Women in Caribbean Society 1650–1838* (London: James Currey, 1990).

Bush, Barbara, 'History, Memory, Myth: Reconstructing the history (or histories) of black women in the African diaspora', in Stephanie Newell (ed.), *Images of African and Caribbean women: Migration, displacement, diaspora* (Stirling: Centre for Commonwealth Studies, University of Stirling, 1996).

Bush, Barbara, 'Hard Labour: Women, childbirth and resistance in British Caribbean slave societies', in D. Barry Gaspar and D. Clark Hine (eds), *More than Chattel: Black women and slavery in the Americas* (Bloomington: Indiana University Press, 1996).

Butler, Kathleen Mary, *The Economics of Emancipation: Jamaica and Barbados, 1823–1843* (Chapel Hill: University of North Carolina Press, 1995).

Bynum, Victoria, *Unruly Women: The politics of social and sexual control in the Old South* (Chapel Hill: University of North Carolina Press, 1992).

Carr, Lori and Walsh, Lorena, 'The Planter's Wife', *William and Mary Quarterly*, 3rd Ser., 3 (1977), pp. 542–571.

BIBLIOGRAPHY

Cecil-Fronsman, Bill, *Common Whites: Class and culture in Ante-bellum North Carolina* (Lexington: University of Kentucky Press, 1992).

Clinton, Catherine (ed.), *Half Sisters of History: Southern women and the American past* (Durham, NC: Duke University Press, 1994).

Clinton, Catherine, *Tara Revisited: Women, war and the plantation legend* (New York: Abbeyville Press, 1995).

Crow, Jeffrey J., *A History of African-Americans in North Carolina* (Raleigh: North Carolina Division of Archives and History, 1992).

Davidoff, Lenore and Hall, Catherine, *Family Fortunes: Men and women of the English middle class, 1780–1850* (London: Hutchinson, 1987).

Davy, Kate, 'Outing Whiteness: A feminist/lesbian project', in Mike Hill (ed.), *Whiteness: A Critical Reader* (New York: New York University Press, 1997) pp. 204–225.

Delphino, Susanna, 'Invisible Women: Female labour in the Upper South's iron and mining industries', in Susanna Delfino and Michele Gillespie (eds), *Neither Lady nor Slave: Working women of the Old South* (Chapel Hill: University of North Carolina Press, 2002).

Delfino, Susanna, and Gillespie, Michele (eds), *Neither Lady Nor Slave: Working women of the Old South* (Chapel Hill: University of North Carolina Press, 2002).

De Pauw, Linda G., 'Women and the Law: The colonial period', *Human Rights* 6:2 (Winter 1977) pp. 107–113.

Dew, Thomas R., 'Dissertation on the Characteristic Differences between the Sexes, and on the Position and Influence of Women in Society', *Southern Literary Messenger* 1:1 & 2 (July & August 1835), pp. 621–632, 672–691.

Douglass, Frederick, *The Life of Frederick Douglass, An American Slave* (London: Penguin, 1986).

Dunn, Richard, *Sugar and Slaves: The rise of the planter class in the English West Indies 1624–1713* (New York: W.W. Norton, 1972).

Dyer, Richard, *Whiteness* (London: Routledge, 1997).

Erickson, Amy L., *Women and Property in Early Modern England* (London: Routledge, 1978).

Eze, E.C. (ed.), *Race and the Enlightenment: A reader* (Oxford: Blackwell, 1997).

Fenwick, A.F. (ed.), *The Fate of the Fenwicks: Letters to Mary Hays, 1798–1828* (London, 1927).

Fischer, Kirsten, *Suspect Relations: Sex, race and resistance in colonial North Carolina* (Ithaca: Cornell University Press, 2002).

Foucault, Michel, *The History of Sexuality* (Harmondsworth: Penguin, 1978).

Fox-Genovese, Elizabeth, *Within the Plantation Household: Black and white women of the Old South* (Chapel Hill: University of North Carolina Press, 1988).

Frankenberg, Ruth, *White Women, Race Matters: The social construction of whiteness* (London: Routledge, 1993).

Frankenberg, Ruth (ed.), *Displacing Whiteness: Essays in social and cultural criticism* (Durham: Duke University Press, 1997).

Freeling, W.H., *The Road to Disunion* (New York: Oxford University Press, 1999).

BIBLIOGRAPHY

Gragg, Larry, *Englishmen Transplanted: The English colonization of Barbados 1627–1660* (Oxford: Oxford University Press, 2003).
Griffis Johnson, Guion, *Ante-bellum North Carolina: A social history* (Chapel Hill: University of North Carolina Press, 1937).
Hall, Kim, *Things of Darkness: Economies of race and gender in early modern England* (Ithaca: Cornell University Press, 1995).
Hall, Richard, *Acts Passed in the Island of Barbados, 1643–1762*, Vol. 1 (William Clowes and Sons, 1875).
Helper, Hinton Rowan, *The impending Crisis of the South: How to meet it* (New York: Burden Press, 1957).
Hill, Mike (ed.), *Whiteness: A critical reader* (New York: New York University Press, 1997).
Hirschon, Renee (ed.), *Women and Property, Women as Property* (Kent: Croom Helm, 1984).
Hodes, Martha, *White Women, Black Men: Illicit sex in the nineteenth-century South* (New Haven: Yale University Press, 1997).
Hodes, M. (ed.), *Sex, Love, Race: Crossing boundaries in North American history* (New York: New York University Press, 1999).
Hurmence, Belinda (ed.), *My Folks Don't Want Me to Talk About Slavery: Twenty-one oral histories of former North Carolina slaves* (Winston-Salem: John F. Blair, 1984).
Jacobs, Harriet, *Incidents in the Life of a Slave Girl* (London: Oxford University Press, 1988).
Kay, Marvin L. Michael and Cary, Lorin Lee, *Slavery in North Carolina, 1748–1775* (Chapel Hill: University of North Carolina Press, 1996).
Lambert, David, 'Liminal Figures: Poor whites, freedmen and racial reinscription in colonial Barbados, *Society and Space* 19 (2001), pp. 335–350.
Lerner, Gerda, *The Grimke Sisters from South Carolina* (Oxford: Oxford University Press, 1998).
Ligon, Richard, *A True and Exact History of the Island of Barbados* (London: Frank Cass, reprinted 1970).
Lockley, Timothy, J. 'Crossing the Racial Divide: Inter-racial sex in Antebellum Savannah', *Slavery and Abolition* 18:3 (December 1997), pp. 159–173.
Lockley, Timothy J., 'Public Poor Relief in Buncombe County, North Carolina', *North Carolina Historical Review*, 80:1 (January 2003).
McLintock, Anne, *Imperial Leather: Race, gender and sexuality in the colonial contest* (London: Routledge, 1995).
McCurry, Stephanie, *Masters of Small Worlds: Yeoman households, gender relations and the political culture of the antebellum South Carolina low country* (Chapel Hill: University of North Carolina Press, 1995).
Momsen, Janet, 'Gender Ideology and Land', in Christine Barrow (ed.), *Caribbean Portraits: Essays on gender ideologies and identities* (Ian Randle Publishers: Jamaica, 1998).
Morgan, Jennifer L., ' "Some Could Suckle Over Their Shoulder": Male travellers, female bodies, and the gendering of racial ideology 1500–1770', *William and Mary Quarterly*, 3rd Ser., 54 (January 1997), pp. 167–192.

BIBLIOGRAPHY

Morgan, Jennifer L., *Laboring Women: Reproduction and gender in New World slavery* (Philadelphia: University of Pennsylvania Press, 2004).

Morton, Patricia (ed.), *Discovering the Women in Slavery: Emancipating perspectives on the American past* (Athens: University of Georgia, 1996).

Oxley, Geoffrey, *Poor Relief in England and Wales 1601–1834* (London: David and Charles, 1974).

Puckrein, Gary, *Little England: Plantation society and Anglo-Barbadian politics, 1627–1700* (New York: New York University Press, 1984).

Rawick, George P. (ed.), *The American Slave: A composite autobiography* (North Carolina Narratives) Vols. 14 and 15 (Connecticut: Greenwood Publishing Company, 1972).

Roberts, Dorothy, *Killing the Black Body: Race, reproduction and the meaning of liberty* (New York: Pantheon Press, 1997).

Rose, Willie Lee (ed.), *A Documentary History of Slavery in North America* (University of Georgia Press: Athens, 1999).

Saunders, Col. W.L., *Colonial Records of North Carolina*; ten volumes, 1886–1890. Col. Recs., II., p. 889. cited in J.B. Spencer, *Slavery and Servitude in the Colony of North Carolina* (Baltimore: The Johns Hopkins Press, 1896).

Scott, Ann. Firor, *The Southern Lady: From pedestal to politics, 1830–1930* (Chicago: University of Chicago Press, 1970).

Shepherd, Verene, *Women of the Caribbean: The British colonised territories* (Jamaica: Ian Randle Publishers, 1999).

Shepherd, Verene et al (eds), *Engendering Slavery: Caribbean women in historical perspective* (London: James Currey, 1995).

Sheppard, Jill, *The Redlegs of Barbados: Their origins and history* (New York: KTO Press, 1977).

Spelman, Elizabeth, *Inessential Woman: Problems of exclusion in feminist thought* (London; Women's Press, 1990).

Stoler, Ann Laura, *Race and the Education of Desire: Foucault's history of sexuality and the colonial order of things* (Durham, NC: Duke University Press, 1995).

Supplee Smith, M. and Herring Wilson, E., *North Carolina Women: Making history* (Chapel Hill: University of North Carolina Press, 1999).

Thompson, Roger, *Women in Stuart England and America* (London: Routledge, 1978).

Ware, Vron, *Beyond the Pale: White women, racism and history* (London: Verso Books, 1992).

Watson, Alan, 'Women of Colonial North Carolina: Overlooked and underestimated', *North Carolina Historical Review* 58 (January 1981), pp. 1–22.

Welch, Pedro, *Slave Society in the City: Bridgetown, Barbados 1680–1834* (Kingston: Ian Randle Publishers, 2003).

White, Deborah Gray, *Ain't I a Woman?: Female slaves in the plantation South* (New York: Norton and Norton, 1985).

Whitehead, Anne, 'Women and Men; Kinship and Property: Some general issues', in Hirschon, Renee (ed.), *Women and Property, Women as Property* (Croom Helm: Kent, 1984), pp. 176–192.

BIBLIOGRAPHY

Wilson, Carol and Wilson, Calvin D., 'White Slavery: An American paradox', *Slavery and Abolition* 19 (April 1998), pp. 1-19.

Wood, Kirsten, *Masterful Women: Slaveholding Widows from the American Revolution through the Civil War, 1790–1860* (Chapel Hill: University of North Carolina Press, 2004).

Wright, Phillip (ed.), *Lady Nugent's Journal of her Residence in Jamaica from 1801–1805* (Kingston: Institute of Jamaica, 1966).

Zipf, Karen L., *Labour of Innocents: Forced apprenticeships in North Carolina, 1715–1919* (Baton Rouge: Louisiana State University, 2005)

INDEX

Note: unless otherwise indicated, references relate to *white* women.

abandonment and desertion
  of husbands and families 56, 91
  legislation to prevent 36
  of wives and children 35–36,
    211–213
abolition and abolitionism 121,
    124–125, 131–132, 143–145
adultery
  of white males with enslaved
    women 58, 60
  of white women with black men
    44–46, 54–55, 58
African women
  European representations of
    21–23
  legal distinctions from white
    women 66
  sexual abuse of 28, 48
  as tithables 66
alimony, petitions for 91
alliances between enslaved people
    and poor whites 19, 26
apprenticeship 13–14, 34, 38–39,
    47–48
  see also children

bastardy and elite women 54
benevolence and charitable
    associations 13–14, 113–114
  see also Raleigh Female
    Benevolent Society

children
  education of 30–31, 66
  forced separation from parents 34,
    37–39, 47–48
  illegitimate concealment of 46,
    55, 60
  legal status of 28, 50
  orphans, care of 32, 34, 100
  see also apprenticeship
clothing
  as marker of racial status 113
  value as property 113
colonialism
  as civilising process 23
  enhancement of women's status
    and 81
  women as active agents of 2–3
  women as passive victims of 2–3,
    224
coverture 86–88, 94, 179
critical white studies 3–4

degeneracy and poor whites 210
devaluation of and invisibility of
    women's extra-domestic
    labour 75
displacement of poor whites from
    plantation economy 16–17,
    168
distribution of slave ownership by
    gender 173
divorce and separation
  married women's rights and
    90
  petitions for 16, 56–60
  poor women and 92
domestic servants
  free black women as 149–150
domesticity, ideology of 66
  poor women and 66
  see also separate spheres, ideology
    of
dower 93, 97, 107, 198
  see also widows

INDEX

Dulaney, Alice Ward Loomis
  administrator of deceased husband's estate and 189
  femme sole as 196–198
  impropriety of field labour and 187, 194
  independent plantation mistress 185–198
  insanity and 185–198

economic agents
  elite women as 81–89, 93–115, 155–181, 185–197
  poor white women as 17, 53, 64, 68–76, 104, 157, 167–168
elite women
  legal assertions of property rights and 85, 88–89, 160, 174
  economic dependency of 66, 75
  family roles and 65–67
  as feminine representatives of patriarchal state 65
  inter-racial sexual relationships and 15, 55
  privileges of whiteness and 2–5, 151–152, 215, 219, 224
  support of pro-slavery ideology and 81, 143–144, 160, 179, 223
  as subjects of patriarchal authority 15, 29, 68, 81, 84
employment creation schemes 17, 63–65
enslaved people
  defined as real estate 80–88
  as inheritable property in wills 104, 108–112, 159, 172–178
  as marriage portions 138–139, 179
  as troublesome property 147
  women's ownership of 115–179
enslaved women
  denial of rights to motherhood and 159–160, 175
  as plantation labourers 161
  relations with mistresses and 207–210
  as reproducers of enslaved labour force 159, 175, 176–177
  as reproducers of enslaved status 50–51
  resistance and 175, 209
  sexual relations with white males 28, 60
  slave-owning women's preference for 173

female education 30
femme coverts 86
femme soles 86–87, 101, 103, 106
field labour
  poor white women and 17, 69–70
free black men
  restrictions on conveyance of property to children 62
  sexual relationships with white women 46–48, 53
  see also inter-racial relationships
free coloureds
  demands for political power 28
  as potential threats to white hegemonic rule 62
  property rights and 62, 80, 223
  as targets of control 28
  as threats to existing racialised property relations 62

gender and property rights 85–101
gendered identities
  of black women 22–23, 70, 159–160
  intersections with race and class and 151–153
  of white women 22–23, 26, 159–160

hotel, tavern and ferry keepers, women as 73, 83, 167
homosexuality 213
Howard, Leah
  apprenticeship and 14
  conformity to standards of white womanhood 40

[234]

INDEX

historiography, poor women in 14
marriage portion and 13–14, 40
hucksterism 17

ideal and ideology of white womanhood
  elite women and 21, 67–68, 108–109, 111–112
  nonconformity of poor women to 27, 40–41, 49, 69
illegal possession of estate 104–105
illicit trading between whites and blacks 72–73
indentured servants and servitude
  legal status of 52
  socio-sexual regulation of 47, 51–52
industrialisation, southern
  expansion of opportunities for women's waged labour and 74
infanticide 44–46
  see also Wiggins, Sarah Herring
inheritance
  children's share of inheritance by gender 111
  of enslaved people 91, 159–160, 163, 168, 172, 174–175
  male attitudes to women as executors 87–88, 104, 107–110
  mechanism for deceased husbands' control of widows as 108–110, 172–173
  primogeniture and 107
  as route to property ownership 106–110
  unmarried daughters/single women and 112–113
inter-racial marriage 15, 27, 51–52, 61–62
inter-racial relationships
  elite women and 29, 44–46
  poor white women 15, 27, 29, 48–49, 52–53

proscriptions against and regulation of 15, 27, 47–48, 50–51
  as threat to boundaries of freedom 29, 50
  as threat to property relations 62
  as threat to white purity 26–27, 29
  as threat to sanctity of white family 48
  as threat to white hegemony 48
inventories, household 99, 105

land
  as basis of wealth and status 49, 80, 104, 127, 132, 199
  routes to ownership of 103–105
  significance of ownership for women 103
  transactions by women 95–96, 98–99, 104, 165
  usage of 98–99, 104

manumission of enslaved by gender 178–179
marital property, disputes over 89–90, 164, 199–200
marriage as natural destiny of white women 56, 67
marriage settlements 88, 95, 198–199
married women
  as *femme soles* 92–93
  property rights 86–92
  as testators 110–111
mulattoes *see* free coloureds

'other', white women as 22–23, 26

Phillips, Ann
  exploitation of enslaved women's reproductive capacities and 159–160
  slave-ownership and 155–160
physical and sexual abuse of wives 55–56, 58–60, 90

[235]

INDEX

poor relief
  apprenticeship and 32, 38–39, 48
  criteria for eligibility 33–34, 36
  mechanism for socio-sexual control of women and young girls as 15, 31–32, 49
  poor white families and 15, 37
  reproduction of boundaries of whiteness and 15, 31–32
  role in maintenance of social order 31–32, 34–36, 53
poor white women
  as carers of parish poor 34–35
  challenges to socio-sexual regulation and 37–41, 51–53
  dependence on enslaved labour and 167
  elite representations of 24, 27, 49, 53
  importance of enslaved labour to economic survival 71, 167
  incorporation into white cultural sphere 31
  innate blackness of 26
  participation in illicit market economy and 167
  as potential threat to purity of whiteness 27
  as potential threat to social order 29
  as recipients of benevolence 13–15, 63–66
  resistance to charitable interventions and 64–66
  resistance to patriarchal authority and 37–41
  rights of access to enslaved labour and 164, 167–168
  as sexually immoral 26–27
  tenuous claims to whiteness of 26
poor whites
  economic and material conditions of 16–18, 32
  elite attitudes towards 16–19

power, exercise of by women over enslaved peoples 3, 10, 29, 158–161
property deeds, as sources 81
property ownership as marker of whiteness 179
property relations and gender 80–81
property rights
  legal protection of women's 87–89, 91, 157, 163–166
  of married women 86–92, 107, 110
  of unmarried women 101–102, 112
  of widows 92–101
  women's, legal and social basis of 88–102, 106–110
public and political sphere, women's exclusion from 66–69

race, discourses of 20–27
Raleigh Female Benevolent Society 63–65

Saint John School for Female Industry 13–14, 36–40
separate spheres, ideology of 66, 199
sexuality
  regulation of 15, 27–29, 40, 46, 53, 58, 62
  white males' appropriation of black female 28, 60
slave-holding women
  appropriation of enslaved women's reproductive capacities and 159–160, 175–176
  attitudes towards enslaved 129, 131, 137, 151
  dependence on enslaved labour and 149, 161–168, 204, 210–212
  domestic responsibilities and 139–143, 201–206
  management of enslaved people 141, 147, 149–150, 209
  punishment of enslaved and 206–209

INDEX

relations with enslaved and 129, 131, 205–209
slave trade and slave trading, women's involvement in 165, 169–170

textile manufacturing, women workers in 74–75
tradeswomen 16–18, 70, 72–73

unmarried women
  as *femme soles* 101–102
  importance of economic independence and 179
  inheritance and 112–113
  as lone mothers 102
  threats to ideology of dependent womanhood 68, 102
unproductive consumers, white women as 8
unwaged labour, women's participation in 70
  see also slave-holding women; yeomanry

vestries
  St John 13, 31, 34–40
  St Michael 31–32, 34

waged labour, forms of participation in 16–18, 64, 70, 73–75
wastage and theft of women's property
  by husbands 8–9, 58–60, 89, 166
whiteness
  gendering of 21–23
  instability of 21–22
  invisibility of 4
  origins of 20–24
  privileges of 2–5, 151–152, 215, 219, 224
  racial purity of 24
  relationship to freedom and 160
  reproducing the boundaries of 24–25

social and historical construction as 4
symbol of terror as 5
theories of 4–5
variability by class, ethnicity and gender of 21, 23–25
women as the biological reproducers of 2
white superiority and supremacism, ideology of 24, 27
widows
  economic agency and 98, 165, 169–170, 184–198
  economic vulnerability of 93–97, 99
  independence of 92, 96–97
  remarriage and 95, 100–101
  responsibilities of estate administration and 93–94
  responses to widowhood 93–94, 96
  vulnerability of elderly 99
Wiggins, Sarah Herring
  allegation of rape by enslaved male and 44–45
  infanticide of illegitimate mulatto child and 44–46
Williams, Sarah Hicks
  acculturation as a southern matron 126–153
  anti-slavery sentiment and 119–123
  evolution as pro-slavery sympathiser 141–146, 150
  management of domestic slaves 141–143
  problems of free labour in civil war era 150–151

yeomanry
  economic importance of women in
    yeoman households 69–72
  female yeomanry 71–72

[237]

EU authorised representative for GPSR:
Easy Access System Europe, Mustamäe tee 50,
10621 Tallinn, Estonia
gpsr.requests@easproject.com

www.ingramcontent.com/pod-product-compliance
Ingram Content Group UK Ltd.
Pitfield, Milton Keynes, MK11 3LW, UK
UKHW021835140426
5217IPUK00021B/1468